"Could Do Better"

DATE DUE

MARCH 12 -03 FL: 2864530			

"Could Do Better"

Why Children Underachieve and What to Do About It

Harvey P. Mandel, Ph.D.
& Sander I. Marcus, Ph.D.
with *Loral Dean*

John Wiley & Sons, Inc.
New York • Chichester • Brisbane • Toronto • Singapore

LC 4691 .M315 1995

Mandel, Harvey P.

"Could do better" : why
children underachieve

Library of Congress Cataloging-in-Publication Data

Mandel, Harvey P.
    "Could do better" : why children underachieve and what to do about it /
Harvey Mandel and Sander Marcus with Loral Dean
        p. cm.
    Includes bibliographical references (p.   ) and index.
    ISBN 0-471-15847-X
        1. Underachievers—Education—United States.   2. Underachievers—
Education—Canada.   3. Motivation in education—United States.   4.
Motivation in education—Canada.   I. Marcus, Sander I.   II. Dean, Loral.
III. Title
    LC4691.M315   1995
    371.92′6—dc20   95-21521

Printed in the United States of America

10 9 8 7 6 5 4 3 2 1

To Dorothy,
and Christine, Ellen, Kathy, Anita, and Anne

Contents

Acknowledgments

We wish to thank Donald Lawson, President, and Elizabeth McTavish, Executive Director, of the Counselling Foundation of Canada for their long-term financial support of the Institute on Achievement and Motivation, York University.

We are grateful to our staff for their support, and greatly appreciate the willingness of many underachieving students and their parents to share their struggles.

We owe a special debt of gratitude to Dr. Dorothy Mandel for her insights on families and children that appear throughout the book.

We are especially grateful to Dr. Jotham Friedland for his perceptions about underachievement in the workplace, and for his leadership in the development of the Achievement and Motivation Profile (AMP), an objective test for distinguishing different types of underachievers, published in 1995 by Western Psychological Services of Los Angeles.

A colleague of ours, psychologist Dr. Jim Davison, provided thoughtful and helpful comments about the manuscript.

We also wish to thank Dr. Robert M. Roth for his contributions to our early professional development, and especially for his knowledge in the area of academic underachievement.

We appreciate the support and guidance of Herb Reich, senior editor at John Wiley & Sons, New York, whose appreciation of our research in underachievement resulted in our scholarly text in 1988.

The three authors wish to pay special tribute to the personable and witty high achiever who brought us together. Nancy Colbert, former publisher of HarperCollins, was the first to recognize the potential in this book, and was our guiding inspiration throughout its writing.

A happy team of three sounds like an oxymoron. It was not. Although the technology of the '90s smoothed the efficiency of our collaboration, our personal chemistry as a working team was our real achievement. Our thanks to Nancy Colbert, a true professional, for creating this successful triad.

And our thanks to Iris Tupholme and Susan Broadhurst, our editors at HarperCollins, and to Carole Hall, our editor at John Wiley & Sons, who so skilfully coordinated the editing and production of this book on both sides of the Canada–U.S. border.

"Could Do Better"

The Underachievement Myth

- "My son used to be an A student. But this year, for no reason I can figure out, he's become lazy and unmotivated and his average has dropped to a C. I have no idea what's happened to him."
- "My daughter is squeaking by with Cs and Ds and it doesn't seem to bother her a bit. She's so unmotivated. How can I make her want to do better?"
- "I know my son is bright. He has so much potential. So why doesn't he care about doing so poorly at school? Why is he so lazy and unmotivated?"

We've been working with underachieving kids and their parents for more than 25 years, and we have heard these cries of bewilderment and despair—and dozens more like them—thousands and thousands of times. All of them reflect a common misconception that we call The Underachievement Myth.

The Underachievement Myth presumes that underachieving students are lazy and unmotivated and need some kind of incentive to get them going. They need a push. They need to be inspired to achieve, according to the Myth.

Parents are not the only people misled by The Underachievement Myth. Far from it. Teachers, guidance counselors, psychologists, friends, grandparents, even underachievers themselves accept it as Truth. "Yes, I *know* I'm lazy and unmotivated." Or, "We *know* this kid is lazy and unmotivated. What can we do about it?" they say.

According to The Underachievement Myth, your job as a parent (or teacher or counselor or friend) is to motivate the lazy and unmotivated underachiever, tap all that under-used potential, and awaken their inner, dormant desire to achieve.

So frustrated parents try to motivate "lazy and unmotivated" underachievers in vain by:

- promising rewards;
- imposing punishments;
- trying to help make school work more interesting or entertaining;
- emphasizing the importance of education for their future;
- helping them achieve so that they will experience the rewards and joys of success;
- tutoring them or hiring a tutor;
- having heart-to-heart talks;
- encouraging them to talk with successful people whose sterling role model *surely* will motivate them;
- encouraging them to talk with unsuccessful people to awaken them to the pitfalls of underachievement;
- changing schools so that they'll be in a more disciplined, competitive, caring or otherwise more encouraging environment for achievement;
- shifting courses or academic programs to ones they like better or are more interested in;
- and on and on and on. . . .

*   *   *

Have you torn your hair out trying these or other ways to motivate or inspire your child, only to become discouraged—over and over again—because nothing seems to have a lasting effect?

Well, allow yourself a moment of relief, because you are not alone. You are in the company of thousands of frustrated parents who have had exactly the same experience as you are having. And this company of strangers includes more than parents. It includes many, many professionals, too. In fact, the dilemma posed time and time again by educational and psychological literature on academic underachievement is the daunting challenge of finding ways to motivate underachieving students.

Why do none of these methods work? Why does it seem so impossible to motivate "lazy and unmotivated" underachievers? No one can deny that underachieving kids are lazy and unmotivated—well, can they? We all know the telltale patterns: Underachievers put things off until it's too late. They cut classes. They promise to do better: "Don't worry, Mom. I'll make a clean start next term." They have to be reminded to study. They have to be prodded to do their homework. They have to be told that the deadline for their project is looming.

Does this not *prove* that they're lazy and unmotivated?

No, it does not!

We have worked with thousands of underachievers from all kinds of backgrounds. *And we have yet to find an underachiever who is truly lazy and unmotivated.*

We have come to the overwhelming conclusion that underachievers are, in fact, highly motivated—in directions other than getting good grades. And finding out precisely where their motivation lies is the key to helping them turn around and become achievers at school.

The key to unlocking their motivation lies in understanding what kind of underachiever they are. And once you've found that out, you'll also find you have shattered another assumption embedded in The Underachievement Myth—the assumption that all underachievers are alike.

During our many years spent working with underachievers, we have observed over and over again that although all underachievers arrive at the same destination—underachievement—each of them takes a different journey to get there. Underachievers are *not* all alike. They come in all shapes and sizes and colors. And recognizing what really motivates each type of underachiever is essential to understanding underachieving kids and helping them fulfill their potential.

The six most typical underachiever styles are:

- *Coasters*: They are the ultimate procrastinators, usually described as easygoing and unmotivated. Coasters are the most frequent type of underachiever.

- *Anxious Underachievers*: They *want* to do better but are too tense and uptight to work effectively.

- *Identity-Searchers*: They are so wrapped up in trying to figure out who they are that they become distracted from their school work.

- *Wheeler-Dealers*: They are impulsive, charming or intimidating, manipulative, self-seeking and so intent on instant gratification that they see no percentage in doing well at school.

- *Sad Underachievers*: Their depressed mood, low self-esteem and difficulty making decisions rob them of the energy they need to concentrate on school work.

- *Defiant Underachievers*: They underachieve as an act of rebellion.

These are underachiever prototypes, of course, each of whom is motivated in a different way. In the chapters that follow, we will describe each kind of underachiever in detail. We will list their defining characteristics, provide a checklist to help you compare your child to the prototype, take a searching look at each underachiever's *real* motivation, provide a list of ways to help, take a realistic look at what parents can expect when they implement our practical suggestions and look at what happens to each kind of underachiever as an adult.

We will also briefly discuss underachievers with learning disabilities, gifted underachievers, "combination" underachievers (mixes and matches of the six prototypes) and underachievers who don't seem to fit any profile. And we will look at your child's achievement in the future that faces us all.

CHAPTER 1

How Do I Know If My Child Is Underachieving?

We've been working with parents and kids for more than 25 years now and we have yet to meet a parent who thinks their child is doing as well as he or she is capable of doing at school.

Does this mean that *every* student is underachieving? Of course not. It merely reflects most parents' hopes and dreams about their children's success.

So how do you know if your child really is underachieving? How can you separate The Underachievement Myth from the reality of underachievement?

The place to start is with a solid definition of underachievement itself.

The Achievement Gap

The basic definition of underachievement is pretty simple. *Underachievement means that there is a significant gap between a student's potential and performance.* In other words, high IQ, low school marks. Picture two people facing each other on opposite cliffs. Call one person Potential, the other Performance. Between them is the Achievement Gap. The underachieving kid brings home a report card that says something along the lines of "Jake is a lively, bright child. He could do much better."

"Could do better" is the mantra parents and teachers repeat about underachieving children. Underachievers frequently pick up the phrase and use it to describe themselves. "Could do better" is—in a nutshell—the definition of underachievement. How so? Because anyone who could do better is achieving below their potential. In the late 1960s, aptitude tests were developed to statistically measure gaps between student potential and student performance. Ten to 15 percent of all high-school and university students were labeled underachievers according to these statistically based tests.

But there's been a lot of disagreement about the measuring standards used on these aptitude tests. For example, norms developed for Caucasian students may not be valid for those of African, Hispanic, Asian or other origins. And all students—no matter what their culture or background—may underachieve at some point in their academic career, even if it is only in one course or in one grade or for a few months.

So how do you know when to start worrying? As a responsible parent, how do you know when a few low marks are just a passing phase and when it's time to press the alarm button?

To answer this question, consider our Principles of Achievement.

The Seven Principles of Achievement

Principle 1: School marks are determined by many factors.
How children perform at school—like any aspect of their behavior—is the result of a combination of many things, including the school itself—its curriculum and structures, how students interact with their teachers and their relationships with their peers at school. It also includes their environment at home and in their community. It includes their individual makeup. Family, school, friends, personality—everyone and everything may play a part.

Let's focus first on *physical factors*. Let's say your daughter gets the flu and stays home from school for a few days or more. She will miss assignments and fall behind while she is away. And even when she's physically in class, her school work may suffer because she lacks energy or can't concentrate. And if she is suffering from a long-term illness or other significant physical problem, her school performance will suffer more serious consequences.

Poor nutrition can contribute to underachievement, too. Many studies have shown, for example, the benefits of a good breakfast on a student's ability to think clearly. A student whose diet lacks essential vitamins or minerals, or a kid who exists on a steady intake of junk food, or isn't eating enough, or has an eating disorder (anorexia or bulimia, for instance), cannot perform efficiently at school.

Emotional factors in a child's life can contribute to underachievement, too. These may include conflict of any kind—with parents, siblings, friends or teachers. Something as seemingly minor as constant belittlement by another member of the family can affect a sensitive child's achievement at school. Marital problems in the family often contribute to underachievement. An illness or accident affecting anyone close, a death in the family, family violence, alcohol or drug problems all may play a part.

Conflict is a normal part of life, of course, and each child's reaction to personal friction varies. The occasional argument or disagreement between your child and teachers, friends, brothers, sisters, your spouse or you can be a temporary problem with no long-term impact on academic achievement. However, the longer the same conflicts remain unresolved and the more intense and entrenched they become, the greater are the chances they will negatively affect school performance.

Other emotional factors may include significant upheaval in the normal pattern of your child's life. *Children of immigrants*, for example, are at major risk for underachievement, due to culture shock and everything that entails. These kids have endured a change of country and culture that can include a new language and political system, different values, customs, dress, climate, even the kind of house they live in. In addition, the immigrant child often has to cope with his parents' financial pressures or emotional distress.

A *family move* within the same culture can result in similar problems on a smaller scale. North Americans move a lot, and any move—to another city or even to a new neighborhood or school—can cause a sudden drop or improvement in school performance. The new school may have a wider range of courses, fewer students per class, better textbooks and teachers or any number of positive improvements in curriculum that result in a dramatic jump in a child's marks. Or, on the other hand, classes could be larger, teachers underqualified or apathetic and the curriculum unchallenging. Or again: The new school might have a serious problem with gang activity, drug use or racial tensions. And the trauma of being the new kid in class, struggling to make new friends, can cause a sudden drop in any child's academic performance no matter how highly motivated or emotionally well-adjusted he or she is.

Mental or intellectual factors also can contribute to underachievement. These include a child's basic ability to learn, as well as specific learning problems such as learning disabilities, dyslexia or attention-deficit disorders. For obvious reasons, children with specific learning difficulties often do well in courses that do not involve their disability and poorly in subjects that are affected by it. Math, spelling and reading are subjects often affected by a learning problem. Most students with moderate to severe learning disabilities are discovered by the time they reach Grade 5 or 6. But some milder forms of learning disability may remain undetected until well into high school or beyond.

Then there is the impact of *the school itself.* During the 1980s, independent American research teams of sociologists, psychologists and educators (Coleman and Hoffer, 1987; Purkey and Smith, 1983; Stevenson and Stigler, 1992) examined the qualities that distinguished a "good" school from a "bad" school. They wanted to know whether there were any school characteristics associated with high academic achievement, a high rate of graduation, a higher proportion of graduates moving on to university and so on. And to make the comparisons fair and valid, the researchers considered many factors, including family income and parent education, religious background and other demographics.

They found that certain school structures and attitudes enhance high-school student performance. Schools that demand and enforce high standards of student conduct, regular school attendance and meaningful homework each night; that offer a challenging curriculum emphasizing the core subjects of English, math, science and history; and that have a dedicated teaching staff that communicates quickly with parents about potential problems consistently produce students with academic skills approximately two full school years ahead of schools that do not.

So to the degree that your child's school reflects these features, it enhances your child's achievement.

Principle 2: Intelligence is only one of many factors that determine school marks.

Again and again, research shows that intelligence is only one of a great many factors that contribute to a person's grade-point average (GPA).

Our research shows that about 25 percent of a student's grade-point average can be attributed to intelligence. This leaves an astounding 75 percent to be explained by factors other than intelligence. This in turn means that a child's family, school, friends, personality and cultural milieu, taken together, have a much greater influence on your child's GPA than does intelligence alone.

So don't assume for one second that just because your child is intelligent, high marks will automatically follow.

Principle 3: It's normal for a student not to do equally well in every school subject.

Many parents believe their child performs equally across all school subjects. *But research clearly shows that no individual's capabilities and talents are equally distributed across the board.*

Think about your own school history. Did you find every one of your subjects equally interesting or easy to understand? Were you uniformly good at all school subjects? Probably not. If you were, you were in a statistical minority.

Fast-forward to today. As an adult, are you equally talented or, indeed, interested in art, mathematics, languages, music and car mechanics? Not a chance!

By the time we become adults, most of us have learned to recognize our individual interests, talents and aptitudes. If we're lucky, we excel in a few areas. What's more likely is that we accept we're good at some things and not so good (perhaps even hopeless!) at others.

It's easy to forget this when, as parents, we look at a report card and expect to see As or Bs equally distributed across the page.

Principle 4: You can expect temporary drops in school performance during certain transitions within a child's school years.
Academic performance typically drops slightly between Grades 4 and 6, when schools begin to make more serious demands of students. Around this time, students become responsible for a range of new activities—homework, projects, class presentations. Many students take time to adjust to these new demands and their marks may suffer during the change. This drop may occur even for students whose home and school environments are stable and positive.

The second predictable period when marks go down is during the transition to high school. Many forces are at work during this change, including new school structures, puberty and the intense relationships within peer groups that accompany puberty. Instead of a single, stable environment with one teacher and one set of classmates, students are suddenly thrown back on their own resources, required to change classrooms, teachers and classmates all day long. These shifts require a level of maturity and self-discipline not demanded in their earlier grades. Until the student adapts, academic performance may suffer.

Many parents of 12- to 14-year-olds anguish over their youngster's sudden academic slump. Suddenly the child they thought they knew so well is another person. "Sara has suddenly become academically brain-dead," they wail, mystified and unnerved at this change. They worry that the change will be permanent. They are nervous about their child's passage through puberty with all its predictably unpredictable changes. They watch their teenagers become fascinated with body shape and attractiveness, agonize over relationships with their friends and become obsessed with rock music. They worry about them experimenting with sex or drugs or being exposed to gang activity.

A third predictable drop occurs during the transition to college or university. Once again, the student encounters radically different structures, demands and expectations. Moving on to college usually means leaving long-time friends and forging new friendships. College students face more adult concerns and responsibilities, and must assume much more independence. They encounter new issues of intimacy and commitment with the opposite sex, questions about long-term goals and decisions about a prospective vocation.

To summarize: As academic demands increase, beginning in middle-elementary school and continuing through university, each student has to learn how to sustain or improve previous performance levels. All these predictable transitions require time, attention and energy that may detract from school work and affect academic achievement.

But if these drops are predictable, does this mean that, as a parent, you should ignore them? Absolutely not! But neither should you panic. Most of these students, over time, regain their academic equilibrium and return to previous achievement levels.

There is a rule of thumb, however: *A marked decrease in academic performance that lasts for more than one school year is a signal for you to take a closer look.* You can start by discussing the problem with your child. You can consult with school personnel. And a more specialized approach or professional help may be advisable.

Principle 5: Underachievers are not all alike.

We're back to The Underachievement Myth and its assumption that all underachievers are alike. Yes, all underachievers do share one common characteristic: They are all performing at a level far below their potential—a level far below what is expected of them and, usually, far below what they have accomplished in the past. But each of them has taken a different journey to arrive at that destination. And when we uncover the route they have chosen to get there, we can explain what really is motivating them.

Underachievers are vastly different in why they underachieve, how they underachieve, how much or how little support they receive at home, at school or from their friends, and the degree to which they are motivated to change.

Some underachievers are reacting to major problems within their family. Some are responding to difficulties with their peer group. Others are in a head-on conflict with the school system itself. And some may be experiencing problems in all three areas.

Some underachievers are tremendously upset about their falling marks. Others are a bit concerned. Others don't care at all. Some have clear explanations about why they are underachieving. Some are utterly confused and seem to have no idea. Others blame everyone but themselves. Some say they *want* to change and work hard, but do nothing about their stated intentions. And some won't even commit themselves verbally to trying harder.

But, you may be wondering, if underachieving kids are so individual and different from one another, how can I, the parent, possibly decide how to deal with the problem?

The answer is this: Although underachievers *are* different and every underachiever is unique, we can describe the most frequently seen types of underachievers. Based on a number of our research studies, we now can systematically differentiate types of underachievers. In other words, although we are careful not to label individuals, we can categorize *types* of underachievers. This is a great leap forward in our efforts to help these kids turn themselves around.

Principle 6: Different types of underachievers require different approaches to change their achievement patterns.

Now that we know that underachievers are not all alike, it follows logically that no single approach is successful in helping all underachievers.

If your child is underachieving, it is important to determine exactly what factors are contributing to *your* child's underachievement. Only then can you move on to the next step: determining how to help him or her achieve.

For example, if your son has a learning disability in math or spelling, he will certainly require specialized help in that area. And the sort of help he will require will be quite different from the kind of professional help it might take to reverse the academic performance of a child whose parents are going through a divorce.

Professional help is important. But getting the right kind of help requires an informed parent who can provide the professional with essential information about his child's situation.

Principle 7: Changing achievement patterns takes time.

Grades can plummet overnight. But they rarely rise overnight. Why?

All that has to happen for a grade to drop from 80 percent to 20 percent is not do the required work. But getting back up to 80 percent takes not only effort but extra time—time just to catch up. Meanwhile, the rest of the class is forging ahead. The student has to catch up on missed assignments, finish overdue projects and re-establish work patterns. It's like getting back into shape physically. Getting rid of that pot belly takes time, discipline and consistent effort.

But parents usually are impatient. Once their child promises to do better, they heave a sigh of relief and look for massive change right away. We strenuously advise taking a longer view of events. *Expecting rapid improvement is usually unrealistic and will only add tension to an already loaded situation.* And the damage may go further and have a negative effect on your child's improvement.

*   *   *

Those are The Seven Principles of Achievement we have stitched together over our many years working with underachievers and their parents. Let's look over the list:

Summing Up: The Seven Principles of Achievement

Principle 1:   School marks are determined by many factors.

Principle 2:   Intelligence is only one of many factors that determine school marks.

Principle 3:   It's normal for a student not to do equally well in every school subject.

Principle 4: You can expect temporary drops in school performance during certain transitions within a child's school years.

Principle 5: Underachievers are not all alike.

Principle 6: Different types of underachievers require different approaches to change their achievement patterns.

Principle 7: Changing achievement patterns takes time.

The Achievement Gap: Take 2

We have defined underachievement as a significant gap between potential and performance, a major discrepancy between what a student *can* do and what that student *is* doing.

Here's a list many professionals use to identify the gap between can do (potential) and is doing (performance):

1. *High ability, low marks*: This involves a discrepancy between scores on ability tests and grade-point average.

2. *Time*: This means that underachievement has persisted for a long period of time (more than one year, minimum).

3. *Age/performance discrepancy*: This means that achievement is two years behind grade level in at least one major subject and at least one year behind in another.

4. *Any sudden drop in performance*: especially if it is dramatic.

5. *The teacher's opinion*: In their day-to-day contact with students, teachers often form accurate opinions about student potential.

6. *The parent's view*: Your day-to-day contact with your child enables you to form opinions about the extent of your child's achievement gap.

7. *The student's view*: Although some underachievers underestimate their performance and others overestimate it, some underachievers have a clear view of the extent of their achievement gap.

Overachievers, Achievers and Underachievers

We have explained that underachievers are not all alike. They are, in fact, a maddeningly diverse group. In comparison, overachievers and achievers are much more predictable.

Comparing all three, overachievers are the most alike, achievers the second most homogenous group. And underachievers? They're the wild cards of the pack.

Judge for yourself:

Characteristics of Overachievers	Characteristics of Achievers	Characteristics of Underachievers
1. Highly responsible	1. Motivated	1. Submissive
2. Production-oriented	2. Positive self-image	2. Defensive
3. Seek approval from adults	3. Serious-minded	3. Easygoing and unassuming
4. Internally anxious and tense	4. Responsible	4. Considerate
5. Very hard-working	5. Dominant	5. Rebellious
6. Highly organized	6. Leaders in groups	6. Extroverted
7. Highly consistent	7. Self-confident	7. Alienated
8. Unable to relax	8. Self-disciplined	8. Emotionally inhibited
9. Driven	9. Future-oriented	9. Passive-aggressive
10. Self-worth defined by their achievement	10. Independent	10. Hostile and resentful
	11. Self-starters	11. Low aspirations
	12. Organized	12. Depressed, sad or pessimistic
	13. Consistent	13. Anxious or tense
	14. Socially aware	14. Distrustful

As you glance over the list for overachievers and achievers, you will find a certain consistency. *The dominant theme in the overachievers' list is the extreme*—of effort, of focus, of every kind of expenditure of energy, no matter how it is directed. Overachievers don't just work hard, they are *very* hard-working; they are not merely organized, they are *highly* organized.

In the achievers' list, the dominant themes are order and balance, the sense that things are under control but not overly controlled, a feeling that everything is in its place. Each of these two lists could describe a single person. In other words, one person could display every characteristic in each list.

Now look closely at the characteristics in the underachievers' list. Does anything look out of sync? Compare, for example, easygoing and unassuming with anxious or tense. It's impossible to be both at the same time, right? Or how about emotionally inhibited and extroverted? Or considerate and hostile? Not so easy to be both simultaneously.

The reason for these contradictions is that *underachievers are not a homogenous group.* In other words, underachievers come in all shades and colors and shapes and sizes.

Getting a handle on underachievers means looking for the differences among them, not for the things they have in common. We're back to the false assumption embedded in The Underachievement Myth—that all underachievers are alike. On the contrary, *remembering how different underachievers can be is essential to understanding and helping them.*

The Four Steps to Achievement

The key to achievement is motivation. No matter how much ability you have, no matter what kind of family you come from, no matter where you live, where you go to school or where you work, you'll never achieve anything unless you are motivated.

Where does motivation come from?

There is a simple, very strict recipe for motivation that allows no variations. The recipe contains four essential ingredients: *vision, commitment, planning and follow-through.*

- Each of these four ingredients is equally important.
- No substitutes, please.
- Each ingredient must be added in the correct order.

And every underachiever has got stuck somewhere along the way while putting together this simple but unalterable recipe.

Motivation: A recipe.

1. Vision

Motivated people have a vision. A vision of themselves in the world. Call it a goal, call it a mental image if you wish—the word doesn't matter. What matters is the idea. You see how you fit into the world, you can visualize a specific role that you wish to play.

Your vision reflects your values and beliefs. If your goal is making money, then material goods, comfort or perhaps social status are important to you. If your goal is developing a creative talent, then music, literature, theater, art or dance are important in your life. If your goal is finding a cure for cancer, then probing the mysteries of medical science is your abiding passion.

If you are competitive, your vision will incorporate a very particular goal image. That goal image will be one in which you achieve and excel in comparison with the achievements of others. When your vision includes a competitive edge, you gauge your level of commitment, planning and follow-through so that you perform well enough to match or outdo the competition.

If you don't have a vision, your level of motivation will fluctuate according to each situation. When people lack an overall vision, their level of motivation varies widely over time.

The fascinating thing about vision is that anyone is capable of having one—but if you don't have one, finding one seems impossible. We often meet kids in our practice who think finding a vision is an insurmountable task. These kids look lost. They *feel* lost. They think it's going to be impossible to find a vision. The very idea of developing a goal seems hopeless. And they've been looking! Downtown, in the mall, on television. . . .

Without a sense of vision, a student can be easily distracted and manipulated. Not working hard enough at school comes naturally because he or she has no concrete image that connects achievement at school with a future in life.

But for the student who has a vision, it seems the most natural thing in the world. Not that these students can eloquently describe their vision—or even articulate it clearly. But every day they act in accordance with their vision—and people around them readily sense it.

How does one develop a vision?

Some people seem to be born with a sense of purpose, but they're in a very small minority. Most people develop their vision gradually, through the various people and events and influences they are exposed to. They try on different ideas about who they are and want to become, and see what brings them personal satisfaction and what does not. It's a matter of risk and experimentation, over time.

Life is never static and the edges of a person's vision often shift and change. Sometimes more than the edges vary and the change is dramatic: When this happens, the person whose original goal is to be a ballerina ends up as an accountant.

What's important to motivation is the sense of purpose at each stage along the way, *not* possessing an ironclad goal that is impervious to growing and developing as life changes us.

2. Commitment

After vision comes commitment. Motivated people are committed. After they have formed a vision, a goal image, they commit to that goal by translating it into a sense of mission—a reason and purpose for going toward that goal. The mission is specific: getting an 80 percent average in order to qualify for entrance to a particular university; earning math and science credits so that they'll get into the technical college they've chosen; getting the required number of credits to apply to a particular community college.

Once a person is committed, that commitment becomes a powerful, dominating force in his life. It is always present. He may not always be aware of it. But if a buddy comes along and says, "Let's go *eg. boyfriend w/ money*

out to the pub tonight," his answer is likely to be, "I'm sorry, I can't. I have work to do."

A commitment to the vision is strong enough to withstand peer pressure and disapproval. Fellow students may goad her to skip classes, cut back on study time, take drugs. The student who has made the leap from a vision inside her head to a solid commitment to that vision will almost always refuse, even when her friends exert serious pressure. When the heat is on, the commitment to the vision comes to the surface and the message comes back, "I can't. It's there. I can't let it go."

What sustains commitment to a vision? Reinforcement, both internal and external. These students have a powerful internal sense that they will suffer serious personal loss if their commitment wavers. And they are encouraged and reminded of the commitment by parents, teachers and friends. As they progress toward their goal, the committed students will begin to experience the satisfactions of accomplishment. They will be able to see what they are accomplishing. They will be able to feel it. Their sense of commitment is reinforced.

3. Planning

Motivated people have a plan—a concrete plan of action. Their plan is specific, detailed, practical and realistic. It contains the steps that will get them where they say they want to go—as a matter of fact, where they believe they must go.

Any student can say he or she intends to study harder. But it's a safe bet that nothing will happen unless the student sets aside a specific time for studying and breaks down that block of time into specific allotments for individual subjects.

An effective plan includes clear priorities. For example, a student who is failing math probably will choose to tackle math first, not at the end of the evening when fatigue sets in.

An effective plan anticipates problems—both predictable and unforeseen. What if the student forgets to bring home the history textbook? Does he just throw up his hands and do no history homework? Or could he borrow a book from a friend down the street?

What if she's not sure exactly what was assigned? Does that mean she does nothing at all? Or can she telephone a classmate to find out?

An effective plan anticipates interruptions and distractions. Is she going to answer the telephone during her study hours? Has he declared the television off-limits? If not, extra time should be factored into the study schedule to compensate for time lost.

An effective plan includes a realistic, flexible allocation of time. A neat work schedule that allocates 20 minutes for each subject probably won't work. Some subjects always take longer than others. Estimating how long a project or assignment will take is a planning skill, and the student should learn from his past. How long did the last English essay take to research and write? If he stayed up half the night writing it, is it realistic to sandwich the next one between math and chemistry assignments? Wouldn't it make more sense to set aside an afternoon over the weekend to concentrate all his attention on that one project?

4. Follow-through

You can have a vision, you can have commitment, you can have a plan. But unless you follow through, you're just spinning your wheels. Follow-through is the final, crucial step toward achievement. Follow-through means *doing* it.

All the sophisticated vision, commitment and planning in the world won't get you anywhere if you don't act on it. Follow-through has to be focused—focused on your goal, focused on *achievement.*

Underachieving kids are notorious for generating lots of activity but no real action. Follow-through is not activity-oriented. It's achievement-oriented. It means action—specific action that leads to achievement.

How Do I Know If My Child Is Underachieving?

This is one of the central questions you will want to answer. Bearing the four ingredients of motivation in mind (vision, commitment, planning and follow-through), you can begin by answering the following questions:

- Are my child's school marks significantly lower than his or her previous academic performance?
- Has this decrease in marks occurred across most or all school subjects?
- Has this decrease in marks occurred over more than one school year?
- Do I have any solid evidence (e.g., teachers' evaluations) that my child has the potential to do much better?

If you answered "Yes" to any of these questions, your child may be an underachiever.

Before You Read Further, a Note of Caution

As you read the following chapters, it is important to keep in mind a couple of important cautions.

You are concerned about the academic performance of one or more of your children. You know your child better than anyone else. And, yes, you are an important player in your child's life. But you also have your own biases. You may even have contributed, albeit unintentionally, to the problem.

We hope this book will organize your thinking and guide you toward a greater understanding of your child. But you need to consider this: When dealing with underachieving adolescents, professionals are in a luxurious position compared to parents. *It is much easier for a professional to be objective about your child's academic performance because the professional doesn't have the enormous personal investment in your child's achievement that you do.*

Because of this investment, parents often can—and do—misinterpret what is going on with their underachieving teenager. As parents of adolescents, we know this all too well from personal experience. We *know* we cannot be objective within our own families. And one of our studies has borne out our personal experience: Only 40 percent of parents correctly identify the nature of their underachieving child's motivation. Turned around, this means *most parents had difficulty judging the reasons underlying their own child's underachievement.* You know the old saying: You can't drill your own teeth!

So our advice to all parents about to read this book is: Read it, enjoy it, use it to organize your ideas and increase your understanding. *But this book is no substitute for an assessment from a professional in an appropriate discipline. Seek outside, qualified confirmation.*

Two final notes before you read further: First, our descriptions of the different types of underachievers are based, in part, on the widely accepted 1994 classification system of the American Psychiatric Association (APA). However, the underachieving types we describe have many characteristics that are different from the APA system, are specific to the problem of academic underachievement, and do not imply abnormality.

And second, we have recently published a test called the Achievement Motivation Profile (AMP). This test, which we developed over 14 years of research on thousands of adolescents and adults, uses the ideas presented in this book to evaluate motivation and achievement not only of students but of adults in the workplace as well. The AMP identifies the key ingredients of a person's motivation—his or her vision, commitment, competitiveness, planning and follow-through. The AMP and its adult versions, the Sales Achievement Predictor (SalesAP) and the Motivation and Achievement Inventory (MAI), are available for use by qualified professionals from Western Psychological Services, 12031 Wilshire Blvd., Los Angeles, CA 90025-1251. Tel: (310) 478-2061. Fax: (310) 478-7838.

CHAPTER 2

The Coasting Underachiever

- "Everyone did lousy on that test. It's nothing to worry about, really. Don't worry, Mom. I'll do better next time."
- "Okay, you're right. I could have worked harder this term. I'll start fresh next term—get a new notebook, fill out my study schedule, a clean start."
- "It's too early to start studying. The term has just started!"
- "It's too late to start that project now. But it's not worth much, anyway."
- "The teacher is terrible. She doesn't explain anything."
- "I sit down to study .... but then my mind wanders."
- "No, we haven't had any tests yet, but I know I'm doing okay. Don't worry, Dad, I'll be sure to study when one comes up."
- "I remember more if I only study the day before the test."
- "That mark I got in math is a mistake. I'll straighten it out next week when I have a chance to talk to the teacher."
- "I can't do any homework tonight because I forgot my books at school."
- "I don't have any homework tonight."
- "I really hope I'll do better next time."

*   *   *

- "Kevin could do better if only he tried harder."
- "More effort is required if Jennifer is to realize her full potential."
- "Assignments have been handed in late and some not at all. Otherwise, it's a pleasure to have Christopher in my class."
- "It's a shame to waste all your potential, Patricia. Why can't you work consistently throughout the term?"

If ever there was an underachiever who fit The Underachievement Myth, it's this one. Coasting Underachievers*, the world's ultimate procrastinators, are constantly labeled lazy and unmotivated. And they're such an easygoing bunch, they may even call *themselves* lazy and unmotivated. Often as not, the label doesn't bother them a bit. Coasters are kids who got reasonable grades in elementary school without ever really working hard or consistently. They're forgetful about homework, they put things off, they say they fully intend to begin working harder "next time." They have a multitude of reasons (that is, excuses) for slipping grades. Yet in many other areas of their lives, they are good kids—trustworthy, easygoing, sociable.

Are Many Underachievers Coasters?

The Coasting Underachiever is the most common type of underachiever by far. *Thirty to 40 percent of underachievers can be labeled as Coasters.*

At what age do kids start coasting? The telltale signs of this pattern often emerge around the age of 9 or 10 in Grade 4 or 5, when kids start being assigned homework and projects that require planning, disciplined work and follow-through. But parents usually don't become seriously concerned until Grade 7 or 8, when the Coaster's

---

*   We gratefully acknowledge the pioneering work of psychologists Dr. Robert Roth and Dr. H. Arnold Meyersburg, who first identified this type of underachiever in 1963. They called this kind of underachievement The Non-Achievement Syndrome (NAS). Dr. Roth also completed subsequent research on treatment methods specific to this type of problem.

marks begin to slide and the gap between potential and performance becomes more glaring.

Are Coasters more likely to be the eldest, middle, youngest or only child in a family? No. They're distributed throughout families large and small.

Are more boys than girls Coasters? No—the ratio is 1:1.

Are Coasting Underachievers more likely to be Catholic, Protestant, Moslem or Jewish? No. We have found them in every religious group.

Do only middle-class white families produce this kind of kid? No again. We work with Coasters from many diverse cultural and racial groups.

Coasters come from families of all backgrounds and heritages. Coasters can be the first, last, middle or only child in a black, white, brown, Protestant, Jewish, Moslem, Catholic, Buddhist, rich, middle-class or working-class family. And they can come from European, African, Asian, North American, South American or Australian origins.

Coasters are everywhere and they are us. Like death and taxes, they don't discriminate or exclude. The Coaster is the ultimate equal-opportunity employer.

In our 25 years of working with Coasters and their families, however, we have found two common threads.

1. Coasters come from normal families.

We know that definitions of normal families are tricky these days. But the families that produce Coasters display few serious or unusual problems. They usually are not, to use '90s lingo, dysfunctional families. And Coasters are not antisocial individuals. Parents of Coasters often talk with pride about their Coasting child's trustworthiness, their drug-free life, their exemplary behavior socially and their consideration for others.

2. Coasters seem impervious to parental and teacher efforts to get them to achieve.

In spite of prolonged efforts, support and concern by both parents and teachers, Coasting Underachievers maintain their poor grades. This can be very frustrating for anyone who wants to help.

*   *   *

We've put together a long list of characteristics to help identify Coasters who saunter through our office door. Notice we say "saunter." These kids feel good about themselves and about life's possibilities. They're optimists. And they usually have lots of friends in addition to a loving, supportive family.

Let's look at 12 characteristics that set this Coasting optimist apart from other kids who underachieve.

Anatomy of a Coasting Underachiever

1. They procrastinate at home and at school—without concern.

The issue here is not that this kid puts things off. Most people procrastinate to a degree—and then proceed to worry about what they haven't done and what will happen unless they do it.

The Coaster *never* worries. (Well, almost never. We'll get to the "almost" later.) It's the lack of concern about procrastinating—not the procrastination itself—that is one of the hallmarks of the Coasting Underachiever.

"Did you hand in your project today?"
"My project, did you say?"
"Did you mow the lawn?"
"The lawn?"
"Have you done your homework?"
"Uh, homework?"

When you ask a Coaster a direct question about a specific task, the answer that comes back seems to reverberate:

Lawn? *Lawn . . . lawn . . . lawn . . .*
Project? *Project . . . project . . . project . . .*

A Coaster's basic motto is: "If it can be delayed *in any way* until tomorrow . . . or the day after tomorrow . . . or sometime later, then delay it." At the same time, they're masters of verbal compliance. One of their favorite sentences is a cheerful, "Yes, I'll do it later."

These are the kids who buy new loose-leaf notebooks at the beginning of every term and neatly fill in the study timetable at the back of the book. Then, for the first four or six weeks of that term, they do some work. They may even get a few decent grades.

But somewhere around the sixth week, something happens. This six-week period is a constant—in Toronto, in Oshkosh, in Southern California. Between the fourth and the sixth week, these kids just let go.

And they don't worry about it.

2. They give up—without concern. They get low marks—without concern. They lose interest—without concern.

Every once in a while, Coasting students perk up and show genuine interest or even excitement about a school project or course. But then the sledding gets tough and they quickly lose interest. Any sustained involvement over the long haul, any suggestion of having to sacrifice free time in order to complete the project, and the Coaster abandons ship (jumps sled?). And they show no concern about what might happen—or not happen—as a result of giving up.

Here is a typical conversation between a Coaster and her frustrated parent:

Parent:	"I don't understand. You started with such energy. You seemed really interested in that course. And now you can't be bothered with it any more. What happened?"
Teenager:	"I don't know. And besides, I wasn't really *that* interested."
Parent:	"But you did some good work back at the beginning!"
Teenager:	"Yeah, well, I guess I just lost interest."
Parent:	"But what turned you off? Was it the teacher?"
Teenager:	"No, actually the teacher's pretty good."

Parent:	"Was it the other kids in the class?"
Teenager:	"No, they're okay."
Parent:	"Was the work boring? I know that anything boring turns you off."
Teenager:	"No, it wasn't *boring* . . . I really don't know. I guess it's just that I stopped doing my work."
Parent:	"You don't even seem concerned about your change of heart."
Teenager :	(pause)"There'll always be other courses, Mom. Stop getting so uptight!"

There *are* a few select occasions on which a Coaster worries about poor performance. Four of them, to be precise. They are: (1) just before a test; (2) immediately before a deadline for a project or essay; (3) the day the report card comes home; and (4) just before parent-teacher night.

An imminent test or deadline causes the Coaster a brief, sharp moment of inner tension—emphasis on the brief. When their report card is due, Coasters talk openly about the family meeting they know will follow and how uncomfortable it can be. And just before parent-teacher night, they get noticeably uptight. They may even suggest you skip it: "Like, what's the point anyway, Dad, when you only get five minutes tops with any one teacher?"

Otherwise, Coasting Underachievers show little or no concern about their academic problems. As in the following conversation:

Counselor:	"So you barely passed your English course. How do you feel about that?"
Student:	"Oh, I suppose it could have been better. But I know now what happened. You see, I hadn't read a couple of the books. I was praying they wouldn't be on the test. But I got nailed. There were more questions on those books than on the ones I did read."
Counselor:	"How are you going to deal with your parents?"
Student:	"Oh, I'll just explain that next time, I'll try to

> read all the material before the test. They'll be a
> little upset at first. But in the end, things will be
> okay."
>
> Counselor: "So you're not all that worried about their reac-
> tion?"
> Student: "No, not really. They've been pretty good about
> this kind of thing before."
> Counselor: "So overall you don't feel that bad?"
> Student: "No, not really. I know I can do better next
> time."

"I know I can do better next time." For the Coasting Underachiever, hope springs eternal. And in the meantime—*don't worry, be happy!*

3. They have selective memories. They remember what they want to remember—and forget everything else.

Coasters know exactly what movies are showing at which theaters and who's starring in them. They know precisely how much money you owe them to the last penny. They know all the baseball box scores for the local team and they're experts at calculating batting averages.

But they're failing math. In fact, they have no idea what the math test is going to cover. And their assigned chores around the house? Forget it. They can't remember them from one day to the next.

This is not a neurological problem. This is a finely honed, *selective* use of memory.

4. They make sincere-sounding statements of intention— but don't follow through.

This kid's favorite day of the week is Monday. Especially if today is Tuesday, Wednesday or Thursday. Monday promises to be a good day because it will give them a chance to start fresh. A new week, with lots of time to start from scratch.

When Coasters make statements about improving their future performance, they're perfectly sincere. They mean what they say when they say it. But their intentions are written on water.

Consider the following conversation. Does it sound familiar?

Father:	"We were very surprised when we saw your geography mark on your report card. We thought you were doing much better. You say you're disappointed too—am I right?"
Student:	"Yup."
Mother:	"This isn't the first time this has happened."
Student:	"Well, not exactly in the same way. This is the first time for geography."
Father:	"You know what your mother meant. This has happened before in other subjects. This is becoming a familiar pattern and we don't like it. What do you intend to do?"
Student:	"Well, first, I have a plan."
Father:	"What sort of plan?"
Student:	"I'll study much more next term. That should make a mega difference."
Father:	"We've heard *that* before."
Student:	"Yeah, but it's going to be different this time. I plan to study geography every night even when I don't have homework."
Mother:	"Sounds good. I hope you carry through on it."
Student:	"I will. Can I go now?"
Father:	"Hold on a minute. You said you had a plan."
Student:	"You mean about geography?"
Father:	"Yes."
Student:	"Well, if I work more in geography, I *know* that I'll do much better. That's my plan!"

What do you suppose really happened next term?

The Coaster re-registered for geography and worked harder for the first six weeks of the term. Then he slacked off. His final geography mark was only slightly better than it had been before.

The frustrating thing about having a Coaster in the family is that they're very convincing when they promise future change. But their sincere (well, sincere-ish) intentions evaporate because they don't have a detailed plan. "Working more" in geography is a vague commitment, not a genuine plan.

5. They are easily distracted from school work and chores—but concentrate intensely on personal interests.

A phone call from a friend while they're doing their homework, a TV program that *must* be watched—and it's all over. A Coaster's concentration has been broken and he rarely gets back to work.

Here's a typical conversation with a distractible Coaster:

Counselor: "So you weren't able to get to that law project?"

Student: "No, although I really intended to do it."

Counselor: "What happened?"

Student: "Well, I sat down to study, but then I realized that my room was too cold. So I went to adjust the thermostat and the phone rang."

Counselor: "I see."

Student: "Well, it was a friend of mine. I told her I couldn't talk because I had to work on my Law and Society project, but she said it would only take a minute."

Counselor: "And what did you say to her?"

Student: "I let her start, and that was a mistake."

Counselor: "You mean it ended up taking longer than you expected?"

Student: "Actually, much longer. How did you know?"

Counselor: "I suppose because this type of thing has happened before. You don't seem too upset that her telephone call threw you off your plan."

Student: "Well, I figured I could always study later."

Parents often try restricting telephone calls during study hours. This does help. But the distraction problem doesn't go away quietly. Coasters find other things to distract them—their radio, tape deck ("Don't worry, Dad! I can concentrate while I'm listening to music. In fact I *need* it to study!").

And when it comes to non-school activities such as sports or music, Coasters often show remarkable determination and perseverance. They will spend many concentrated hours searching for a particular tape or disc, make detailed plans months in advance for concerts, spend hours playing soccer or hockey or basketball. All of these activities require sustained commitment, planning and action. Coasting Underachievers certainly do not lack the ability to concentrate over long periods of time. They just don't use this ability on school and home responsibilities.

6. They tend to overestimate their academic performance.

Does this conversation sound familiar?

Counselor: "So you got your report card this week. How did you do?"

Student: "I didn't do as well as I expected. It was kind of weird."

Counselor: "Weird? What do you mean?"

Student: "I thought I was doing much better in math. It's got to be a mistake on my report card. Don't worry about it. I'll talk to the teacher—I figure the mark is probably wrong."

Counselor: "How did you do in math?"

Student: "I barely passed it—and I *thought* I was doing much better than that."

Counselor: "How much better?"

Student: "I was averaging around 65 percent before the mid-term."

Counselor: "Okay. And how did you do on that last test?"

Student: (pause)"Actually, now that I think about it, I didn't do real well on that test."

Counselor: "What mark did you get?"
Student: "Not good. I failed it."
Counselor: "And how much was it worth?"
Student: "I guess a lot more than I thought."

7. They offer vague explanations for their poor academic performance.

"How have you been doing this year?"
"Well, if you go by grades, not too well. But in general I'm okay."
"How's French going?"
"French? French could use a little sprucing up, I guess."
"How are you doing in history this term?"
"Oh, history's decreasing."

Note the use of the passive voice: "History is decreasing." (*Right. I can see it over there on the other side of the room and it's definitely gone down.*) Note, too, the vague, generalized language. Coasters rarely provide specific information about the status of their courses. "Everything's okay—don't worry, Mom!" is their refrain. When you press them, details emerge only with a lot of prodding.

8. They have a ready supply of plausible excuses.
We all fall back on excuses from time to time, especially when we're late or haven't followed through on a task we promised to do. And every type of underachiever uses excuses occasionally for poor performance. But the Coaster is a specialist in excuses. Here are some of our favorite Coaster excuses:

- "I can't seem to get up in the morning."
- "I have to be in the right frame of mind to study."
- "I really hope I'll do better next time." (*Underline "hope" and "next time."*)
- "I don't have to work yet—the term has barely started."

And then there's:

- "It's useless to start studying now—it's far too late in the term."
- "I guess I just lost interest."
- "The textbook is terrible. I can't understand it—*nobody* can."
- "I study about 30 minutes a day. That should be enough."
- "I just don't take good notes."
- "Everybody did lousy in that course this time."
- "Other kids don't let me concentrate." *(Message: "The computer put me in a class with my friends. Forget it. It's over.")*
- "I flunked the test because I studied the wrong material."
- "I can't do my homework because I forgot my book at school."
- "I didn't hand in my project because I forgot it at home." *(These last two are known together as the home-and-school theory of underachievement.)*
- "I didn't do well because I must have made some stupid mistakes." *"How did you come to this conclusion?"* "Well, I didn't do well." *(Notice the deep thinking going on here.)*
- "I can't study at home—it's too noisy."
- "I can't study at the library—it's too quiet."
- "Other kids cut class too!"
- "I sit down to study—but then my mind wanders."
- "The teacher never explains things."
- "I know I said I'd check with the teacher. I did go to see her but she wasn't there, so I left."
- "The reason I did poorly is because I never knew we were having a test that day."
- "I don't have to start studying for the exam *yet*. I remember much more if I really cram the day before." *(True—you have much less to forget.)*

- "The reason I failed that course is because I thought I had already dropped it."
- "Somebody stole my book the first week of class, so I couldn't study much for the test."
- "I went to the library to get the book I need for my project, but it was already taken out by someone else."
- "The reason I don't have my essay ready is because my computer crashed."

We've saved our all-time favorite excuse for the end of this list. It's very powerful. It stops everyone who hears it dead in their tracks. Usually some eloquent body language accompanies it. Both shoulders moving is a favorite. It goes like this:

> "How come you didn't do well in math?"
> *"I dunno."*
> "How come you didn't finish your project?"
> *"Beats me!" (Message: "I don't know. And I tell you what. Until I do know, I suggest we drop this subject. When I find out, I'll give you a buzz. Don't wait up.")*

Coasters offer these excuses as *explanations* for their poor marks. The implication is that forces beyond their control have interfered with their sterling intentions.

9. They go through a predictable work cycle each term.

Every term, sure as spring leads to summer and autumn leads to winter, Coasters move through predictable phases and seasons. Every term, they complete a full cycle. And each cycle has eight phases, each with a season of its own.

Phase 1: The Season of Good Intentions

At the beginning of each term, brimming with optimism, Coasters buy new notebooks and appear to be positioning themselves for change. The Season of Good Intentions is characterized by hope, promises and energy. Parents are often excited by this—and pray that this is indeed a new Season of Achievement.

Phase 2: The Season of Early Promise

During the first four to six weeks of each term, Coasters attend classes, take some notes and work on homework and projects. Their initial work is judged acceptable or even above average. If they continued working at this pace, they would do well.

But, of course, they do not.

Phase 3: The Season of Coasting on Accomplishments Past

You know that the Season of Coasting on Accomplishments Past has begun when the student says things like, "I don't have to study that— I did well on it earlier this term." Or, "I won't hand that in. But it's okay because I'm already doing well in that course."

Coasters seem to believe that early accomplishment will automatically continue whether they continue to work or not. During this phase, they miss a few classes, may not hand in all assignments and put off preparing future work.

Phase 4: The Season of Escalating Excuses

For each abandoned project and incomplete assignment, the Coaster offers a companion excuse. An increasing flow of excuses is a clear sign of decreasing effort and plummeting performance.

Phase 5: The Season of Shock/Horror and Soul-Searching

This usually happens when they fail or almost fail a test, or get a sharp warning from a teacher about an overdue project. At first they are genuinely dismayed, realizing they can no longer assume that early efforts are enough to maintain their earlier average.

Phase 6: The Season of Renewed Effort

Now they become frantic and start to cram. Coasters tend to believe that a well-timed (limited) effort can erase weeks of work limbo.

Phase 7: The Season of Resignation
This begins the day the report card arrives. The Coaster can no longer continue to hope that things will improve.

Phase 8: The Season of Amnesia
This follows hard on the heels of the Season of Resignation. Coasters quickly forget the cycle they have completed during the term. They await term break with renewed hope, believing that the next term will bring better marks. But the Coaster is doomed to repeat the same pattern in the new term.

10. They don't respond to rewards or punishments.

The parent dangles the keys to the family car in front of the 17-year-old and says, "It's yours for the asking on the weekend if you pull up your grades to a 65 percent average." The kid begins to salivate as he thinks about cruising around in the car with his friends. For a month or maybe even six weeks, he works. He pulls his average up to 66 percent. But then the old pattern sets in, and his marks plummet. He doesn't like the fact that he can no longer use the car—but he soon shrugs it off and goes back to hitching rides with friends or taking the bus or subway.

Rewards and punishments are effective in changing Coaster behavior only over the short term.

Over the 25 years we've been dealing with Coasters, we've encountered a long list of rewards and punishments imposed by teachers and parents who are frankly desperate to light a fire under the complacent Coaster. Many of the things on this list are not new. In fact, they may remind you of some of the methods your parents used on you or your problem brother or sister.

Here they are:

Rewards and Punishments We Have Known

POSITIVE INCENTIVES (A.K.A. BRIBERY)

By Parents: "You can use the car on weekends if you get just one term's worth of decent grades."

By Parents: "You can't go out until you've done your homework."

By Parents: "Why don't we hire a tutor in math?"

By Teachers: "If you do well on your class assignments during the term, you'll be exempted from the final exam."

NEGATIVE INCENTIVES (A.K.A. PUNISHMENT, NAGGING, GUILT)

By Parents: "You're grounded for life—or until you bring home one decent report card. Whichever comes first."

By Parents: "When *you* start taking some responsibility for your school work, *we'll* stop reminding you about it!"

By Parents: "Do you have any idea what your terrible grades are doing to your father's blood pressure? Do you care?"

By Teachers: "If you fail to hand in your assignment by Friday, you will have a detention. And you will stay right here in this room until you've completed it!"

By Teachers: "No student with incomplete assignments will be eligible to try out for the football team."

By Guidance "How about enrolling in a study-skills program
Counselors: after school?"

Do any of these motivational techniques (or manipulative ploys) work? And if they don't work, what's a parent to do?

Let's go over the list.

- The family car offer: It works for a few weeks, as we've already described. Then student *and* parent return to square one.

- The going-out offer: Coasters will race through their work so that they can go out. And the predictable happens: Quality is sacrificed—big-time—to speed. They finish quickly, but turn out incomplete or inadequate work.

- The tutor offer: Coasters heartily resist the idea of hiring help (*"Oh Dad, I'm sure I can handle it myself!"*), but once they begin working with a tutor, their marks usually do improve. Once tutoring ends, however, the old work patterns return like a bad smell.

- The final-exam exemption: Coasters typically respond with increased effort for the predictable four- to six-week period. Then they slack off, with the usual results.

- The grounding threat: Grounding, cutting back on allowance, curfews, use of TV, audio equipment or telephone are all variations on the same theme. Coasters are not fighters and tend to comply. But their grades rise only slightly.

- The nagging approach: Many parents seem to believe that repeated reminders will have a cumulative effect, and that their Coasting teenager will suddenly spring into action. Unfortunately, the opposite usually occurs. Kids simply tune out and turn off.

- The guilt trip: As kids go, Coasters are relatively sensitive and considerate souls. They notice their parents' discomfort and it bothers them, up to a point. But it doesn't upset them enough to goad them into changing.

- The detention threat: Coasters are not outwardly rebellious. They sit out detentions, albeit a bit grudgingly.

- The course-changing ploy: Coasting Underachievers are notorious for making guidance appointments to drop or change courses they've done little work in. Typically, Coasters deal with the new course the same way they dealt with the one they've just dropped. And now they have an added excuse: They were already behind when they joined the class! How could anyone expect them to do well?

- The study-skills suggestion: This just wastes energy, because many Coasters know full well how to organize their work. But they don't translate their knowledge into action. And those who don't have study skills won't use them if they're taught them.

So what's a parent to do? Does *nothing* work?

Many of the above techniques *do* work—and they work well—for other types of underachievers whom we describe in subsequent chapters. But they do not, in general, work well for Coasters. What *does* work is described later in this chapter under the heading A New Course of Action.

11. They exhibit general contentment with themselves and with life.

Remember the list of characteristics of underachieving kids in Chapter 1? Remember unassuming and easygoing? This is the person we were talking about. This is a teenager without angst. She's happy with herself and with her life in general. Her theme song could be the reggae hit "Don't Worry, Be Happy."

Coasters are not depressed, anxious, angry or argumentative. They're easygoing, considerate people who like to be liked.

They don't complain about their family or their friends. They may even praise their parents for their support and for providing a loving, comfortable home. The only time they get a bit edgy is around examtime, report-card day or parent-teacher night. Otherwise they appear serene and content. Mental-health practitioners would judge Coasters to be psychologically healthy.

12. They are unconcerned about the future.

A teenager walks into our office and we say, "How old are you?"

"Fifteen," he replies. "Add on 10 years," we say. "Zzzzzzt! You're 25 now. What sorts of things do you see yourself doing when you're 25?" A blank look clouds his face. *"Twenty-five?"* (*Message: "I can't tell you about Saturday! How can you expect me to think about 25?"*) So we soften it a bit and say, "Okay, how about five years from now? You're 20. What do you think you'll be doing?"

The face relaxes a bit. He can handle this one, maybe. "Okay. Well, I'll probably still be living at home . . . Uh, how old are you when you graduate from high school these days?"

He's asking us! This kid does not fret about tomorrow.

That's the Anatomy of Coasting Underachievers as we have known them over 25 years. We hope the preceding pages make Coasters as real to you as they are to us.

Let's glance over the list of characteristics.

Summing Up: Anatomy of a Coaster

1. They procrastinate at home and at school—without concern.

2. They give up—without concern. They get low marks—without concern. They lose interest—without concern.

3. They have selective memories. They remember what they want to remember—and forget everything else.

4. They make sincere-sounding statements of intention—but don't follow through.

5. They are easily distracted from school work and chores—but concentrate intensely on personal interests.

6. They tend to overestimate their academic performance.

7. They offer vague explanations for their poor academic performance.

8. They have a ready supply of plausible excuses.

9. They go through a predictable work cycle each term.

10. They don't respond to rewards or punishments.

11. They exhibit general contentment with themselves and with life.

12. They are unconcerned about the future.

And now, as they say at the Oscars, may we have the envelope please? The answer inside will determine where you and your child go from here.

And the question is: How similar are my child's characteristics to those of the Coasting Underachiever?

Parent Checklist

1. Does my child procrastinate about chores assigned at school and at home—without strong concern?

   Yes___ No___ Don't Know___

2. Does my child lose interest quickly or fail to complete tasks at school or at home—without strong concern?

   Yes___ No___ Don't Know___

3. Does my child constantly forget school tasks and home chores—but have no trouble remembering things he wants to do?

   Yes___ No___ Don't Know___

4. Does my child constantly say she intends to improve her performance at school and at home—without following through?

   Yes___ No___ Don't Know___

5. Is my child easily distracted
   from home and school
   chores—but fully capable of
   concentrating on other
   things?

   Yes___ No___ Don't Know___

6. Is my child a master of
   inventive excuses about
   incomplete school and home
   chores?

   Yes___ No___ Don't Know___

7. Does my child explain his
   poor performance at school
   with vague generalizations?

   Yes___ No___ Don't Know___

8. Does my child regularly
   overestimate school grades?

   Yes___ No___ Don't Know___

9. Are rewards and punishments ineffective over the
   long term in changing my
   child's academic performance?

   Yes___ No___ Don't Know___

10. Does my child seem content
    with herself and her life in
    general? (i.e. not anxious,
    not sad, not a behavior
    problem)

    Yes___ No___ Don't Know___

11. Does my child appear
    unconcerned about or
    unaware of the future?

    Yes___ No___ Don't Know___

12. Does my child go through a
    predictable cycle every term
    with good intentions at the
    beginning and poor grades
    at the end?

    Yes___ No___ Don't Know___

If you answered "Yes" to nine or more questions, your child's characteristics may be similar to those of the Coasting Underachiever.

What's Really Going On with the Coaster?

Now that we've described Coasting Underachievers in considerable detail, and you've assessed *your* child in light of our description, let's take a look at Coaster behavior patterns.

As Henry Higgins (of *My Fair Lady* fame) would have said, "What the devil is the matter with her?"

What makes Coasters run (or, more to the point, not run)?

Why does the Coaster drift on down the road, operating on cruise-control, despite rewards, punishments, concern, help, encouragement—and second, third, fourth . . . *10th* chances?

And, you well may be thinking, let's hear some solid evidence that Coasting Underachievers are *not* lazy and unmotivated. Prove to me that The Underachievement Myth holds water when it comes to these kids. Because they sure look lazy and unmotivated to me!

Where Does Coaster Behavior Come From?

Fifty years before Sigmund Freud was born, William Wordsworth wrote, "The Child is father of the Man." The assumption that early childhood experiences determine adult behavior and govern the adult psyche is fundamental to studies of human development.

Because this is so widely accepted, parents of Coasters, quite naturally, tend to beat their breasts with the cry, "What did I do wrong? How have I failed as a parent?"

As we have said, Coasters usually come from caring, stable families. Parents of Coasting Underachievers love their children and work hard to instill in them a sense of responsibility about school, family and life in general. They provide decent role models of behavior for their children.

Because they seem to have done all the right things, parents of Coasters think that everything ought to fall into place. Surely care and decency at home should automatically produce responsible achievers, should it not?

Generally, they are right. The reasons Coasters behave the way they do certainly cannot be explained by lack of support and encouragement at home or by early childhood difficulties. Much more subtle stuff underlies Coaster behavior.

One subtlety is this: *Parents of Coasters tend to be uncomfortable with conflict, direct expressions of anger toward their child, and confrontation.* They may fear this could lead to a break in the relationship or change forever the positive qualities in their families. They also may "hover" a lot—fearing that unless they assume day-to-day, hands-on responsibility for their child's school achievement, their child will slip between the cracks and fail.

"What?" you may be saying. "Fear of conflict and confrontation? That's certainly not our family you're talking about! We experience conflict every day around school issues. I'm constantly asking, reminding, begging, bribing or punishing my daughter for her poor grades!"

Please bear with us. The kind of conflict parents of Coasters avoid is very specific. We will describe this in detail, later in the chapter. And you may find that what we say is pertinent to your situation.

A second subtlety underlying Coaster behavior is this: *The key to understanding the Coaster's present academic problems is the future and the Coaster's reactions to the future.*

"What?" you probably are saying again. "What kind of double-talk is this? The future is a key to my Coaster's underachievement?"

Let us explain.

The Mysteries of Coaster Motivation Revealed, or What Makes Coasters Not Run

Principle 1: Coasters are not lazy and unmotivated.

Coasters are prime fodder for The Underachievement Myth. Observers tend to accept as a given that Coasting Underachievers are lazy and unmotivated. Parents, teachers, counselors, friends—and

Coasters themselves—assume without question that The Under-achievement Myth applies to Coasters.

But labels have a way of taking on a life of their own and losing their connection with what's really going on. You may be so used to labeling your Coasting Underachiever as lazy and unmotivated that you can't see what's really happening.

Stop looking at what your Coaster is *not* doing and look instead at what she *is* doing. A whole new world of understanding is about to open before you.

Principle 2: Coasters are highly motivated. \

Look at what Coasters do. They expend a lot of energy (passive energy, it's true) *not* doing what you and teachers would like them to do. Remember the Anatomy of a Coaster? One characteristic we noted is the Coaster's ability to concentrate when *he* chooses. When it comes to activities unrelated to school and chores, Coasters can be intensely energetic and focused.

And consider this: Do Coasters fail miserably? No! They scrape by with marks in the 50s or 60s. They rarely get into a position where they might be kicked out of school or forced to quit. They try not to make waves. They wish we'd stop bugging them and let them be.

They are, in short, motivated to just get by.

Principle 3: Coasters are achieving their goal.

Coasters are motivated to just get by. *Just getting by is their goal. So they are achieving their goal.*

Novel idea? Consider this: In the face of overwhelming pressure to do better from family, teachers, and even friends, the Coaster doggedly continues to just get by. This is not a sign of *lack* of achievement. It is, rather, an indication of a powerful, single-minded purpose and commitment to resist efforts to get them to change. For the Coaster, low grades do not *cause* a problem, they *solve* one. And what problem do they solve?

Principle 4: The Coaster's goal is to avoid more responsibility.
The problem that low grades solve is the unpleasant prospect of acquiring more responsibility. Achievement inevitably propels the achiever forward to greater challenges. More work, more demanding work, more responsibility, more independence, more adult tasks.

But Coasters are comfortable and warm at night. And frankly, my dear, they *like* their lives as they are. Remember the unassuming, easygoing kid whose theme song is "Don't Worry, Be Happy"?

This brings us to the next, crucial principle.

Principle 5: Coasters don't want to face the future.
Coasting Underachievers wish nothing would ever change. Underachieving gives them a good shot at maintaining the status quo, at slowing down the inevitable consequences of growing up. *Coasters underachieve because they want to postpone the future.*

Graduating from high school means facing up to what comes next. It means making serious decisions. Trailing along with sub-par grades, on the other hand, means that the comforts of dependence can continue.

How so?

Think about it for a moment. When your Coasting daughter produces another mediocre performance at school, do you applaud her for her confident step forward toward greater challenges—or do you wring your hands and decide she needs more help?

You do the latter, of course. And you continue to worry that your son will never be able to stand on his own two feet, despite the fact that he is a pleasant, trustworthy and popular boy. You fret about how he'll *ever* become a responsible adult capable of looking after others when he cannot so much as assume responsibility for his own school work.

Principle 6: Coasters are not fully aware of their goal.
Don't wait for your daughter to say to you, "I'm highly motivated to just get by because I'm trying to postpone the future and the responsibilities of adulthood." She's not fully aware that she has chosen this route in order to avoid the struggle for independence. This is why

Coasters are so filled with ready, plausible excuses for their Coasting behavior. "If only I hadn't misread that question, I would have done better." They believe their own excuses because they are not aware of their real motivation. This is why they seem so sincere when they claim that they want to do better.

Yes, they are hiding the truth even from themselves.

Principle 7: When Coasters abandon their excuses, change is possible.

What happens when Coasters realize they are not helpless bystanders to their underachievement? What happens when they recognize that their excuses are just that—excuses? What happens when Coasters accept responsibility for their mediocre grades?

In short, what happens when they realize that they are *not* lazy and unmotivated and never have been?

The answer is, change is now possible. It's possible because now they cannot escape the knowledge that they are and always have been at the helm—that they *choose* what they will do or not do, they *choose* whether they will study or not, they *choose* how much or how little they will study and in what ways they will study. And ultimately, they choose what their grades will be.

And they now realize that they have *always* chosen how they have studied and what their grades have been.

Confronted with this new knowledge, Coasters are face-to-face with the fact that their Coasting has been a choice.

- *Now* change is possible.
- *Now* it is possible to alter their study habits.
- *Now* it is possible to stop procrastinating.
- *Now* it is possible to find new ways of following through and completing school tasks.

And, most important, it is now possible to develop new achievement goals—and to pursue them.

Principle 8: Coasters may be forced to abandon their excuses through "crap detection." They must recognize their false assumptions and start seeing things in a brand-new way.

This process has been described by two well-known observers of the American educational system, Neil Postman and Charles Weingartner. In their book, *Teaching as a Subversive Activity*, they use the term "crap detection." They describe crap detection as the questioning of commonly held assumptions.

Crap detectors distinguish themselves by not automatically accepting what is commonly considered an unquestionable truth. Crap detectors thereby free themselves from conventional wisdom and can develop new directions and points of view.

For example: Many people assume that grades in school are a direct reflection of a student's intelligence. If you get good grades, you're smart, and if you get poor grades, you're dumb.

A crap detector who questions this assumption and does a little research will find that many intelligent people get poor grades, and many people with average ability get good grades. This opens up new, very different points of view. It is now possible to recognize the roles of effort, interest, organization, study skills, perseverance and other factors.

How does crap detection apply to the Coasting Underachiever?

Well, if Coasters continue to assume that they are lazy and unmotivated, there is little that they can do to change the pattern. But if they "detect the crap" in their excuses, they will begin to question whether they really are lazy and unmotivated. They will have to entertain a new point of view, for example the notion that they already *are* motivated—motivated to avoid achievement and to just get by.

But wait a minute. Are Coasters going to crap-detect their own excuses? Not on your life! So who *is* going to do it? The rest of us: parents, teachers, counselors, friends.

As a parent, you will immediately reduce your frustration level by focusing on your Coaster's behavior and doing a little crap detection of your own.

This parental crap-detection task requires a new course of action. We will get to this later in this chapter.

Principle 9: Coasters who finally abandon their excuses take increasing responsibility for their choices.

Coasting Underachievers behave in very predictable ways until their excuses crumble. But when this finally happens, they become less predictable. They may or may not procrastinate. They may or may not choose to achieve. They may or may not be as polite or cooperative as they were before. They may or may not accept their parents' expectations. They may not or may not be as calm and easy to get along with as before.

Although no one knows exactly what the outcome will look like, only now is it possible for them to choose achievement as a goal.

And the good news is, most do! Both our professional experience and our research show that when Coasters abandon their excuses and take responsibility for their choices, they usually choose to work harder and more consistently in school. And their efforts eventually pay off in higher grades.

But do all these Coasters choose to achieve in school? No, not all. Some decide they have other goals that are more important to them. Here's how one couple described their Coasting daughter's new goals:

Mother: "I still don't like the fact that Susan has decided to pursue a career in tourism. She barely finished high school. But both my husband and I have noticed something: She gives us straighter answers these days than she used to."

Father: "It's true. And the atmosphere at home is much more relaxed. We've also noticed that Sue is putting much more time in on her tourism assignments than she ever did on her high-school courses. (Chuckles.) It's almost as if she's making up for all those wasted hours."

Whether the Coaster chooses to achieve in school or finds other goals, he or she is no longer coasting and The Underachievement Myth is history.

Summing Up: The Mysteries of Coaster Motivation Revealed (What Makes Coasters Not Run)

Principle 1: Coasters are not lazy and unmotivated.

Principle 2: Coasters are highly motivated.

Principle 3: Coasters are achieving their goal.

Principle 4: The Coaster's goal is to avoid more responsibility.

Principle 5: Coasters don't want to face the future.

Principle 6: Coasters are not fully aware of their goal.

Principle 7: When Coasters abandon their excuses, change is possible.

Principle 8: Coasters may be forced to abandon their excuses through "crap detection." They must recognize their false assumptions and start seeing things in a brand-new way.

Principle 9: Coasters who finally abandon their excuses take increasing responsibility for their choices.

A Fresh Look at Coaster Behavior—Now That We Know What Really Motivates Them

Coasting Underachievers have dual goals, their *stated goal* and their *unstated goal*. Their stated goal is to do better, to achieve at higher levels. Their unstated goal is to work just enough to get by, to avoid responsibility and to delay having to face decisions about their future. Their behavior is consistent and persistent, even in the face of mounting adult pressure. They are doggedly committed to mediocre performance. They even have a plan—an unstated one—to allow "external forces" (irresistible forces beyond their control) to keep them from school work.

In light of these contradictory dual goals, let's take another look at Coaster behavior:

Why are Coasters unconcerned about procrastinating and failing to complete school and household chores?
Because, despite denials, they really want to put things off and avoid responsibilities at school and at home.

Why do Coasters constantly make sincere-sounding statements of intention to improve—and fail to follow through?
Because they have genuinely fooled everyone, especially themselves, about their desire to see things change.

Why do Coasters respond with vague generalizations when asked to present their plan of action?
Because their "plan" is written on water. If they really intended to pull up their grades, they would have a detailed plan of action.

Why are Coasters so adept at producing plausible excuses?
Because all excuses imply good intentions. Because excuses sound like explanations when in fact they merely describe what happened. Because excuses imply that Coasters are hapless victims of circumstance, not the architects of their own misfortune. Because excuses allow Coasters to maintain the illusion that they are motivated to achieve.

Why are Coasters not upset at mediocre grades? Why do they show no inner tension, no anger, no frustration?
Because their underlying motivation is to just get by—and they are succeeding in achieving their goal!

And now, let's do something about the Coasting Underachiever we have come to know so well.

A New Course of Action, or How to Make an Achiever out of Your Coaster

Step 1: Abandon The Underachievement Myth. Stop thinking about your Coasting Underachiever as lazy and unmotivated.

It won't be easy to suddenly see your child in an entirely different way. Old perceptions die hard. Until now, lazy and unmotivated has seemed a made-to-order description of your Coaster's all-too-predictable behavior. So expect to take time to get used to your new view.

But do this you must. If you don't, you'll find yourself falling into all the old familiar traps. Like trying to motivate your Coaster with rewards and punishments when you know all too well that incentives and disincentives just do not work.

Once you fully accept the fact that your Coasting kid is already strongly motivated—motivated to just get by—you can step into your new role as crap detector and uncover your Coaster's unstated goals—in other words, his or her underlying motivation.

Step 2: Start with the facts.

You can't expose a discrepancy between what seems to be and what really is unless you are armed with facts. Coasters are not good sources of facts about school work, timetables and so on. For starters, they haven't made it their business to stay on top of the facts. Second, their version of the facts about homework, term-paper dates and so on is probably incomplete and flawed.

So where do you go for the facts?

Step 3: Inform your Coaster that you will be getting the facts from the school.

Now you're going to encounter some real energy—the energy of resistance. *This* from your agreeable, lackadaisical child! As you embark on your forthright attempt to find out exactly what your child is responsible for in each course—plus what he is actually doing and not doing—your child will not be pleased.

However, open conflict with your Coaster will not accomplish anything and it *certainly* will not transform him into an achiever. To prevent serious friction between you and your child at this stage, you might broach the subject like this:

"You know I've been concerned about your school marks for some time. You continue to say you would like to do much better, and up until now, I've relied on you to get all the information about each of your courses and take full responsibility for your work. But for whatever reason, you've had trouble doing it accurately and consistently. So I've decided to help you in a new way—by getting the information directly from the school. This way, when we sit down to check your homework or talk about a project coming due, both of us will have our facts straight. I want you to know I'm not doing this to punish you or to embarrass you. I'm doing this because you say you want to do better and I want to help you do that. I promise you that once you really are able to shrink the gap between what you say you want and what you actually achieve, I'll be more than pleased to back off and let you carry the ball."

Step 4: Set up a structure to get the facts.

There are many ways you can get accurate information from the school about how your Coasting child is doing. Some high schools prefer to coordinate all information through one person, usually a guidance counselor. At other schools, you may have to talk to each teacher separately. Whatever you have to do, the idea is to get as much accurate information about course requirements, deadlines and the current status of your child's work as you can.

Be prepared for frustration. Teachers and guidance counselors usually are overloaded and under great pressure. Many are overwhelmed with serious problem students. They may not consider your Coaster much of a problem on the general scale of things: "Oh, she could do better, of course, but she's such a pleasant kid—a real pleasure to have in my class!"

Persist. This is *your* child. Do whatever needs to be done, spend the time, leave *another* telephone message that you called, until you get the information you need.

And what facts do you need? To effectively monitor your child's work, you need to know the following about each course:

1. *What are the course requirements?* This includes a complete accounting of marks for tests, projects, class assignments and so on. This is not as daunting as it sounds. Most teachers provide a detailed overview at the beginning of each course—which many Coasters conveniently misplace.

2. *What are the deadlines for each project, term paper, assignment, homework, etc.? What are the penalties for handing things in late or not at all?*

Allow your Coasting child to be part of the information-gathering system—at the beginning. But make sure you have a backup system. *Remember: Your child's main aim*—the force that drives him, the force that is always there—*is to just get by.* Put yourself in your child's shoes: If that were your aim, wouldn't you tend to "forget" about getting all the facts? Of course you would! So be prepared to bypass your child if the information-gathering system turns into information-gathering breakdown.

And don't get too upset if this happens. It's entirely predictable. Having a backup system ready will decrease tension.

Another key part of this home/school information network: You need a quick method of finding out when your child has not handed in a project or when she's done poorly on a test, before it's too late. A schedule at your fingertips will do the trick.

And, although you should persist because your child is important, don't set up the teacher or the school as your enemy. This too will defeat your purpose. Instead communicate with the guidance counselor or teachers about what you are trying to do for your child. If you approach them in the right spirit, they'll accept you as a partner, not an opponent, and even welcome your interest.

Step 5: Set up regular checks at home.

Now that you have a system for gathering the facts, you have what you need to set up a regular monitoring system at home. Ideally, this should occur every evening after your Coasting child finishes homework or projects. Sit down with your child and review both the quantity and the quality of the work done.

If two parents are at home in the evening, share this quality-control chore. If you are a single parent, you'll have to do this on your own. If you are separated or divorced, try to share all school facts with your former partner to maintain consistency when your child is visiting. Consider suggesting he or she read this book to give you the strength of a team approach.

Step 6: Learn the keys to Constructive Confrontation.

All roads lead to Constructive Confrontation, a term first defined in 1969 by Dr. Gerard Egan, a professor of psychology at Loyola University of Chicago and a specialist in human-relations training. Unlocking the keys to Constructive Confrontation is at the heart of our approach to turning the Coaster around and pointing her in a new direction.

What is Constructive Confrontation?

A confrontation is a face-to-face challenge of another person, one that is not easily avoided. It demands that the other person address a discrepancy in his thoughts, feelings or actions. And it requires an immediate response.

The distinction between Constructive Confrontation and the destructive confrontation most of us are much more familiar with is this: A person faced with a Constructive Confrontation will be forced to clarify the inconsistencies in his behavior. And it will result in greater closeness between the two individuals involved in the confrontation. This is, of course, in direct contrast to the perilous destructiveness of negative confrontations.

Secrets of Constructive Confrontation
(1) BE SURE YOUR MOTIVATION IS CONSTRUCTIVE.
Confrontations occur every day in every part of the world and every

segment of society. The vast majority are overwhelmingly negative. The confronter is mightily pissed off at someone and damn well wants to show them up. The confronter isn't interested in changing behavior. The confronter wants to get back at someone. He is motivated by revenge.

Consider the following confrontation:

Coaster:	"I said I was going to speak to the teacher. Well, I went—but she wasn't there."
Father:	"You've used that line before and you know it! Spare me the crap, pull-ease! I'm sick and tired of listening to your empty promises!"
Coaster:	"*What* crap? I went, didn't I? I did exactly what I told you I was going to do!"
Father:	(sarcastically) "So *now* what?"
Coaster:	(sullenly) "So now nothing. I can't do the assignment because I don't have the information."

Compare it with this one:

Coaster:	"I said I was going to speak to the teacher. Well, I went—but she wasn't there."
Father:	"So?"
Coaster:	"So I left."
Father:	"Okay. So you tried—but it didn't work out."
Coaster:	"Right."
Father:	"So I guess that means the ball game's over?"
Coaster:	(slowly) "Well . . . what else do you expect?"
Father:	(in a firm, controlled voice) "What else do *I* expect?"
Coaster:	"Okay, okay! What I meant was, what else could I have done?"
Father:	"Nothing—unless you *really* wanted to get the information from the teacher."
Coaster:	(in a conciliatory voice) "I *did*, but she wasn't there."

Father: "So what were your options?"
Coaster: "Well . . . I guess I could have gone back later."

In the first confrontation the confronter immediately blows up. He is frustrated and angry about his son's broken promises and he lets his anger rip. The Coaster's response is entirely predictable. First he becomes defensive. Then he retreats, shedding responsibility for his own actions as he does so. The confrontation ends with an impasse: Father and son are farther apart than they were when the confrontation began—and nothing has been accomplished. The immediate issue—getting an assignment done—has been neither addressed nor dealt with.

The second confrontation begins with the parent calmly but firmly mirroring back the information his son gives him. He continues this until his son tries to shift the responsibility for seeing the teacher from his own shoulders, where the responsibility belongs, to his father's shoulders. His father immediately zeroes in on this manipulative attempt. Still calm—but also firm—he refuses to let his son get off track, again by mirroring back his words ("What else do *I* expect?"). The son, confronted head-on, has to respond head-on, which he does ("Okay, okay . . . what else could I have done?"). The confrontation ends with the student, of his own accord, taking more responsibility for his actions.

(2) FOCUS ON THE FACTS.
Compare the following exchanges:

Exchange No. 1:
Father: "So how did the test go?"
Coaster: "Okay, I guess."
Father: "Okay? I thought you said you were going to do brilliantly, that you were really prepared this time."
Coaster: "Well, I was much better prepared. You *saw* me study."

Exchange No. 2:

Father:	"So how did the test go?"
Coaster:	"Okay, I guess."
Father:	"Tell me more about what happened, specifically."
Coaster:	"Well, I answered all of the questions."
Father:	"Sounds good. So why did you sound so unsure about it?"

The first exchange is much more likely to result in a defense of what the Coaster did "right" and not focus on the details of what actually happened. The second exchange allows the father to gather more facts before deciding how to proceed. Without facts, chances for accurate assessment and effective action decrease.

(3) INVITE YOUR CHILD TO JOIN IN SOLVING THE PROBLEM.

The message from you to your teenager should be: "Okay, you're having a problem. Let's try to figure it out together."

This is an invitation, not an accusation. Both you and your child recognize a problem and *together* you'll find a way to solve it.

Watch how the mother in the following exchange both confronts her daughter and invites her to discuss a problem:

Mother:	"I don't understand. Was the project due last week or not?" *(Mother confronts facts.)*
Daughter:	"Yes—*originally* it was, but the teacher gave us some extra time to hand it in."
Mother:	"Okay, so you have another shot at it. Do you really want to get it in?"
Daughter:	(somewhat annoyed) "What do you mean, do I really want to get it in?"
Mother:	(coolly) "Just what I said. Are you really interested in finishing this project? I just want to know where *you* are. If you don't want to hand it in, let's drop it."

Daughter: "No, no. I *do* want to get it in." *(Daughter takes responsibility for her own problem.)*

Mother: "Well, is there a problem with getting it done?" *(Mother invites daughter to explore the nature of the problem.)*

Daughter: "I guess I'm just finding it hard getting started." *(Daughter explores causes of her problem.)*

Mother: "How can I help?" *(Mother places onus on daughter to suggest solutions.)*

Daughter: (with a wicked smile) "How about writing it for me?"

Mother: (returns the smile) "Aside from that, how can I help?"

Daughter: "I guess if we talked about it a bit, I might be able to get started." *(Mission accomplished: Daughter proposes solution to problem.)*

(4) CONFRONT PROBLEMS WHEN THEY OCCUR: DON'T LET TENSIONS BUILD.
Confronting a problem when it's happening isn't easy. Most of us avoid confrontations whenever we can, because they require a lot of effort and they're emotionally draining. And, subconsciously, we hope the problem will go away if we ignore it.

Because we dislike confronting others, we avoid doing so when the issues seem minor. At the same time, we diligently store the things that bother us in our memory banks. And usually the situation does not improve, mainly because we haven't given the other person feedback about how we're affected.

As we continue to store rather than confront, resentment builds up inside. When we finally confront, the intensity of our reaction is often way out of proportion to what's really happening. So the focus of the confrontation becomes our *overreaction*, not the problem that triggered our reaction.

Think of the times in your marriage you chose not to say something about little things that bothered you. Instead you let them pass. Later, when something really upset you, you let loose. Whereupon your spouse pointed out how unreasonably you had reacted. *By delaying minor confrontations, we invite ineffective major ones.* The following exchange between a mother and her Coasting son is a good example of an overblown confrontation:

Mother:	"Max, I want to talk with you now about school."
Son:	"Do we have to right now? There's a basketball game on. How about waiting till later?"
Mother:	"I said *now!*"
Son:	"Gee, sounds real serious. What's up?"
Mother:	(heavy sarcasm in her voice) *"What's up?* I'll tell you what's up. I promised myself when this term started that I wouldn't say anything to you about your school work. And I've kept that promise for about a month now. But I can't stay silent *any longer.*"
Son:	"What's the problem?"
Mother:	(her voice rising) "What's the *problem*? You just said you have no homework. But when I asked you whether you were up to date in your courses you said you were behind in some."
Son:	"So?"
Mother:	"*So?* Are you serious? How can you be so calm about your school situation? You promised to do better and you're behind already. I should have said something to you earlier, but I kept my mouth shut. You sounded so convincing at the beginning of the term. But nothing has changed! In fact, if the amount of homework is any measure, you've probably slid even more. You're not doing *anything* right this term, nothing!"
Son:	"That's not true! I'm doing okay in *some* subjects."

The intensity and sweeping nature of the mother's accusations are the result of keeping her observations to herself. She hoped that the situation would improve. But it did not, and she got more and more frustrated. So when she finally dealt with the issue, her pent-up frustrations exploded in a torrent of generalized accusations. And her son reacted just as you would expect, defensively and combatively. And nothing was accomplished or solved.

Some wives and husbands are experts at this. Once a heated confrontation begins, both parties haul out unsaid, long-ago grievances for an airing: "And not only did you not follow through as you promised, *you did the same thing 14 years ago in Texas on our vacation.*"

It's emotionally satisfying at the time—what the ancient Greeks would call cathartic—but it doesn't accomplish anything. Usually what happens next is a heated argument about the facts—what *really* happened 14 years ago in Texas. People's memories play havoc with what happened way back when and the real, present problem is lost. Coasting Underachievers have trouble remembering what's happening with their *current* courses. What they did last term or two years ago is forgotten history. It's okay to point out patterns from the past but don't get stuck on these. *Stay with the facts right now or in the immediate past.*

(5) Confront strengths, not weaknesses.
Focusing on strengths that are not being used is a much more effective motivator than focusing on your child's academic weaknesses. Addressing your daughter's lack of follow-through, for example, might be handled as follows:

> "You know, dear, it's amazing to me. You've followed through on so many things in your life—like your dancing, for example. And in your English course. But in history, it's not the same. You don't follow through. It's really puzzling."

Now compare this:

> "You *never* follow through in history. What's wrong with you?"

Both examples confront the student with the fact that she is not completing her history assignments. But the first focuses on her *strength*, her proven ability to follow through in other situations, and contains an *invitation* to solve a problem ("It's really puzzling, I'm confused. Can you help me sort this out?").

The second confrontation not only focuses on her weakness, it implies there is something fundamentally wrong with her ("You *never* follow through . . . What's *wrong* with you?"). This parent is going for the jugular and attacking the daughter's fundamental sense of herself, not just her performance in one subject.

The importance of focusing on a person's strengths is a basic psychological truism. Children who are constantly criticized start to really believe there is something essentially wrong with them. On the other hand, children who are praised for their accomplishments start to feel good about themselves and believe in their own potential. Applying this to a confrontation with an underachieving child is just one illustration of how it works.

(6) BE SELECTIVE ABOUT WHEN AND HOW OFTEN YOU CONFRONT.
Like any extreme method of dealing with an unwanted situation, confrontation should be used judiciously. Don't confront your child on every issue. If you do, it will quickly lose its impact and effectiveness or, even worse, become negative.

And, too, if you can avoid it, don't confront when your son or daughter is feeling down or upset about something else going on in his or her life. Choose a day when things seem fine. Sure, there is never a perfect time to confront, but doing so when your daughter is distraught about breaking up with her boyfriend is not fair. And, conversely, don't spoil a special day—like your son's birthday or the day of the spring prom.

(7) BE PREPARED FOR THE CONFRONTATION TO INCREASE TENSIONS—OVER THE SHORT TERM.

Confrontations tend to heighten tensions—temporarily. And that's exactly what they are supposed to do. Nobody accomplishes anything without some inner tension. Done properly, confrontation is intended to increase Coasters' inner tensions just enough to propel them off their comfortable chairs.

Most of us avoid confrontations because of the anger and resentment they will force to the surface. Perhaps you have avoided confronting your Coasting Underachiever for this reason. Perhaps you are reluctant to create resentment in your child, especially since *you* will be the target of that resentment.

If this is true, spend some time thinking about exactly what it is that makes you uncomfortable about your child's anger. Are you afraid of being the bad guy? Are you worried that your Coasting child will reject you? Fears like this are overblown. Sure, your child will grumble and complain and possibly even lash out at you, but he's not going to reject you holus-bolus over your legitimate and realistic assessment of his school situation. In his heart, he knows you're right. The tension created by this confrontation will be constructive—and short-lived.

Step 7: Be clear about who owns the problem.

Coasting Underachievers are such masters at not following through that their parents often fall into the responsibility trap. How many times have you felt responsible for reminding your Coasting son about his homework or about a deadline for a project? How many times have you rescued your Coasting daughter at the last minute by typing her half-finished paper? How many times have you got so excited about your child's project that you did most of the research?

These are examples of shifted responsibility—responsibility shifted from one person's shoulders to another's. It is all too easy to let this happen. How can you not rescue your Coasting son when you have worked so hard to get him this far in his project? Surely the least you can do is finish the last section.

The problem with this approach is that *you're* assuming responsibility for your son's school performance. And *he* is not.

And who should own the problem? *He* should.

Does this mean you should refuse to help if your Coasting child asks for your assistance? Of course not. But helping doesn't mean taking over. Nor does it mean being held hostage to half-baked efforts, total lack of planning, last-minute scrambles.

Here is a rule of thumb to determine whether you are taking on too much responsibility for your Coaster. Ask yourself the following question: Who is more worried about this project—my son or me? If the answer is yourself, you are taking possession of a problem that your child should own.

Step 8: Don't accept pat answers at face value—keep probing!

"Did you do your math homework?" you ask. "Sure," your Coasting daughter replies. *Ask to see it.* Chances are she has done some of it. She may even have finished it. But she probably hasn't checked it for errors. Check both the quantity and quality of each assignment.

Checking up on your child's assignments is not the same as nagging (which is *not* effective). Checking up is a clean, one-time exercise. You look over what your child has done and see whether or not it is complete and whether or not it is a quality effort, one likely to pull in better marks.

Here is an example of a work-assignment check-up confrontation:

Mother:	"Okay, what's up with that math homework?"
Daughter:	"It's fine. I'm finished. I'm done for the night."
Mother:	"How good is the work?"
Daughter:	"It's fine."
Mother:	"Okay, I'd like to see it please."
Daughter:	"I *said* it was done. Why do you need to see it?"
Mother:	"That was our agreement. You said that you wanted to do better in math. So I'm checking your work."

Daughter: (in a resigned voice) "Oh, okay. I suppose I'll get it."

Mom checks the math homework and realizes her daughter has not completed every example. And she has made several errors. Here's how she *constructively* confronts her daughter:

Mother: "Okay. You haven't finished the exercise. And you've made several mistakes."

Daughter: "Right. I was going to finish those few examples tomorrow morning before class—and check everything through then, before handing it in."

Mother: (in an unruffled tone of voice) "Okay. So it wasn't totally finished as you originally said." *(She confronts a factual discrepancy.)*

Daughter: "Stop being so picky. What's the difference if I do it tonight or tomorrow morning?"

Mother: "Nothing, really, except that it sounds a lot like you operated before. But you know what? That's okay with me if you don't really want to get better marks in math."

Daughter: "I do. I said I would go over them!"

Mother: "You sound like you're getting annoyed at me. What did I do? All I did was ask you to tell me straight about what you already agreed to do. I'm even saying that if you don't want to do better in math, then I don't need to see your work. Just tell me that you *don't* want to do better and we'll drop the whole thing."

Daughter: (somewhat exasperated) "Okay, okay, I'll do those extra examples now if it makes you happy. Sometimes you get so picky!"

Mother: "Hold it! I'm only doing what we'd agreed to do. You sound like I've laid something on you—like I'm *forcing* you to do what we already had agreed

to do." *(Mother refuses to let her daughter shift*
responsibility onto her shoulders.)

Daughter: "Forget it, I'll do the work! Let's just stop talking about it."

Probing inevitably uncovers facts that don't wash. Once the factual
inconsistencies are laid bare, the parent's next task is to confront the
gaps in the facts, as the mother in the above exchange does so well.

Notice how this confrontation increases tension between mother
and daughter. It increases tension, but it does not cause an explosion,
thanks to the mother's cool and reasoned approach to the situation.
As we said earlier, a short period of increased tension resulting from
a confrontation is a good sign. Coasters need this elevated tension to
nudge them forward.

One of the most constructive aspects of the above confrontation is
the way the mother separates her aspirations for her daughter's performance from her daughter's own responsibility for her school work.
Parents often find it very hard to make this separation. This is why so
many parents of Coasters tend to take over for their children—with
predictable results.

Step 9: Approach every school problem by asking a systematic list of problem-solving questions.

In your new day-by-day relationship with your Coaster, you will
become a master of the art of gentle persistence. As problems arise,
you should be prepared with a mental checklist approach to problem-
solving. Here's a list of sample questions to ask your Coasting
Underachiever whenever a problem comes up. It's intended as a general guide to help you sort out particular problems.

1. Are you getting the grades that you want this term?
Your Coaster's answer will almost always be a resounding "No."

So why ask?

You need to keep asking this question because it exposes your
Coaster's dual goals—stated and unstated.

Coasters talk about their *stated goals*: to do better in school. In marked contrast, their behavior reflects *unstated goals:* to just get by and avoid taking on additional responsibility. And if you keep reminding them of their stated goals, it's easier to expose the discrepancy between their stated and unstated goals.

In our experience, parents of Coasting Underachievers *also* have two sets of goals. A parent's stated goal is to help their Coasting Underachiever become whatever their child wants to become. The parent's unstated goal usually involves their own aspirations and expectations for their Coasting child.

Parents *also* talk about their stated goals, while their behavior often reflects their unstated goals. It is very difficult for parents, especially parents of Coasters, to remain focused on their *child's* goals and not interject their own unstated goals.

The father of a 17-year-old Coasting Underachiever told us about a phone conversation he had with his son's prospective employer, a person the father knew through his business. The employer had called because he was seriously considering offering the son a summer job. The father, who was well aware of his son's Coasting pattern, took the phone call. Here is how it went:

Father:	"Thanks for calling, but my son isn't here at the moment."
Employer:	"Could I leave a message?"
Father:	"Sure."
Employer:	"Would you please have Brent call me as soon as possible? He has my number. It's about the summer job."
Father:	"Give me the number anyway. I'll make sure he calls you back."

Brent's father reminded him three times about returning the call, but Brent never did. And naturally he became increasingly angry with Brent because *he* had promised Brent would return the call.

The father's *stated goal* was to give his son a message and to have his son return the call. But he also had two *unstated goals:* (1) to ensure his son got a summer job, and (2) to avoid looking irresponsible in the eyes of his son's prospective employer.

And what about Brent's dual goals?

Brent's *stated goal* was to get a summer job. His *unstated goal* was to postpone returning the phone call, because he didn't really want the job.

We pointed out to Brent's father the dual set of goals both he and his son held. If Brent's father had recognized his own goals, and if he had asked Brent about *his* stated and unstated goals, he would not have allowed himself to get detoured by promising the prospective employer that his son would call.

And how would he handle the call in light of these new perceptions? we asked Brent's father. His reply:

> "Brent isn't in right now, but I'd be pleased to give him a message that you called."

Then he would say to Brent:

> "Mr. Smith called. I told him that I would pass the message on to you."

What else might Brent's father do, remembering that in this case, the goal is a job, not school grades? He might say to his son: "This looks like an opportunity for a summer job. If you call him promptly, you'll have a better chance of getting the job."

You may have a clear perspective on how crucial good grades and timely action are to your child's future. But you must keep firmly in mind that it is *his* goals, not yours, that determine his achievement. He owns the problem—and he ultimately must solve it. Trying to impose your goals is a waste of energy. It's his life—he's in charge, whether you like it or not. Your job is to advise and suggest, not take over. This means confronting your Coaster on the gap between stated goals (doing better in a course) and unstated goals (lack of follow-through).

2. If you're not happy with all your grades, which courses in particular are you not satisfied with?
This allows you to focus on *stated* areas of dissatisfaction. Let your Coasting child make the selection. Don't do it yourself. *Her* commitment is the issue. She must choose.

3. Do you want to do anything about any of these courses?
To answer this question, your Coaster must state—out loud—an achievement goal. Don't expect this to be a rock-solid commitment. The important thing is you have an definite, spoken statement on the record. In future confrontations, you can keep referring to this state- ment and use it as a focus for discussion.

4. If so, what's happening in these courses that you want to change?
This question ushers in the most tedious and time-consuming phase of the problem-solving process. It's called *taking stock.* You will have to laboriously seek out all relevant facts about each problem course, one by one.

Don't expect Coasting Underachievers to have these facts at their finger tips. Quite the contrary. Every time you ask them for informa- tion they'll have to dredge up facts they should have had long ago. Steel yourself for generalizations and vague answers to every specific question you ask, such as the following:

Father:	"Okay. So what are the requirements in math this term?"
Son:	"I think we have two term tests and a final exam. We also get some marks for homework."
Father:	"Did the teacher by any chance hand out a course description in which she listed the exact course requirements and breakdown of marks?"
Son:	"Oh yeah. The first day, I think."

Father:	"Where is it?"
Son:	"Let me think. (Pauses.) Probably in my math notebook."
Father:	"And where's that?"
Son:	"In my locker at school."
Father:	"Okay. Can you remember the breakdown of marks without looking at the teacher's handout?"
Son:	"No, not really, but I have a pretty good idea."
Father:	"And what's that?"
Son:	(long pause) "I guess I have to look at the course sheet."
Father:	"Okay. What do you suggest you do about that?"
Son:	"I'll get the sheet from my notebook tomorrow at school."
Father:	"Okay. Then tomorrow night we'll look at it together?"
Son:	"Sure."

Perhaps you can't repeat this drawn-out interrogation for *every* course that you and your Coaster identify as a problem. But in our experience with Coasting Underachievers, we've found that every bit helps. Focusing even on one course can carry over.

5. Don't accept vague statements. Pursue facts by asking specific questions.

Ask a Coasting Underachiever how she is doing in school and she'll often reply that she doesn't know because she hasn't got any grades back yet. Yes, she *does* know what the course requirements are. But there's no way of assessing how she's doing—you see, it's too early in the term!

This kind of exchange often affects parents just the way Coasters intend it to. They're frankly flummoxed. "Well," they muse, "I suppose that *sounds* reasonable enough."

But think for a moment about what the Coaster is really saying:

Just because the teacher hasn't graded the work yet doesn't mean that the student can't estimate how she is doing. How hard has she been working in that course? Is she behind the class? If so, how far behind? Does she understand the material? *All* of it? How many classes has she missed? What has she done about the material she doesn't understand? Anything? How much homework is incomplete? How good is the homework she has done? Have any projects been assigned? If so, how much work has she done on these projects? Is she studying the course material taking into account the type of tests the teacher said would be given?

Now *there's* a list of questions to ask your Coaster when she says it's too early in the term to judge how she's doing!

6. *What specifically do you need to do to get the grades you want?*

This is another intensely time-consuming phase of the problem-solving process. It is not enough for Coasting Underachievers to promise to do better or work harder. They need a detailed plan of action. And you'll have to repeatedly confront them to help them generate this plan. Remember, even though they say they want to do better, their unstated goal is diametrically opposed to any such thing. By exposing how little they actually have planned, you'll be in a position to question the validity of those plans. Then they'll *have* to choose whether or not to do more. As in:

Father: "Okay, you said you had a plan for your history course. What is it?"

Daughter: "I said I was going to read more."

Father: "When?"

Daughter: "What do you mean, when?"

Father: "When do you plan to read more history? During your free periods at school? At home after school? Before supper? Late at night? When?"

Daughter: "Dad, I can't tell you *exactly*. It changes every day. Sometimes it'll be after school, sometimes

	at school—*I* don't know!"
Father:	"Okay, so you don't know from day to day when it will be. How much time do you plan to spend each time you read history?"
Daughter:	"I don't believe you! How can I tell how much each time? That's impossible!"
Father:	"Well, each time you get together with one of your friends, you can tell approximately how much time you're going to spend with them. How come that's easy?"
Daughter:	"That's different. I know I have to be back at a certain time, that's all. Otherwise I'd spend more time."
Father:	"Okay, so you have some limits and you're able to stay within them. What limits can you set for history?"
Daughter:	"I told you. I plan to read more—but I can't say when or how long."
Father:	"So you don't have any set plan for when or how long. Do you know what material you'll be reading in history?"
Daughter:	"Sure. Whatever the teacher assigns."
Father:	"And you can't say what that will be yet. So I guess you can't say how much reading you'll be doing?"
Daughter:	"Right."
Father:	"And do you have any plans for the way you will read?"
Daughter:	(clearly annoyed by now at her father's persistence) "What do you mean—*the way I'll read?*"
Father:	"Well, do you plan to take any notes as you read?"
Daughter:	"Yeah, well, I thought about that . . . but actually I haven't decided yet. Depends what I'm reading."

Father:	"So let me see if I have this straight. You plan to read more in history, but you don't really know when . . . or where . . . or for how long—or in what way you will do this. Sounds to me like you really don't have much of a plan. Sounds almost as if you *think* it will happen, but you don't have any clear way of making sure it will happen. And that's okay if you really don't want to do much more reading in history anyway."
Daughter:	(frustrated) "That's not fair, Dad. I do, I do!"
Father:	"But you've done nothing different this term to guarantee it will happen. So . . . my guess is that it won't happen. Just don't keep telling me you have this plan. I don't hear a plan. I hear a hope."
Daughter:	(at her wit's end) "What do you want anyway, Dad? Do you want me to study night and day? Well, I won't do it!"
Father:	"I don't want you to study night and day and I certainly don't *expect* it. What I want is for you to stop telling me about this great plan to read more in history when you have no specific structure to follow. I'll be prepared for another 50 in history at the end of term."
Daughter:	(cornered at last) "Okay, okay. I'll start to set some time aside each night to read history. Satisfied?"
Father:	"I'm not asking you to do anything. Just be straight with yourself and me. If you say you want to read more, then set out a definite plan. Nothing gets done without a plan anywhere, in any kind of job. If you don't want to read more, for heaven's sake don't promise you will."
Daughter:	"Okay, I'll read each night."

Father: "Seven days a week?"
Daughter: (sarcastically) "Sure thing, Dad! That's proba-
                  bly what you'd want me to do. (Pauses.) No
                  reading on Friday and Saturday nights."
Father: "Okay, that sounds clear."
Daughter: "Can I go now?"
Father: "You sound as if I've been holding you prisoner.
                  I thought we decided to talk about school in
                  order to help you some."
Daughter: (sulkily) "That's true. But can I go, now, please?"
Father: "Well, I do have another question."
Daughter: (pouting) "I thought you would."
Father: "How long will you read each night?"
Daughter: "About half an hour. Okay?"
Father: "Will that get you the mark you want in his-
                  tory?"
Daughter: "Yeah, I think so."
Father: "Will you do anything with the material you
                  read in history?"
Daughter: "You mean like take notes or underline?"
Father: "Yeah, things like that."
Daughter: "Yeah, I guess so."
Father: "I *guess* so?"
Daughter: "Oh, *Dad*. There you go again. I *said* I'd do it!"
Father: "I really don't understand why you're getting so
                  annoyed with me. All I'm asking about is your
                  plan for history. I guess it's hard to deal with
                  because you really didn't have a detailed plan."
Daughter: "I *had* a plan. I just hadn't thought it out
                  clearly."
Father: "Okay. How will we be able to tell if the plan is
                  working?"
Daughter: "Well, we'll see at the end of the term, I guess."
Father: "And what if the plan didn't work—or you
                  didn't follow it?"

Daughter:	"Right. I know what you're getting at. You want to check it out before the end of the term, don't you?"
Father:	"What do you think about that?"
Daughter:	(resignedly) "I don't like it. But I guess it makes sense."

If just reading the above exchange gave you a tension headache, you're beginning to understand the kind of draining, demanding persistence that Constructive Confrontation requires. There are no shortcuts—sorry.

To analyze the above: The father confronts his daughter on her lack of a specific plan. He refuses to allow her to remain general and vague. By doing so, he heightens her inner tension by exposing the gap between her *stated* and *unstated* goals—without taking over or demanding that she fulfill his wishes. She is left with *her* problem. He has helped her confront it. Now *she* has some decisions to make. He has also increased the probability that she will confront her Underachievement Myth.

7. *What do you predict could go wrong with your plans?*

If you turn this question around and ask Coasters how *well* they are likely to do or how much they plan on doing, they'll protest that they couldn't possibly predict such a future event accurately. They'll say something like, "You never know what the teacher will throw at us."

When we asked how much work he was going to do for the remainder of the current semester, one Coaster replied as follows:

Coaster:	"I don't know what grades I'm going to get."
Interviewer:	"Yes, but I didn't ask you that. I asked how much work you're going to do for the rest of the term."
Coaster:	"Well, I can't predict that."
Interviewer:	"Why not? What could keep you from doing the

work you are planning on doing?"

Coaster: "Because you can't predict the future. I could
                walk outside right now and get hit by a truck."

Ask a Coaster to predict things that could go wrong with his newly
minted plans to do better and he'll tell you that everything will be fine
if he tries harder. Press further and he'll suddenly behave like a veteran crystal-ball gazer. Why, there are *dozens* of events that could
interfere!

Coaster: "I know I can do better next semester if I study
                more."
Interviewer: "Is there anything that could go wrong?"
Coaster: "Well, I could kind of get bored in English 4,
                just like I did in English 1, 2 and 3."

Make no mistake: Coasters know *exactly* how they are going to
behave, despite their claim that they can't predict the future.

*8. Given your stated goals, how can you counteract negative
forces standing in the way of your academic success?*
First, crap-detect by exposing any illogic in the Coaster's explanation
about "unavoidable" blocks. Then request solutions. As in:

Mother: "You say that one of the reasons you didn't do as
                well as you wanted to in history is because you
                kept forgetting when your assignments were
                due." *(False assumption: Memory loss hinders
                performance in history.)*
Son: "Right."
Mother: "Well, you're taking history again. What do you
                think will happen this time round?"
                (Requesting a prediction of the future.)
Son: "I guess I have to watch out for those due dates.
                Otherwise it'll happen again."

Mother:	"Right. Do you want it to happen again?" *(Requesting verbal commitment.)*
Son:	"Mother, be serious! Of course not."
Mother:	"I *am* serious. I just wanted to know where you stood. So what is your plan so that you don't forget all those due dates?" *(Request for a solution.)*
Son:	"I guess I'll just have to figure out a way of making sure I remember."
Mother:	"Take a crack at it now."
Son:	"Well, I suppose I could post it on my bulletin board."
Mother:	"Interesting idea. And if you do that, what do you think might go wrong?" *(Predicting what will go wrong with the solution.)*
Son:	"I guess I'd have to look at the bulletin board from time to time. Otherwise I'd forget the due dates again."
Mother:	"Right. So?"
Son:	"What do you think I should do?"
Mother:	"Remember the last time I suggested something about due dates?" *(Good move, Mom—don't take over.)*
Son:	(smiling) "Yeah, and it didn't work."
Mother:	"Right. So . . . "
Son:	(pauses) "I suppose I could use that daily calendar that you and Dad gave me . . . (With an impish grin) But I just hate to start looking like you and Dad, forever marking things down in your appointment books!"
Mother:	(laughing) "You know, you're right! It would be such a shame for you to end up like your Dad and me—always remembering things like when it's time for your allowance and stuff like that."
Son:	"Okay, okay. I'll try and get into the habit of

	using the calendar. I'll check it every day and mark down when things are coming due."
Mother:	"Okay, sounds like a good idea. What do you think will go wrong with that plan?" *(Predicting what will go wrong with another solution.)*
Son:	"Mom, enough already! Nothing will go wrong!"
Mother:	"What if you lose your daily book or forget it at school?" *(Predicts possible roadblocks.)*
Son:	"Mom, I can keep it permanently in my school bag and only take it out to write something or check something."
Mother:	"Sounds good. Let's check this out in about a week. (She writes this down in her appointment book.) One more thing."
Son:	"Aw, come on. I told you everything you wanted to hear."
Mother:	"That I wanted to hear?" *(Who owns the problem?)*
Son:	"Okay, okay. What else?"
Mother:	"You plan to write all those details about deadlines in your daily calendar. Do you know all the deadlines for each of your courses?" *(Further exposure of flaws that exist in the new plan.)*
Son:	(smiles a bit sheepishly) "Actually, now that you mention it, I'll have to check when my English essay's due. And my history assignment, too."
Mother:	"Okay. Remember, we'll be checking the new system a week from tonight."

We regret to say *there are no shortcuts*. Initially, each problematic school course will require this time-consuming, repetitive, exhausting, point-by-point review. Gradually, however, your systematic approach will start to take hold and your Coasting child will begin to become his or her own Crap Detector.

Summing Up: A New Course of Action

Step 1: Abandon The Underachievement Myth. Stop thinking about your Coasting Underachiever as lazy and unmotivated.

Step 2: Start with the facts.

Step 3: Inform your Coaster that you will be getting the facts from the school.

Step 4: Set up a structure to get the facts.

Step 5: Set up regular checks at home.

Step 6: Learn the keys to Constructive Confrontation.

Step 7: Be clear who owns the problem.

Step 8: Don't accept pat answers at face value—keep probing!

Step 9: Approach every school problem by asking a systematic list of problem-solving questions.

What Results Can You Expect after Implementing a New Course of Action?

1. Expect change to occur much more slowly than you would like.

2. Expect that when changes in behavior begin to occur they will not produce higher marks immediately.

3. Expect some tension and even resentment when you confront Coasters.

4. Expect to feel anger and resentment at the Coaster both for not changing rapidly enough and for requiring that you continue to confront.

5. Expect at times to feel as if your child's poor marks are a reflection of your failed parenting efforts.

6. Expect to feel that the excuses will never end.

7. Expect to have neither time nor energy to confront every excuse in every course.

8. Expect—just when you are about to give up hope—that you will begin to see small changes in your Coaster's behavior.

These changes will include (miracle of miracles) increased crap detection, a clear sign that your child is beginning to internalize the problem-solving method.

9. Expect, as your child assumes greater personal responsibility, that you will not agree with some of his or her choices, that you will have decreasing control over some of those choices and that this is something you'll have to live with.

10. Expect that as the Coaster assumes more personal responsibility, you will need to confront less.

11. Expect a dramatic change in your role as a parent. It doesn't mean abandoning your responsibility but it does mean profoundly redefining it.

The Coaster as an Adult

Coasters as adults tend to look a lot like Coasters as kids—with all the positives and negatives that implies.

Like their younger counterparts, they're nice folks—caring, decent people. They're loving spouses and parents, reliable, even-tempered friends. They're emotionally well-adjusted people—but they aren't fulfilling anything close to their potential.

Some marry high achievers. This is an interesting phenomenon: As we well know, Coasters are *not* hustlers, which is to say they don't *pursue* high achievers. They just lie low in the bushes and wait for one to come along.

And the attraction is magnetic: Some high achievers *like* the steadying influence of a calm, easygoing partner. For these achievers, marrying a Coaster seems to bring a sense of balance. The Coaster lets his partner confront the world—and discipline the children. Coasters tend to be uncomfortable pushing their children too hard: "I did okay. They'll do fine too."

In our professional experience, we have sometimes seen this kind of marital arrangement cause problems. The problems arise when the achieving spouse, tired of carrying all of the family burdens, demands change from the Coaster spouse. If the Coaster refuses to budge and change his or her ways, this leads to increased tension.

In the work world of 10 and 20 years ago, Coasters and others who just did their job reliably and loyally were highly valued employees. They didn't put in 12-hour days but they got the job done . . . eventually.

Alas, the volatile work world of the '90s is not so kind. Motivation, productivity and flexibility are more highly prized in the workplace than the old virtues of loyalty and reliability. In a world where no business can be sure what tomorrow holds, Coasters, once described by employers as "the bricks and mortar of our organization," now often find themselves viewed as deadweight.

Companies are being downsized by the thousands today. And when adult Coasters lose their jobs, they often react the way the student Coaster we know so well reacts to a bad report card—with incredulity, denial and excuses.

Tim, 47, had a comfortable, middle-management job in the personnel department of a large company's branch office. His job had not changed appreciably in 15 years. Suddenly faced with large losses, the CEO decided overnight to consolidate by doing away with personnel managers in the branch offices. Tim was given 30 days' notice and offered outplacement counseling and a year's severance pay.

Tim was stunned—to put it mildly. How could they do this to him, after 15 years of loyal service? During his last 30 days on the job, Tim spent all his time tying up loose ends for the company and no time focusing on the enormous task that lay ahead of him. The day he handed in his keys and identity card, Tim withdrew a chunk of his severance pay from his bank account—and took a vacation. "After this happening," he sighed, "God knows, I need a holiday!"

Tim's story illustrates classic Coaster behavior. Unable to accept what had happened, he went into a state of denial. He didn't want to face up to the hardship of a new world. He was unrealistically optimistic and assumed he would find another job quickly. But the hard truth was that it took him 21 months to find another job—at two-thirds the salary of his previous one.

Sometimes, however, the threat of termination from a job acts as an effective incentive for change in adult Coasters. When confronted by a supervisor or manager about slow or inadequate performance, many Coaster adults suddenly pull up their socks.

The compelling incentive for rapid change in these situations is often the fact that the Coaster's livelihood—and family—depends on it. This can result in a level of energy and drive that Coasters may never have experienced before.

> By the time Joe came to our office, he was ready to face up to hard truths. His wife had begun to confront him, pointing out lovingly but firmly that he was not the salesman he used to be. He had let things slide, she said. He was, in a word, Coasting.
>
> "You know, she's right," Joe admitted. "I haven't been making the calls I used to make." Ten years back, he had been a personable, highly motivated salesman. Joe decided to change.
>
> Within six months Joe had turned his sales performance around. He gave his wife a large part of the credit. "She motivated me to change," he told us. And just what had his wife done? She had constructively confronted Joe on his lack of follow-through.

Like Joe, Coasters who *do* manage to assume more responsibility attribute the change to significant others who cared enough to call them on their lack of follow-through. Coasting adults who have made this change are pleased and proud that they have done so, and describe the change as a shrinking of the gap between their intentions and their actions. We believe it is not coincidental that caring and constructive confrontation are key factors that caused them to change.

CHAPTER 3

The Anxious Underachiever

We give the kids we see lots of specialized tests to help us understand what motivates underachievers. One test is based on the way the student interprets a picture.

The picture shows a little boy sitting facing a table with a violin on it. The violin is flat on the table and the bow is beside it, also flat on the table. The little boy's face is sober, perhaps a little contemplative. His elbow is on the table and he's resting his hand flat against his cheek.

We ask the student to make up a story based on this picture. Coasting Underachievers make up stories like this:

> "This boy is looking at his violin because he's supposed to practice it. His parents want him to learn how to play the violin. But he'd rather be outside playing and having fun with his friends."
>
> "How do you think this situation will turn out?" we ask the Coasting Underachiever.
>
> "Oh, he'll probably begin practicing soon."

Note "probably" and "soon." Our favorite procrastinator is behaving according to type.

Now contrast the following story told by the underachieving type we call the Anxious Underachiever:

"This young boy has been having trouble practicing his violin. He has been trying to get ready for a concert and he's been putting in extra time. But he still hasn't been able to get it right. He's worried that he won't be ready for the concert and that he will disappoint his parents."

"And how do you think this situation will turn out?" we ask.

"Well, he continues to practice really hard. And when he performs at the concert, everyone tells him he did very well.

"But he didn't—not really. Oh, he got through all his pieces and he didn't freeze up on stage the way he thought he would, but he didn't do nearly as well as he should have. The reason everybody told him he did well was because they were trying to make him feel better."

The contrast between these two kids' stories is about as stark as it gets. The first doesn't care about learning to play the violin. Oh, he'll do it . . . *maybe*. When he gets around to it. And when he does, *if* he does, he'll do just enough to get his parents off his case.

The second kid earnestly wants to perform well. He desperately wants to please his parents. He works really hard at preparing for his performance. But it's not good enough. He knows it and everybody else knows it, even though they're too nice to say it.

These two kids are about as different from each other as it is humanly possible to be. And yet the end result is the same: Both the Coaster and the Anxious student are achieving at levels far below their capabilities. Each could do better.

But the Coaster is almost entirely anxiety-free, apart from a brief burst of nerves the day before an exam and another mini-attack the day he brings his report card home. The Coaster is a walking advertisement for The Underachievement Myth.

The Anxious Underachiever, in telling contrast, is tense almost all the time. She worries that the project she's working on won't be good enough. She worries that she's studied all the wrong things for the exam. Even when she gets a perfectly acceptable grade for an assignment, she worries. "Was it okay? Was it good enough?" she asks her teacher, her face a mask of anxiety. She earnestly, prayerfully, wants things to change. She asks for help. And when she finds someone willing to help her tackle her problems, she becomes her helper's eager partner. Unlike her Coaster classmate, she's more than happy to put in hours of hard work. Truth is she's already putting in the hours. But they don't seem to be getting her anywhere. Lazy and unmotivated? No way.

The Anxious Underachiever is willing to go down into the trenches shoulder-to-shoulder beside you. He's ready to follow orders on the double. Whatever you tell him that might enable him to win the battle, he's willing—and eager—to do. Contrast this with the Coaster who says comfortably, "Now that you mention it, it *would* be nice if my marks improved. Feel free to go ahead and work on them—I'll join you later."

Coasters have forgotten yesterday and think today is fine. And tomorrow? It hasn't even crossed their minds. Anxious Underachievers are tied up in knots about the mistakes made yesterday. They're paralyzed with fear about what might happen tomorrow. And they're immobilized by inner tension today.

And, believe us, these kids are not faking. Life is real and life is earnest for the Anxious Underachiever.

Are Many Underachievers Tense and Anxious?

Anxious Underachievers come next in line—in numbers and prevalence—to Coasters. *Ten to 20 percent of underachievers fit the Anxious, uptight profile.* It is the second most common pattern of underachievement.

What about a socio-economic, cultural, racial or ethnic profile? Just as with the Coaster, there *is* none: You're just as likely to find an Anxious Underachiever in an Asian immigrant family as you are in a sixth-generation Caucasian family.

One family characteristic does show up, however. *The parents of Anxious kids tend to be criticizers.* When this student brings home 85 percent on an essay, the parents focus on the missing 15 percent. And these kids suffer because of their parents' negative attitude. They feel their disapproval as keenly as a sharp pain. They are convinced that nothing they do is good enough. They believe that they will never please their parents.

Male/female ratio? One to one. However, Anxious girls tend to seek help earlier for this problem than uptight boys do. Anxious boys are more likely—at first, anyway—to fall back on classic male defensiveness: "I don't need any help. I'm supposed to fix this myself."

When does this pattern appear? It can happen at any age through the school years. It appears whenever inner tension becomes overwhelming and interferes with the student's performance.

And incidentally, this pattern frequently is found among achievers and overachievers. The difference with the Anxious Underachiever is a matter of degree: The achiever and overachiever are often very tense and anxious, but their anxiety does not engulf them so entirely that they are unable to function. Think of anxious achievers and overachievers as swimming in anxiety that buoys them up and even propels them forward. Whereas Anxious Underachievers are drowning in it.

Anxious Underachievers are in some ways the easiest kind of underachievers to help. Why? Because they're eager to change. And they respect—even revere—authority. They're willing and eager to take direction. They want to please you. They sincerely want to achieve—because the prospect of failing scares them. (This fear of failure is a key to understanding what underlies the Anxious Underachiever's tension. More on this later.)

Let's look at the Anxious Underachiever prototype more closely.

Anatomy of an Anxious Underachiever

1. They are tense and unable to relax.

These kids become so anxious and worried just before a test that they go blank and can't remember anything about the material they've spent days or even weeks studying. Or they become so panicked about the amount of material they have to study, and the limited time available between now and the exam, that their minds race and they can't concentrate on a thing. They may look at one chapter and think, "Oh, I can't waste time on that. Chapter 5 is the one I should be looking at." So they look at Chapter 5—and almost immediately mentally shift gears. "No," they think. "Chapter 6 is the one I've got to get to." And so on. By now, they may have spent hours with the book open— but the whole time, they're so overwrought and anxious that they can't focus on anything.

2. They avoid or put off school work because they're terrified they won't be able to do it well enough.
When Anxious kids procrastinate, it's not because they've pushed school work to the back of their minds. Quite the contrary. They put things off precisely because they can't stop thinking both about the work and about the terrifying possibilities of what might happen if they screw up. Instead of just plunging in and starting to study material they feel uncertain about, they become so anxious they simply cannot open the book. They feel overwhelmed by what they *imagine* they'll be confronted with if they do open the book. So they find other things to do rather than study.

This means that even the Anxious Underachiever can be a victim of The Underachievement Myth. Even Anxious kids sometimes are labeled lazy and unmotivated. But what looks like procrastination— and therefore the lazy-and-unmotivated syndrome—is, in fact, this kid's way of avoiding an anxiety-arousing situation.

While they're avoiding school work, they don't enjoy a moment of peace. Every moment they're not studying, they worry. And still they can't get down to it. (This is in marked contrast to their Coaster schoolmates, who have no problem, thank you very much, utterly erasing from their minds the work they should be doing when they're hanging out with their friends or stretched out on the couch watching their favorite TV show.)

3. They worry excessively and unrealistically: about competence, about mistakes made in the past, about anticipated calamities in the future.

Anxious Underachievers are their own harshest critics. Anything they do that disappoints other people, or fails to meet the highest standards, bothers them. Even when they do well in something, they rarely allow themselves the satisfaction of succeeding because they feel that somehow, it wasn't quite good enough.

To make matters worse, Anxious Underachievers are afraid they won't be able to change this pattern, which is why they worry about possible failures, disappointments and inadequacies in the future. They spend so much time ruminating about their past, present and future that they have little time, energy or confidence left over to do anything concrete that might help solve all these potential problems. And because they're making zero progress, their parents may conclude that their kid must be lazy and unmotivated.

When we talk with Anxious Underachievers, we often notice the vividness with which they recall many painful details of past difficulties and anticipate the agony of future failures. The past and present seem to merge in their minds in a way that suggests they've been continuously ruminating about both. Here's an Anxious Underachiever discussing his so-called current academic problems at university:

"My grades would be better if I handed in more papers on time. It's not like I don't work on them! If you look at my report cards from Grades 1, 2 and 3, I tended not to hand in a lot of written work. And I took remedial reading. It wasn't so much that I couldn't read. I read slowly, but I understood more than most people. Half the time the reading tests were timed. I guess I was terrified of reading out loud. It was the judgment of others, and it still goes on. It's like a permanent record. I have a presentation to give next week. Each student will only get 15 minutes. I don't know if I can get all the facts in."

Here's a first-year university student discussing his first three years at elementary school as if they were last week! He switches from present to deep past back to present without so much as drawing a breath. And his comments are highly detailed. There's a panicky undercurrent to his ruminations, too.

4. They need constant reassurance and approval, especially from adults and authority figures.

Most adolescents look much more to their peers for approval. Anxious Underachievers look much more to their parents and their teachers for positive reinforcement. "Was it okay?" she asks when she hands in a project to her teacher. "Yes, it's fine," the teacher replies. And the student says, "Oh, that's great"—and looks tremendously relieved. And then, a couple of minutes later, the brow furrows and she says, "But was it *really* okay?"

Even when she's done something just fine, this tied-up-in-knots kid can't seem to believe that she really did do something right. Words of reassurance never seem to last. And the moment she's finished one task, she starts worrying about the next one—which she's sure she'll never do well enough.

Anxious Underachievers are capable of fretting for days when a teacher makes a sharp comment (even some off-the-cuff remark that the teacher has probably forgotten almost immediately) or even if the teacher throws the student a quizzical glance. They're so worried about impressing people in authority that they're always on edge, fearful that a single mistake—one wrong word or action—will lose them the approval of those who matter. They seem to need a stamp of approval from others merely to exist.

5. They complain of physical ailments, particularly headaches and stomach aches.

Physical complaints may show up when Anxious Underachievers are quite young and still in elementary school. Your eight-year-old son complains that he has a stomach ache and can't possibly go to school. But your parental antennae tell you this stomach ache is almost certainly psychosomatic. Nothing else fits. He doesn't have a fever. His color is good. He doesn't *look* at all sick. And he wasn't sick last evening or during the night. This illness mysteriously occurs just after he's awakened in the morning. "Are you worried about something, dear?" you ask. "No!" he replies, a little too quickly. And then, if you probe a little, he may tell you he's worried about school. Or about a project. Or about a game that's going to be played during recess that he's not good at.

6. They become fearful about attending school from time to time.

This may be the corollary of the mysterious stomach ache or headache. Something has happened—or is about to happen—at school that they're worried about. So they may seem to play sick—although "playing" sick is not entirely fair. Anxious Underachievers are not manipulative or devious. More than likely they've convinced *themselves* they're really sick. And this is what psychosomatic illness is, after all—an illness with real physical symptoms but no apparent physiological cause. The cause is in the brain, not the body.

When Anxious Underachievers skip school or miss a class, it's almost always because they're nervous that they won't be able to perform adequately in some upcoming event—a test or a class presentation, for example. They rarely just goof off, the way most students who regularly cut classes do.

7. They are painfully self-conscious.

All you have to do is look at her and she's embarrassed. She may even be a blusher. She's reluctant to put up her hand in class, even when she knows the answer. When she has to give a speech or presentation in front of the class, she's paralyzed with fear. She has a horror of looking silly or stupid in any situation.

Don't look for Anxious Underachievers trying out for the lead in the school play!

8. They seem more mature than their years.

Teenagers frequently drive their parents crazy because they're afraid to be different from their peers. They slavishly ape whatever crazed fashion statement or slang happens to be the rage. Anxious Underachievers suffer from none of the above. Instead, they try to behave exactly like adults—and well-behaved, conservative adults at that.

Your friends love your son because he's so amazingly socially adept—unlike their teenager. He's easy to talk to, he answers their questions (sometimes in great detail) and he even seems genuinely interested in talking with them—in contrast to their own kid who grunts "Hi" and flees the room.

He dresses neatly (although without flair) and, wonder of wonders, his hair is clean and short. In fact, he looks and behaves a lot like a miniature you. All of which is very flattering, but hardly typical adolescent behavior. Psychologists call it *pseudo-maturity*.

Most adolescents constantly prod and challenge adult norms as they try on various personal identities for size. They frequently look odd—dreadful even (and we haven't even broached the way they behave!). But bizarre and socially unacceptable though they may sometimes be, *they're* in charge, not you—which is the way the universe is supposed to unfold while the typical adolescent is experimenting with approaches to life.

But Anxious Underachievers? They conform to the expectations of others, especially adults.

9. They are perfectionists.

She starts a term paper and rips up page one because the first three words that came out of her head weren't perfect. She cannot accept anything less than perfection. She can't meet this impossible goal, of course. So she gives up.

Anxious Underachievers sometimes develop paralyzing fears of school assignments such as writing essays. Writing something from scratch (as opposed to answering questions with specific right and wrong answers) means you can't seek refuge in the safety of absolutes. There is no prescribed right way or wrong way to write about a broad subject, and the anxiety of this ambiguity can overwhelm Anxious Underachievers and immobilize them.

In our practice, we have encountered many Anxious Underachievers who, for years, either have entirely avoided courses that required essay-writing or have made the following anxiety-avoiding decision: "I won't do the essay [worth 20 percent]. I'll concentrate on class work and the final exam instead." When these students talk about writing essays, they talk about being terrified to show their written work to anyone, as if the writing were carved in stone. And the message is, "I know it's not perfect so I can't do it."

10. They become lost in unimportant details and lose sight of the big picture.

Paying attention to details is an important part of attaining excellence and achievement. Being master of the telling detail enables the lawyer to win a case, the surgeon to operate successfully, the politician to best an opponent in a debate, the researcher to make a scientific advance—and the student to get good grades.

Anxious Underachievers focus on details to the detriment of the overall project. They feel that all details are equally important. They appear to be unable to differentiate between relevant and irrelevant information. They are obsessed with having every detail accounted for perfectly. They may expend all their time and energy on unimportant details and never get to the main body of the work.

Some Anxious kids are so focused on details that they fool you into believing they're not anxious at all. On the surface, they may appear motivated and in control and not particularly tense. In fact, their unnatural focus on details is the conduit for their anxiety. They zero in on picayune details—details that lead nowhere. What they're really doing is spinning their wheels.

Consider the following Anxious detail-fixated student. Does he sound familiar?

Ted is assigned to prepare a detailed chart for his world history class. It's due the following day. The chart is supposed to briefly list major events in politics, economics, the arts, science and other categories for each year from 1940 to 1945.

Ted starts the project the moment he gets home from school, beginning with politics. He sets out to make a list of events but gets hopelessly mired in the details of World War II geopolitics. He looks over the list he's started—and decides it's no good. He tears it up and starts over again. He does this five times—and he hasn't got beyond politics. On the sixth try, he gets through the first two years but, as he starts 1943, he suddenly realizes he's forgotten a crucial event in 1941. He goes back to the beginning.

When his mother calls him for dinner, he tells her he's too busy to join the family downstairs and besides, he's not hungry anyway: "I'll make myself a sandwich later." By 11:30 p.m., he's faint with exhaustion and lightheaded with hunger, and he's finding it hard to think. He's finished politics at last, but he's worried he's left too much out. His head is spinning and he can't concentrate, so he decides to go to bed and get up at 5 a.m. He can't get to sleep because he's so tense and wound up by now—and he's worried he might sleep through his alarm.

And he hasn't even *looked* at all his other homework.

Ask detail-obsessed Anxious students a simple question and they'll start telling you all kinds of details, as if only by knowing every little thing about the subject can you possibly understand what it's all about. And as they tell the story, they get so bogged down in their own accounting of the details that they may get confused about the ultimate point they're trying to make. This frustrates them and makes them even more nervous.

11. They are overly concerned with what is right and acceptable—and, conversely, with what is wrong and unacceptable.

Anxious Underachievers are constantly looking for guidance from others, for someone to tell them the "right" way to do something. They can't seem to trust their own instincts or judgment. They feel they have to be given direction from someone in authority, someone who understands the *proper* method of doing it, *somebody who knows the rules.*

Anxious Underachievers live in a world of endless shoulds and shouldn'ts. They can't even allow themselves to feel certain emotions unless they conform to the "proper" feeling. Classical psychoanalysts call the part of your psyche that is forever supervising and judging what you are doing the *superego.* The rigid view of right and wrong, good and bad, acceptable and unacceptable that these kids have burdened themselves with invariably corresponds to the one they think the authority figures in their lives subscribe to. They're simply trying to be good people so that they will be accepted. Because they know that when they don't feel accepted, it makes them feel anxious, personally attacked and, sometimes, resentful. Often they cannot express this frustration openly and must suffer privately, which makes the suffering worse—and can lead to sadness or depression.

Summing Up: Anatomy of an Anxious Underachiever

Let's glance over Anxious Underachievers' characteristics:

1. They are tense and unable to relax.

2. They avoid or put off school work because they're terrified they won't be able to do it well enough.

3. They worry excessively and unrealistically: about competence, about mistakes made in the past, about anticipated calamities in the future.

4. They need constant reassurance and approval, especially from adults and authority figures.

5. They complain of physical ailments, particularly headaches and stomach aches.

6. They become fearful about attending school from time to time.

7. They are painfully self-conscious.

8. They seem more mature than their years.

9. They are perfectionists.

10. They become lost in unimportant details and lose sight of the big picture.

11. They are overly concerned with what is right and acceptable—and, conversely, with what is wrong and unacceptable.

That's it, then. Do you know this kid? Not every Anxious Underachiever will display all 11 of these characteristics, of course. For example, some Anxious kids may be masters at masking their tension, at least on the surface. And many Anxious students *never* avoid or put off school work. On the contrary, you can't stop them from working.

But let's not focus on unimportant details! The overall list should give you a pretty fair profile of the Anxious Underachiever.

Armed with this lengthy description, it's time to pause and see how similar your child's characteristics are to those of the Anxious Underachiever prototype.

Parent Checklist

Two important points: Specific events (a traumatic event such as a serious accident or the death of someone close, or the minor upsets that can happen anytime to anyone) can trigger anxiety in any student and cause a temporary drop in marks. Don't jump to instant conclusions or make snap judgments based on your child's behavior over a few weeks or even a couple of months. *Your child must exhibit at least five of the following characteristics over a minimum of six months to be similar to this prototype.*

1. Does my child seem tense and unable to relax much of the time?	Yes___ No___ Don't Know___
2. Does my child express serious and repeated doubts about adequacy or competence in academic or social areas?	Yes___ No___ Don't Know___

3. Is my child excessively worried about past or future negative events (e.g. not getting into university, failing an exam, not making the school basketball team, not being invited to a school social event)?

Yes___ No___ Don't Know___

4. Does my child constantly seek reassurance and approval from parents and from other adults?

Yes___ No___ Don't Know___

5. Does my child complain of aches and pains and other physical problems that seem unfounded, vague or without any clear cause?

Yes___ No___ Don't Know___

6. Has my child ever not gone to school or a particular class because of anxiety about performing adequately?

Yes___ No___ Don't Know___

7. Is my child extremely self-conscious or easily embarrassed or humiliated?

Yes___ No___ Don't Know___

8. Does my child set perfectionist standards?

Yes___ No___ Don't Know___

9. Does my child often become immersed in details and lose a sense of the overall task?

Yes___ No___ Don't Know___

10. Does my child continually worry about what he or she "should" be doing or not doing?

Yes___ No___ Don't Know___

If you answered "Yes" to five or more of the above questions, your child's characteristics may be similar to those of the Anxious Underachiever prototype.

What's Bothering the Anxious Underachiever?

First and foremost, it's important to understand that Anxious Underachievers are not playing games. What you see is what you get. They seem tense because they *are* tense. They look worried and they *are*.

At least half of these kids show some signs of depression—in addition to being tense and anxious. This makes sense when you consider the reasons underlying the Anxious kid's tension. What's more, they genuinely want to do better—and they're *trying* to do better. The Anxious Underachiever is tied up in knots because he's set himself up as his own stern judge. And he's decided he doesn't make the grade. In fact, he comes down so hard on himself that he neither sees, recognizes nor acknowledges any of the considerable abilities and talents he in truth has.

Let's look at the reasons underlying the Anxious Underachiever's tension.

The Inner Life of the Anxious Underachiever

Why is the Anxious Underachiever overwhelmed by his anxiety?
A certain amount of anxiety is necessary in order to achieve anything. In fact, an optimal level of anxiety is important in life. Healthy anxiety gets us going, gives us an edge, keeps us alert. It propels us ahead, encourages us to put forward our best effort. Think of a goal you have striven for. You *needed* some tension to motivate you to aim for that goal. But if the tension you feel gets out of control, it can freeze you in your tracks. It can immobilize you, paralyze you, render you unable to do anything. You become so worried you simply cannot function.

This is what happens to Anxious Underachievers. Their anxiety about doing well overwhelms their ability to function.

And why does the Anxious Underachiever's anxiety level run amok?

The Anxious Underachiever's inner tension is fueled by a paralyzing sense of personal inadequacy. This triggers a crushing fear of failure. Anxious Underachievers are consumed with insecurities and feelings of personal worthlessness. They cannot separate doing well or badly on a school assignment from their self-worth as people. Anxious kids blow their academic performance way out of proportion in their minds. Mediocre performance on a test or project is not just that—a mediocre mark. It's definitive evidence that they're worthless, inadequate human beings.

Anxious kids tie their entire sense of themselves to their level of achievement. They have no inner anchor, no still center to draw upon that says, "Okay, all right, enough already. You messed up that assignment. Let's go on to the next one and see that it doesn't happen again."

Why do Anxious Underachievers need constant reassurance from others? And why are they so concerned about "doing the right thing"?

Anxious Underachievers are what psychologists call "other-directed." This relates to the still center we referred to above. Anxious Underachievers do not look inside themselves for a sense of direction. They can only look outside, to others, for direction, guidance and support. They're so dependent on others for approval and guidance that they ignore their own feelings, perceptions and needs. They look at the world almost exclusively from the point of view of the people in charge: the expectations, wishes, needs and goals of others.

This is why they are so concerned with doing the right thing. They're looking for rules, principles, role models—an authority they can look to, take direction from, rely upon.

Anxious kids are looking for certainty in an uncertain world, which is why they try so hard to please adults and to conform to their standards. They are afraid to trust their own instincts because they believe they aren't good enough. They believe they aren't worthy of that trust.

Why are Anxious Underachievers satisfied with nothing short of perfection?

In the same way that Anxious Underachievers cannot separate an individual task from their entire sense of personal self-worth, Anxious kids believe that if they do not perform a job to perfection, they have not only failed this particular task completely (instead of seeing it simply as having done a merely adequate job this time round), they conclude they've failed as persons.

Consider the reasoning that underlies perfectionism: The perfectionist decides that nothing short of perfection will suffice. Perfectionist Anxious Underachievers have two choices: a perfect job (in other words, acceptable) or an imperfect job (in other words, unacceptable). The slightest flaw, the smallest mistake, the tiniest inadequacy places the project—and them—in the imperfect category. Which then makes the project—and them—totally unworthy. There is no middle ground. It's all or nothing and, since human beings are less than perfect, the result can *only* be dissatisfaction and failure.

Let us be very clear: Striving for excellence is noble. But defining one's entire self-worth on attaining unrealistically high expectations is fraught with danger.

Why does the Anxious Underachiever focus on details and miss the overall picture?

Obsessive attention to detail is a logical corollary of perfectionism. When you aim to be perfect and nothing less than perfect, every detail of every task becomes equally important. There's no broad canvas to consider, no dark and light shading. Every tiny detail has to be right in order for the whole picture to be right.

Summing Up: The Inner Life of the Anxious Underachiever

- Anxious Underachievers are overwhelmed by inner tension because they feel personally inadequate and are terrified of failure.

- Anxious Underachievers need constant reassurance from others because they have no confidence in their inner direction. They have to look outside themselves for guidance and a sense of certainty.

- Anxious Underachievers cannot distinguish between unimportant details and the overall picture because they have set themselves an impossible goal—perfection.

- Anxious Underachievers are satisfied with nothing short of perfection because they tie their entire sense of self-worth to every task.

So what's a parent to do?

*   *   *

As we said earlier, the good news is that helping Anxious Underachievers can be an extremely rewarding endeavor. This is because Anxious Underachievers really *want* help. They accept guidance. Once you convince them that you're really concerned and genuinely willing to hang in and help them improve their achievement levels, they'll usually do everything in their power to make the joint effort a success.

Helping the Anxious Underachiever Clear a Path to Achievement

1. Help your Anxious Underachiever learn a practical way to relax during a normal school day.

Tension involves the whole person. It's not physical and it's not mental—it's both. When you're tense, your mind *and* your body are involved. Your mind focuses on a particular situation that worries you and, as you do so, your body tenses.

When anxiety is overwhelming, you quickly stop focusing on your specific problem and succumb to a generalized state of worry. One thing leads to another and, in seconds, your head is swimming with an undefined panicky feeling. And as this happens, your body tenses up.

We suggest a simple, brief method of relaxation to Anxious students we counsel, which they find enormously helpful. This method goes straight to the heart of both the physical and the mental components of anxiety. It goes like this: You simply focus your attention (your mind) on your breathing (your body). By slowing down your breathing, you reduce physical tension. And by mentally focusing on your breathing, you clear your mind of the generalized feeling of worry that is occupying your mind. It takes only a minute or two. Here's how:

Focused Breathing

1. Close your eyes and focus your attention on your feet and toes. Notice the normal sensations of relaxation that are already there—sensations such as a tingling feeling on the surface of the skin, a pleasant inner feeling of warmth or numbness and other similar sensations. Pay close attention to these sensations for a moment. Notice the normal feelings of relaxation in your body.

2. Now shift your attention to your breathing. Notice the normal sensations of breathing. There are subtle differences between inhaling and exhaling that you will notice once you focus on this simple, normal, constant process. The differences are both physical and emotional. Follow three or four breaths, noticing these subtle differences as you do so.

3. Don't try to take deep breaths. Instead, take a normal, relaxing breath, like a sigh—and notice the relaxation that naturally occurs.

4. Open your eyes and go about your business.

Anxious kids we have counseled find this relaxation technique very effective because it's simple, quick and doesn't rely on complicated procedures. It can be done any time, anywhere—and it only takes a minute or two. It doesn't even require any change in a person's normal state (apart from closing the eyes). Instead, it uses relaxation already present in the body and it uses the person's own attention, which is already there but is focused on other, anxiety-arousing things.

The Anxious student can, of course, supplement this with any number of more involved, time-consuming methods of relaxation. There are literally hundreds of them out there, offered in classes, seminars, books and workshops (to name a few: yoga, meditation, biofeedback, imagery, tai-chi, self-hypnosis). But this simple breathing exercise is something Anxious students can use any time during a busy day. And they can use it during moments of great tension—before an exam, for example.

2. Help your Anxious Underachiever find a physical outlet for tension.

As we just said, it's impossible to separate physical from mental tension. One contributes to the other. They're inextricably linked, the same way that a horse and carriage and love and marriage are in the old song.

It follows that vigorous physical exercise releases mental tension, clears the mind and calms the spirit—precisely what Anxious Underachievers need. Bookstores, magazine racks, newsstands, television channels and radio air waves are filled with information about the therapeutic benefits of regular exercise. So if your Anxious child does not exercise regularly, explore various possibilities. Noncompetitive activities may fit best: You don't want to add another worry for your child about whether he or she is measuring up to group standards.

A few suggestions: running, swimming, bicycling, a personalized training program in an exercise gym. Or consider walking: It's the kind of solitary activity that can reduce stress, clear the head and give the Anxious student space to think in an unpressured way. An hour of vigorous walking a day is an excellent tonic for both mind and body.

Steer Anxious Underachievers toward a physical activity that (a) they enjoy and (b) they can easily fit into their daily routine. Most authorities recommend an hour-long workout three to five times a week. If the school has well-equipped sports facilities, a daily workout in the gym or swimming pool or track before or after school might work well. Or if you're within walking distance of school, they could simply walk to and from school each day. Or bicycle to school. Or jog. Or rollerblade.

The important thing is that it's something they enjoy and that the activity is not demanding in a way that contributes to anxiety.

3. Help your Anxious Underachiever learn how to break up each task into manageable parts.

Anxious Underachievers don't take anything a day at a time. They're constantly looking ahead, imagining the worst. When a school year begins, they don't simply attend each class, get a copy of each course outline and then start with the first assignment. That would be too simple. What they do is look at the course outline, listen to the teacher's pep talk about the year ahead and think, "I can't do it. There's just too much. I won't have time. There's far too much to fit in. I won't be able to do it." Every task becomes a mountain and every mountain is Mount Everest.

You can help them see the mountain ahead as a series of small steps. Show them how to break the monumental task ahead into manageable steps. One step at a time. Like this:

How to Break Up a Task into Manageable Parts

1. Make a list of assignments and tests, including the deadline for completing or preparing for each.

2. Rank each task in order of priority. The most important project is No. 1, the second most important No. 2 and so on.

3. Under each assignment or upcoming test, list the specific activities necessary to complete or prepare for it.

4. Under each heading, write the deadline, the materials needed to accomplish the task and the estimated amount of time needed to complete the work.

5. For each activity, write "T" beside it if you need to do at least some work on it TODAY.

6.   Take a deep breath and get to work. Start with No. 1T, proceed to No. 2T and so on.

4. Help your Anxious Underachiever learn when to stop.

Anxious Underachievers often need to learn not only when to start projects but also when to stop working on them. They tend to get bogged down in the middle of an assignment. They lose their grip on the overall shape of the project, they're not sure where they're going, they don't seem to be getting anywhere—and they're afraid to stop: "But Dad, if I *stop*, I won't finish it!"

One way to help Anxious Underachievers get out of this quagmire is to set a time limit for each task. Setting an hourly alarm might help. Students decide before they start that they'll concentrate on this particular assignment for one uninterrupted hour. If, at the end of that hour, they find they're not getting anywhere, they go on to another assignment.

Anxious Underachievers may need some convincing about this approach: "But Mom, I'll never get anywhere if I keep dropping things!"

There is some truth to this argument—but only later on in a project when these students are on a roll and need to maintain momentum until the task is completed. When they're just beginning an assignment, dropping it for the moment and turning their attention to something else not only frees their tense mind from descending into a spiral of worry, it also gives them an opportunity to go on thinking about it subconsciously—without the stress that conscious thought often brings them.

How often have you "slept on" an important decision or problem and awakened with a solution? The same principle applies to any ongoing project. You return to it renewed and with an infusion of fresh ideas that your mind has worked on quietly, below the surface, while you scarcely knew it was happening. Explain the concept of "sleeping on something" to your Anxious child. This is something he may not have experienced yet.

Follow up with a brief explanation of the 80 percent/20 percent principle, which is this: *We accomplish 80 percent of our work in 20 percent of our working time.* This means that when your mind is well-rested and clear, you are capable of proceeding much more surely (without making mistakes) and much faster than you can when you are tired, worried or frustrated. By pacing yourself—setting time limits on tasks—and by varying tasks, you have a better chance of maximizing your efficiency on each task. You actually spend less time working and accomplish just as much—or more.

5. Steer Anxious Underachievers away from perfectionism by helping them learn how to set realistic expectations—and accept realistic results.

We already know that Anxious Underachievers are card-carrying perfectionists. Not only are they perfectionists, they also feel they have to do *everything*. Skipping or skimming over a couple of things isn't good enough. They must do it *all* and they must do it perfectly or it's not worth doing at all.

Here is a typical conversation with an Anxious perfectionist:

Parent:	"Why aren't you working on your term paper?"
Brenda:	"Well, I understand the topic and all that. But when I tried to write the first sentence, it just didn't come out right. I've written it and rewritten it and I seem to be getting nowhere. You see, the teacher says that the whole essay will flow from the first sentence, so when we write it, we should make sure it says exactly what the essay is going to be about. Well, like I said, I do know what I want to say. But I've worked and worked on that first sentence and I just can't seem to get it right! I *know* my teacher will be disappointed."

The teacher's remark about the first sentence of the essay was meant to help the students get started and keep a tight focus on the topic. It was meant as a kick start, not an engine staller! But Brenda turned her teacher's good intentions inside out and made them into an impossible demand for perfection. And since she can't do it perfectly, she can't move on.

What can you do if you have a Brenda?

Try countering her unrealistic expectations with something along the lines of the following:

> "Instead of trying to make the first sentence perfect, why don't you just write down a few sentences about what your essay is going to be about? Don't think about how the sentences look or sound. Just say out loud what the essay is going to be about and then copy down what you've said on the page. It can be very rough—you can always go back later, after you've finished writing the rest of the essay, and polish it up a bit. But for now, just write down a rough idea of what it's going to be all about. And then move right on into the details of what it's about—you know, the body of the essay."

If she replies with something like, "But Dad, the teacher said the first sentence was really important!" you can continue in this vein:

> "You know, when the teacher said what she said about the first sentence, I don't really think she meant it had to be perfect. Probably she was just trying to help you get the essay started. In fact, she probably was trying to get you *past* that first difficult sentence by trying to stop you worrying about it being fancy or brilliant. I'm sure that what she really wants you to do is stick to the topic and tell us what the essay is going to be about in clear, simple language.
>
> "And since you understand the subject, you're way ahead of the game already! Just writing down what it's about shouldn't worry you at all. In fact, I bet you'll find it really quite easy. Once you forget about it being perfect, that is."

When you break down your child's unrealistic expectations in this calm, logical way, you're sending this message: Moving on to the rest of the project is more important than perfection. Concentrate on the large picture. You can always fill in the details later—and polish things up then. But always remember that the polishing part is just the final touch. It's not what the project is really all about.

This does not *mean encouraging Anxious Underachievers to settle for second best.* Assure them that of course, you want them to aim high, of course you want them to strive to do the best they can. But then show them the folly of perfectionism, the no-win, impossible situation they set up for themselves when they arbitrarily decide something either has to be perfect—or it's worthless.

A short sermon on the inherent imperfection of the human condition is in order here—if you can restrain yourself from becoming too preachy! You might use yourself as an example of someone who hasn't always achieved the goals you have set for yourself.

Help your child understand the value of process as opposed to product. Explain why the quality and integrity of the journey is as important as the destination.

6. Help your Anxious Underachiever learn how to concentrate on the forest, not the trees.

As we know, Anxious Underachievers tend to concentrate on details and lose sight of the larger picture. They find it difficult to discriminate between important and unimportant details and, in the process, lose sight of the larger picture entirely.

Each time they start a new project, they're susceptible to this tendency. So the way to guide them away from this trap is to help them confront the problem each time they tackle a new assignment.

Every time your child starts a new assignment, encourage him to write down in a single paragraph (or, even better, in one or two succinct sentences) the overall purpose of the assignment. Next, suggest he make a "quick-and-dirty" outline of the requirements of the project.

Encourage him to do this quickly before he has a chance to think of all the niggling details and potential roadblocks to his progress—all the obstacles he's sure to think of soon.

Then go over the rough outline and help critique it. Ask the following questions:

- What are you trying to accomplish in this project?
- What is its purpose?
- What questions is it supposed to answer?
- What material is it supposed to cover?

Your Anxious child may find it easier to discuss the project verbally at first. This is fine: You can hash it out orally and then write down what you've discussed, together. You can do the actual writing down if you choose—but only if your child dictates to you. *Do not take over or do it for your child.*

If you fall into the trap of taking over for your child, if *you* think it out instead of letting him do his own thinking, he will not think through the meaning of the project and he won't be able to organize and work with the material himself. Remember that these kids *like* to lean on adults. Unlike most underachievers, they look to you for approval. They're eager to depend on you. Feel free to give them guidance and support, but don't take over.

Once you and your child have written down a rough outline of the assignment, you can help him fine-tune it. This does *not* mean filling in the details. It means organizing the material under clear, simple headings, subheadings and a numbered list of steps to proceed with the work.

Next, suggest to your Anxious child that he pin the outline on the bulletin board and refer to it often. This will serve as a constant reminder of the overall parameters of the task. And your Anxious child will be much less likely to get mired and lost in the details.

7. Avoid harsh criticism. Be supportive.

The art of Constructive Confrontation, so useful with Coasters, has to be soft-pedaled to a fare-thee-well with Anxious Underachievers. Yes, their impossible expectations of themselves must be brought to their attention, as we outlined above. But gently, gently. You are dealing with sensitive people, people who are ridiculously easy to hurt. You can, in fact, knock them over with a feather.

You don't have to worry about whether this type of underachiever will actually listen to you and take what you say to heart. Not only will they hear you, they'll rerun the tape inside their head over and over again after the conversation is over. The last thing you want to do is *increase* this kid's anxiety level. Anxious Underachievers' first instinct when criticized or confronted in any way is to conclude that they have lost your approval. This will send anxiety levels soaring—and marks plummeting.

So how can you give feedback? One suggestion: Preface your comments with the caution: "You know, I'm worried about bringing this up. You know why? Because I'm afraid you'll hear it in a very negative way. And that's *not* the way I mean it."

Then proceed. Carefully.

8. Don't encourage your Anxious Underachiever to become overly dependent on you.

Yes, be supportive. But don't be excessively protective and encourage an unhealthy dependence. You *do* want to protect Anxious Underachievers from harsh criticism. And you don't want to abandon them as they struggle to improve academic performance. But you're not doing them any favors by catering to their every bleat. Your purpose is to help them learn to trust their own judgment, believe in their own efforts and think for themselves. If you allow them to come to you to approve every tiny step along the way, they will never achieve their full potential.

So. When he asks, "Did I do this right? Can you check this for me? Can you show me how to do this? Is this what the teacher wants?" try to strike a balance between support and independence.

Try this: Go over the requirements for an assignment together before your child begins working. Then say, "Okay. Now you have a pretty good understanding of what's required. Go ahead with it on your own and keep at it until you're finished—even if you come across a few things that you don't completely understand or that you're not entirely sure you're doing right. When you've gone all the way through and finished a first draft, we'll look over the whole thing together."

This approach has several underlying pluses: It helps your child learn to keep going even when it's not done perfectly or it's incomplete. And it will help your child learn to look at the project as a whole, rather than get mired in details along the way.

9. Give generous praise for specific accomplishments. But keep it brief and low-key.

Anxious Underachievers respond to praise the way a drowning person gasps for air. They want it, they *need* it. So give it to them—but be careful. When you stroke a kid who's uptight, the last thing you want to do is increase anxiety. Anxious Underachievers want parental and teacher approval, but they can't handle a lot of attention without it raising their performance expectations again. It'll make them nervous and start the spiral of worry anew.

So don't overdo it. No surprise parties, no lavish gifts, no big session of praise in front of the grandparents. When parents get carried away with excitement, Anxious Underachievers begin to feel the pressure of parental expectations: "Now he's going to expect me to do the same *next* term. And I'm not sure I can do it *again*."

And be careful of profuse *generalized* praise. Anxious Underachievers have antennae that pick up insincerity fast. They sense very quickly when you're just trying to make them feel good. So don't say, "You're such a good girl!" or "What a good student you are!" or "You're really doing better and better." And, of course, don't give backhanded compliments like: "It's about time you did something right!"

Instead, stick to specifics—and keep it low-key. As in:

"You did a nice job on that paper."

"I'd say you have a good, solid understanding of this subject now."

"This paper looks good."

"You have a nice, neat handwriting style."

10. Seek professional help, if necessary.

Anxious Underachievers lack self-confidence. And this lack of self-confidence may be rooted in low self-esteem. If your child wants to explore the root causes of his or her problems, you might seek help from a psychologist, psychiatrist or family counselor.

And . . . is it possible that, as a parent, *you* may have contributed to your child's low sense of self-worth? Think about this—and be honest with yourself. Are you the kind of person who always sees the bottle as half-empty rather than half-full? Do you always point up the 25 or 30 percent your child *didn't* get on that exam when he brought home 75 or 70 percent? Even though you may feel this is the best way to motivate your child, your critical attitude may very well have contributed to a negative spiral. If that's the case, family or parental counseling might be the best solution.

Summing Up: Helping the Anxious Underachiever Clear a Path to Achievement

1. Help your Anxious Underachiever learn a practical way to relax during a normal school day.

2. Help your Anxious Underachiever find a physical outlet for tension.

3. Help your Anxious Underachiever learn how to break up each task into manageable parts.

4. Help your Anxious Underachiever learn when to stop.

5. Steer Anxious Underachievers away from perfectionism by helping them learn how to set realistic expectations—and accept realistic results.

6. Help your Anxious Underachiever learn how to concentrate on the forest, not the trees.

7. Avoid harsh criticism. Be supportive.

8. Don't encourage your Anxious Underachiever to become overly dependent on you.

9. Give generous praise for specific accomplishments. But keep it brief and low-key.

10. Seek professional help, if necessary.

What to Expect When You Help Your Anxious Underachiever

1. Expect that your child may initially become even more dependent on your opinion, and bug you every time some minor worry comes up.

2. Expect your child to resist letting go of perfectionist ways.

3. Expect that as your child learns to let up on internal pressure, he or she will become happier and more relaxed and will actually have more energy to devote to learning.

4. Expect it will take time for your child to change and adjust.

5. Expect ups and downs. Your child probably will experience swings in self-confidence as he or she moves along the road toward increased self-esteem.

6. Expect your child's debilitating tension to decrease. And as the tension diminishes, physical complaints and other signs of anxiety and nervousness will decrease as well.

7. Expect your child to learn not to judge everything on an all-or-nothing basis.

8. Expect gradually to learn to be gentler with your child and to learn how to let up on some of your demands and expectations.

9. Expect to recognize more clearly your *own* perfectionist tendencies.

The Anxious Underachiever as an Adult

Anxious Underachievers who do not conquer their anxiety sufficiently to achieve often limp along in the workplace locked into lower- or middle-level jobs well below their true capabilities.

There are several predictable reasons. First, they are affected by the stresses of the job to a degree that the stress blocks their performance. Second, they may become so bogged down in the details of a job that they don't get the job done within reasonable time limits. Third, they may put in unnecessarily long hours to perform routine tasks. Fourth, their perfectionist nature may make it impossible for them to delegate authority. Or they may get lost in petty details. Or they may be so psychologically dependent on approval from their superiors that they are fearful of taking on more responsibilities and, therefore, become trapped in low-level positions.

Even when they seek and get help, Anxious Underachievers are rarely transformed into laid-back, easygoing personalities. They live with tension.

Larisa, a classic Anxious Underachiever in her mid-30s, recently came to us for help. The stress of her work had become so debilitating she was seriously considering quitting. She had a job that required making many decisions. She couldn't take the pressure of constantly running the gauntlet of other people's close-up analysis and criticism.

Years earlier, she had applied to graduate school but had been turned down. Her specific problem was that she became immobilized by fear when she had to take standardized tests. Her level of anticipatory anxiety was so great when it came to writing tests that she was unable to pass them. She had been turned down for graduate school for precisely this reason: She couldn't get through the Graduate Record Exam (GRE), a standard exam that potential graduate students must take.

Now she wanted to try to qualify for graduate school once again. Larisa's immediate problem traveled in a straight line back to her undergraduate days at university. Then she was a classic Anxious Underachiever with an average GPA, when she was clearly capable of above-average work.

And classic Anxious Underachiever that Larisa was, she

took it all personally. "Maybe I'm just not good enough to get into graduate school," she would say—knowing full well that all kinds of people not nearly as bright as she was regularly got in. Still, she took it as a reflection on her worth as a person. The unfortunate part of Larisa's story, of course, is that she is intellectually capable of—and educationally prepared for—a much more challenging job than she will allow herself to take on.

But she had saved enough money to take two years off and return to school. (More classic Anxious behavior: A *Coaster* would never analyze a problem at work, plan to go back to school and then save enough money to live for two full years without employment!)

So Larisa quit her job, but she didn't get into graduate school. Instead she was accepted in a related post-graduate program that was not her first choice.

If Larisa had sought professional help early, during her school days, she might have overcome her problem with anxiety—at least enough to get her through graduate school and into the job she had dreamed of. Like Larisa, when Anxious Underachievers do not overcome their problem early on, they carry an extra burden into adulthood.

CHAPTER 4

The Identity-Search Underachiever

- "I'm so confused. I don't know what I want to do with my life. I don't know what my future is going to be. I have no idea about where I'm going. *So why should I study?*"

- "There's no point in studying a meaningless subject! Physics has absolutely no relevance to my life."

- "He just reads from the text, writes a few things on the board and that's it! I mean, he doesn't even make eye contact with anybody in class. So I decided, forget it. English isn't high on my list anyway—and it's sure not going to help me through the night!"

- "I'm interested in *writing*—not grammar! The way she teaches is useless. I've decided to drop the course."

- "He expects us to memorize everything in the textbook. That's not education! It's a waste of time."

- "What I need is my own space. I've got to find my own place. Don't worry—I can pay for it. My job at the restaurant will cover most of it—and I can always get a student loan."

- "How can I concentrate on my school work when I don't even know who I am? I mean, I don't know what I want out of life. I don't know where I'm going to be in three years. I don't know what I want to do. I don't even know what there *is* to do out there."

- How could *you* possibly understand what I want? You've had the *same* job for 18 years! Like, I mean, that's been your whole life! I just can't imagine going to the same office day after day, week after week *for 18 years.*"

- "If you'd just listen to me—listen for one second—maybe we could get along. I'm 17 years old. I'll be able to vote six months from now. So give me a break—I can handle my life."

These are classic remarks made by kids trying to figure out who they are. Their search for themselves is so intense and requires so much energy, it takes a serious toll on their school work. And all this energy diversion, from the outside, looks like that familiar bugbear—The Underachievement Myth. To many onlookers—parents and teachers in the front row—these kids look lazy and unmotivated.

Nothing could be further from the truth. These students are far from idle. They're engaged in a tortuous inner struggle, a struggle with the big questions. Questions like, "Who am I as a person? Where am I going? What should I choose to do with my life? What sort of person do I want to be? How am I going to get there? Is there anyone out there worth traveling with? And when I get there, *if* I get there, will the effort have been worth it?

"Is *anything* worth the effort? And what am I looking for anyway?"

Little wonder they don't have much energy left over for memorizing geometry theorems. *Excuse me, but did you say geometry? What possible relevance could geometry have to Life?*

If this sounds familiar to you, you shouldn't be surprised. Most of us have wrestled with the Big Questions at some point in our lives. Some of us never stop confronting these issues. But usually they hit us full force only once or twice in our lives: First, when we're on the cusp of adulthood, and later when we're about halfway through our adult lives.

The latter, of course, has been labeled Mid-Life Crisis. But there are differences between adolescent identity crises and mid-life identity crises. The young person struggling with these issues is doing so *before* making the journey. And the middle-aged person is looking back as well as ahead.

The adolescent is saying, "How do I want to jump? When do I want to jump? What terrible things will happen to me if I commit myself totally to one direction? Will I close the door on other directions? Maybe I shouldn't jump at all. Because jumping will probably turn out to be too . . . *limiting.*" Young identity-searchers are focused on defining themselves. Whereas mid-life identity-searchers aren't so much concerned with defining themselves as they are with choosing meaningful activities.

The middle-aged person says, "I thought I knew what it was going to be like! And now that I've been in it for 15 or 20 years, it hasn't turned out the way I thought it would. The way it was *supposed* to turn out. *Why* hasn't it turned out the way I thought it would? What am I going to choose to do with the time I've got left?"

If you've experienced a mid-life dark night of the soul, you'll be able to empathize with your child's struggle. But always remember that the two crises are not, cannot, be identical. You're at different stages of your lives.

Are There Many Identity-Search Underachievers?

Not enough hard research has been done to tell us how many kids there are out there who are underachieving specifically because they're struggling with a search for identity. But in our experience and in the literature to date, *roughly 5 to 10 percent of high-school under-achievers and 10 to 15 percent of college and university under-achievers fit this pattern.* This prototype appears most frequently in mid to late adolescence, with the emphasis on late.

Overall, *the sex ratio is about 1:1.* But at the high-school level, we tend to see more girls immersed in these questions than we do boys. It's long been a truism that girls mature earlier than boys, especially in early adolescence. This probably is one reason we see girls confronting issues of identity and direction earlier than boys. Another contributor is the rapidly changing, and constantly shifting, role of women in modern life. The delicate balance among marriage, child-bearing and career may affect young women's thoughts and emotions more than it does young men's.

What kinds of families do these kids come from? There's no cultural, socio-economic or ethnic profile. But they appear to be members of caring families. They have parents who say, "Hey, Bill, we're with you. We understand what you're going through. You can go to Tibet and become a guru if that's what you need to do in order to find yourself. We'll even kick in with some of the airfare. *After* you've graduated, that is. Get your diploma—and *then* concentrate on who you are. It may even give you more of a self to work with! But seriously, you can become anything you want to become—whatever makes you happy. But please, *get your diploma first.*"

How do you know if you are the parent of an underachiever who is similar to this prototype? Look through the following list and see if it fits.

Anatomy of an Identity-Search Underachiever

1. They are intensely self-absorbed. They are constantly struggling with questions about who they really are.

These kids spend a lot of time thinking about themselves. But they're not introverted, withdrawn, quiet or uptight. Ask and they will tell you—probably more than you ever wanted to know. They're not the least bit inhibited about revealing their innermost thoughts and feelings. On the contrary, they're eager to share them with you. They'll tell you *exactly* how they feel—and at some length! (Unlike, for example, Anxious Underachievers, who may be defensive about how they feel, or try to hide things for fear of embarrassment or not measuring up.) It usually never occurs to Identity-Searchers to be embarrassed about anything. They're too involved with the inner struggle to worry whether or not it "looks" right.

Identity-Searchers are in a perpetual state of self-analysis. They examine every move they make, hoping to learn something that will help them define who they are. They analyze the way they brush their teeth, the exact number of minutes and seconds it took them to run

3-3/8 miles, the *real* reason they had a particular dream last night. And amazingly, they also manage to be very sensitive to what's going on around them—although they do tend to see everything in relation to themselves and how it affects *them.*

Identity-Searchers want to find a role in life that *matters.* They want to make a difference. They want to be different from others who have gone before. They're aware of the world of possibilities ahead of them and they long to sample the full range of choices. They want to create a different self.

2. They are intense about almost everything—from the debate about abortion rights to the price of milk.

Don't look for passivity or apathy in this kid. You name it, they've got an opinion about it. And they *care* about issues—passionately.

They are ready to philosophize on virtually any subject that comes up. They may engage in endless discussions about religion, politics, the environment, the state of the world, family, values, ethics, the future and the meaning of life.

They stay up all night agonizing with their friends about the fate of Planet Earth and our doomed environment. They talk endlessly about who they are, about their plans and dreams and fears. They rarely resolve a thing. Not that it matters. The debate is all—they can't get enough of it. They thrive on it.

Sometimes they can look too intense. This may worry some parents. In fact, some professionals may interpret the Identity-Searcher's intense self-absorption as clinical depression, obsessiveness or a mood problem. In our experience, this type of underachiever is *not* abnormal. They're just more intensely involved than most in a normal search for self.

3. They are determined to be independent. They take full responsibility for their actions, behavior and decisions.

Identity-Searchers face up to things. They rarely shy away from the consequences of their actions. They're honest with themselves and with others. They never blame somebody else for things that have gone wrong. They see themselves as the agent of all their decisions.

And they don't want (or need) a lot of parental interference. In fact, they often just ignore parents, teachers or other authority figures who try to tell them what to do. They're not openly defiant. They're not looking for a fight. They just want to be left alone to make their own decisions, do their own thing, live their own life.

4. They are often uncertain—about what they should do, about what they believe, about how they really feel, about making the right decision.

She may have strong opinions about just about anything, but when it comes to making up her mind whether she wants to apply to university or take a year off to travel, she's stymied. And she agonizes over whether it would be ethical to accept an invitation to the formal with a guy whose intellect she doesn't respect.

Another Identity-Searcher feels strongly about the state of democracy in the new Russia and then wonders if he should worry about that so much when there are street-people working the corner at the end of his block. He works himself into a perpetual state of confusion and ethical angst.

Yet another Identity-Searcher can't decide whether or not to drop physics, let alone what she wants to do with her life. She's interested in a lot of fields, but finds it impossible to focus on any of them as a possible career.

5. They experiment with opinions, value systems, beliefs and groups of friends.

Identity-Searchers may bounce among dramatically different groups of friends at school—preppy kids, the grunge set, bikers—and, amazingly, appear to be accepted by every group. Their relationships with peers become a sort of experimental laboratory. They try out different roles not just as a way to socialize but to find out who they are. This experimenting may include a wide variety of issues: sexuality, education, lifestyle (such as manner of dress), politics, religion, culture and especially peer relationships.

When it comes to school work, they may be highly motivated to achieve in some school subjects and not in others. How well the Identity-Searcher does in a course is often determined by whether or not the course is "relevant." In other words, whether or not the course really means something, which teachers deserve respect, whether or not the teacher is intellectually stimulating or whether or not the subject is going to be important to his or her future.

And just because he has chosen to achieve in, say, math this year does not guarantee that he will make the same decision next year. Next year, math may find itself relegated to the "irrelevant" heap.

6. They question adult values and lifestyles.

Identity-Search Underachievers can be very judgmental. They're comfortable questioning adults with searching questions that to the adult on the hot seat may seem impertinent or unduly candid.

He questions how you, his parents, are raising his younger brother.

She buttonholes a teacher about what she labels his unfair or unethical teaching practices.

He lets you know that he's happy to work for Teacher A—because he agrees with her values—but he will *never* lift a finger for Teacher B because he respects nothing about her—her teaching style, the way she disciplines the class, her political beliefs.

Identity-Search Underachievers are not doing this to put you on the spot. They're far too tied up in their own thought processes even to think of that. They're simply trying to figure things out for themselves. Asking uncomfortable questions of other people is all part of their own search for identity.

Summing Up: Anatomy of an Identity-Search Underachiever

If we had to sum up the Identity-Search Underachiever in one word, it would be "introspective." Does "introspective" describe your child? Let's glance over the rest of the list of characteristics.

1. They are intensely self-absorbed. They are constantly struggling with questions about who they really are.

2. They are intense about almost everything—from the debate about abortion rights to the price of milk.

3. They are determined to be independent. They take full responsibility for their actions, behavior and decisions.

4. They are often uncertain—about what they should do, about what they believe, about how they really feel, about making the right decision.

5. They experiment with opinions, value systems, beliefs and groups of friends.

6. They question adult values and lifestyles.

But hold on a minute, you may be saying, doesn't every adolescent go through a period of intense self-evaluation? Isn't this a normal part of growing up?

Yes and no. Yes, most adolescents go through a period of self-evaluation. No, it's not always so intense that it interferes with their achievement or their relationships. The stereotypical view of adolescence as the stormiest period of one's life does not always hold true. Remember the Coasting Underachiever? Coasters often remember their adolescence as the best (i.e., most serene) years of their lives. Or consider Anxious Underachievers. They don't agonize over who they are. They're much too concerned about the authority figures in their life.

So it's normal to ruminate about who you are and where you're going somewhere between the ages of 15 and 25. But Identity-Search Underachievers go over the top in this department. Their internal struggles cause them intense distress about decisions in a number of major areas. These include decisions about:

- school and education
- long-term goals
- career
- friendship patterns

- sexuality
- religious beliefs
- value systems
- family relationships.

Their internal search may surface in one or more of these areas. How long this battle has been going on—and how much it is interfering with your child's academic achievement—is the key to helping you decide how to intercede in this battle.

To help you determine the extent to which your child's pattern of underachievement is similar to the Identity-Search Underachiever prototype, answer the questions in the Parent Checklist below.

1. Is my child self-absorbed, focused on inner thoughts and feelings about who he or she is?

Yes___ No___ Don't Know___

2. Does my child have intense feelings about school, friends, careers and long-term goals, the family or values and beliefs?

Yes___ No___ Don't Know___

3. Does my child insist on making his or her own decisions about school, friends, careers and long-term goals, the family or values and beliefs?

Yes___ No___ Don't Know___

4. Does my child seem to change his or her mind, or to be uncertain or confused about school, friends, careers and long-term goals, the family or values and beliefs?

Yes___ No___ Don't Know___

5. Does my child continually   Yes___ No___ Don't Know___
    express or try out new opin-
    ions, likes and dislikes, ideas,
    attitudes or experiences?

6. Does my child question or   Yes___ No___ Don't Know___
    challenge parental or societal
    values?

Parent Checklist

If you answered "Yes" to four or more of the above questions, your child's characteristics may be similar to those of the Identity-Search Underachiever type.

Why Do Some Identity-Searchers Underachieve?

Many novels have been written about the inner lives of people struggling with questions about their own identity. This is not a subject up for discussion here. But if we had to compress the struggle into a single phrase, we would have to say that the Identity-Search Underachiever is experiencing a prolonged struggle with *defining the self.*

> Who am I? How do I go about deciding who I am?
> What am I going to do with my life? How will I ever be able to decide?
> I've lived my life as a child up to now. My future is going to be as an adult. Who is that adult? Who do I want that adult to be?
> What am I going to do now that I really am independent?

Identity-Search Underachievers experience intense doubt. Doubt is one of those rare states that involves the mind *and* the emotions in more or less equal parts—which helps explain why the Identity-Searcher is both intellectually combative and prone to bouts of anxiety or sadness as well.

"But you're only hurting yourself."

"I know, but if this is what school is, I want to do some-thing else."

"What do you mean?"

"Why should I keep going to school if it's meaningless? Everything about it is meaningless—the teachers and their attitudes, the subjects, especially the required courses. Required for what? Not for anything I want to do."

"What is it you want to do?"

"I don't know yet. But listen, I know I could do better in chemistry—if I wanted to. But why should I spend hours and hours memorizing formulas when they have nothing at all to do with my life?"

Unlike many other types of underachievers, Identity-Search Under-achievers make a conscious and deliberate choice *not* to achieve. And that choice revolves around an intense need not only to do what is meaningful, but to *avoid* what is meaningless.

Summing Up: What the Identity-Searcher Is Looking For

- The Identity-Search Underachiever is looking for a sense of identity that he can call his own. He wants to be sure that he himself is the person who defines who he is, and nobody else.

- The Identity-Searcher is wracked with agonizing doubt—doubt about who he is and where he is going, and uncertainty about the world at large.

- Either the intensity of the Identity-Searcher's inner turmoil is so overwhelming she has no energy left over to devote to school work, or the Identity-Search Underachiever makes a deliberate choice *not* to achieve at school because she rejects the values, attitudes or standards of the school and its teachers.

Life is as real and as earnest for the Identity-Searcher as it is for the

The Identity-Search Underachiever experiences both *self-doubt* (doubt turned inward) and *doubts about the world at large* (doubt turned outward).

Self-doubt explains their experimentation with different belief systems, kinds of friends and modes of life. *Generalized doubt about the state of the world* explains their endless late-night discussions, arguments, questioning of authority, debates about moral, ethical and religious values, heated arguments about things trivial and mundane, and dramatic swings in passions and opinions.

Two scenarios help explain why the Identity-Searcher underachieves. Most Identity-Search Underachievers fit one or the other scenario. And some fit a little of both.

Scenario 1: Lost in the whirlpool.

The inner emotional world of Identity-Search Underachievers can be compared to a whirlpool. At the center of the whirlpool is the Identity-Searchers' struggle to define themselves as independent beings. All of their energies, goals, thoughts, emotions and perceptions are swept up in the whirlpool and drawn into its center. Nothing else matters or is even remotely important. At the same time, the whirlpool is so busy and confusing, Identity-Search Underachievers find it impossible to pull any sense from it. Every ounce of their energy is swept up into the swirl. There is little energy left over for what Identity-Searchers see as the mundane, meaningless task of getting good grades in every course.

In short, Identity-Search Underachievers have devoted so much energy and intensity to the search for self that they have neither time nor energy left over to concentrate on school work.

Scenario 2: By deliberate choice.

"How come you're doing poorly in math?"
"I don't agree with the way the math teacher treats the kids in that class. It's not what education is supposed to be. I just don't want to be a part of it."

Anxious Underachiever. There is nothing phony or fake about the Identity-Searcher's quest. Nor is there anything false about the angst. But helping Identity-Search Underachievers is a much trickier matter for a parent than helping Anxious Underachievers. Identity-Searchers' cries for help are muffled by their protests that they can handle this just fine by themselves, thank you very much. So to come to their aid, you must first learn how to approach them. This requires sensitivity, patience and a willingness to listen.

Helping the Identity-Search Underachiever

1. Take stock of your attitude toward your underachieving child. When you approach an Identity-Searcher with an offer of help, you risk rejection. "Thanks Dad, but I can handle this myself." Or, "Why can't you just leave me alone? I've got enough problems without you poking your nose into my life!"

Broaching the subject of help is a delicate matter. To learn how to approach your Identity-Searching child, consider the following:

Take a deep breath and try to approach your child with an attitude of openness, acceptance and appreciation of his or her genuine struggles.
Swallow your own opinions for a moment. Keep quiet and try to tap into your child's inner turmoil.

Approach your child as an equal.
This may take many deep breaths—and silent reminders to yourself: "Don't talk down! He's becoming an adult and needs to be treated like one."

Treating your child as an emerging equal may require a conscious pulling back on your part. Your relationship up to now has been a parental one, as, of course, it always will be. But there is a new quality entering your relationship. Your son or daughter is no longer a child, and you need to add an adult-to-adult element to your communication. This requires you to deliberately distance yourself in order to see

him as an independent, separately functioning human being. As a way
of helping yourself do this, you might try mentally imagining him as
someone you work with—a particular colleague or client whom you
respect and whose views and expertise you value.

*All of the above is an exercise in learning to let go as a parent
of a child who is maturing.*
Identity-Search adolescents are stepping out into the unknown on
their own. They're ready to take full responsibility for their own decisions and actions. And there's no turning back. All you can do now is
stand back and offer encouragement, empathy and wisdom from the
sidelines.

Because for better or worse, they're launched into their own future.

2. Learn how to listen.
The key to helping the Identity-Search Underachiever is *listening*.
Non-judgmental, empathic, caring, open-ended, appreciative, non-
controlling, probing, helping, reflective listening.

The only way you can help Identity-Search Underachievers find
their way is by climbing into the labyrinth of their minds with them.
Together you can gently probe the confusion within and *maybe* find
a few signposts pointing toward the way out. But all you can do to
help find those signposts is listen to what's on their mind.

Here's how:

*To encourage the Identity-Search Underachiever to open up,
ask general questions that steer clear of specific problems or
situations.*
Usually parents or teachers approach low or failing marks (or, indeed,
sub-par performance of any kind) by firing a volley of confrontational
questions. For example:

"Why did you fail math?"
"Why didn't you start studying sooner for the test?"
"Why don't you bring your books home more often?"

And usually, the answers they receive are short and not so sweet. For example:

"Why did you fail math?"
"I hate math."

"Why didn't you start studying sooner for the test?"
"I don't want to talk about it."

"Why don't you bring your books home more often?"
"There isn't much in them anyway."

Why does it happen this way?

Because asking questions, especially specific questions like the ones above, *closes down communication rather than opens it up.*

Ask a simple question, you get a simple answer.

For example: "What was your mark in Spanish?" *"Thirty percent."*

You asked, she answered. End of discussion—because the hidden agenda within your question is, "I want to know what your mark is and I'm not interested in reasons or excuses. All I want to know are the facts."

The most damaging kind of specific or "directive" question is the "why" question: "Why did you get such lousy grades?" "Why don't you study more?" "Why can't you get your act together?"

The hidden agenda for all three of those questions is: "What's the matter with you anyway?"

A non-specific question sends out a completely different message. The message is, "I'm interested in *you,* all of you. I'm interested in what you think, how you feel, how *you* see the problem or the situation. I'm not looking for a simple yes or no."

Non-specific, "non-directive" questions are questions like the following:

"What happened?"
"How do you feel about that?"
"What do you think?"
"What are you going to do?"
"What do you think of your grades?"

Whenever possible, open up channels of communication by making statements instead of asking questions (even the non-specific questions above).

There is a specific kind of statement that opens up communication. It's called a *reflective statement*.

Reflective statements are just what they say they are. They reflect back—or mirror—what the person you are talking with is saying or thinking or feeling.

You come into the kitchen after work and find your teenage son sitting at the kitchen table, shoulders slumped, staring into space. Here's how to find out what's wrong using reflective statements:

Father:	(with surprise and genuine concern in his voice) "Gosh, David, you look really down!"
Teenager:	"Naw, not really." *(He's not exactly dying to tell his father all about what's bothering him. Dad's going to have to earn David's confidences with some sensitive probing.)*
Father:	"Not really." *(A simple reflection of what David has said, repeated straight—without using irony, sarcasm or a judgmental tone.)*
Teenager:	"Well, I'm not exactly what anyone would call happy." *(Hearing his statement mirrored back makes him feel as if his father understands a little about how he feels. Feeling understood gives him the courage to risk telling his father a little bit more about how he feels.)*
Father:	"You're not exactly happy right now." *(Ditto, as above. Note that Dad does not "parrot" David's statement. He simply repeats a slight variation on it, in a concerned tone of voice. This encourages David to open up a crack more.)*
Teenager:	"Yeah. I don't know why. I guess I just don't know if school is worth it. I mean, who cares?"

Father:	"You're not sure if school is worth it."
Teenager:	"Yeah, I mean, like, we're studying stuff I'm *never* going to use. So what's the point?"

Dad now has a fair stab at (a) getting to the heart of what's really bothering David (which could be something as simple as a specific incident that day at school that has upset and depressed him) and (b) helping him cope with it.

The secret to success in situations like this is learning to quell your fears for the moment that the child is rejecting everything you've tried to instill in him about the value of education. If you can resist imposing your opinion for the moment, you will find that although your child is uncertain now, he eventually will use many of your values to solve his dilemma. So . . . have faith.

Now contrast the above with the way these kinds of situations usually occur:

Dad walks into the kitchen, tired after work and sees his son slumped over the kitchen table. Doing absolutely nothing—zip—when he should be doing his homework.

Father:	"Why aren't you in your room doing your homework?"
Teenager:	"Oh, for God's sake, leave me alone! You walk in here and you don't even bother to say hello."
Father:	"Now you look here, sonny. I walk in here after a 12-hour day, exhausted, and I find you sitting here on your behind, goofing off—as usual! What do you expect me to say? Frankly, I'm sick of your lazy, self-centered, layabout ways."
Teenager:	"I can't stand this." (He walks out, slamming the door behind him.)

Father and son now are at each other's throats—even further apart than when Dad walked in. What's more, Dad has no idea about what's going on inside his son's mind. He just assumes he's lazy and unmotivated. And his son is so angry and upset, he sits in his room all evening, brooding—and does no homework at all.

*   *   *

Contrast the following two conversations:

CONVERSATION A

Mother:	"Why did you get such a lousy mark in math?"
Daughter:	"I dunno."
Mother:	"Well, there must be a reason."
Daughter:	"I told you—I don't know! And I don't want to talk about it either."
Mother:	"Now you look here. You can't just dismiss this and say, 'I don't want to talk about it.' Your mark in math is important to your future—and you know it!"
Daughter:	"God, Mom. Why can't you just leave me alone?"
Mother:	"Don't you *want* to get good grades?"
Daughter:	(with a deep sigh) "Oh, I don't know."
Mother:	"How can you keep saying, 'I don't know?' You sound like a broken record! You're going to have a rude awakening one of these days, young lady, when you realize how you're ruining your future!"

CONVERSATION B

Mother:	(in a mildly concerned tone of voice) "I see you got a D in math."
Daughter:	"Yeah."
Mother:	(looks her daughter directly in the eye, but her facial expression is soft) "You don't look too happy about it."
Daughter:	(dejectedly) "I'm not."
Mother:	(gently) "Tell me about it." *(A general statement*

> *that allows her daughter a lot of leeway about how she chooses to approach the subject.)*

Daughter: "I don't know what happened. I guess I didn't study enough or . . . I don't know. I don't even like math."

Mother: "You don't like math." *(A reflective statement. It implicitly encourages her daughter to open up the subject of why she doesn't like math.)*

Daughter : (with feeling) "Yeah, I hate it! And I *know* I need it to get into science at college. And that's two years away! How can I study something I hate so much for *two whole years?*"

The floodgates have opened. The conversation could take any direction from here—including the daughter's current problems with her boyfriend or anything else that happens to be on her mind—because an atmosphere of trust and acceptance has been established. And more to the point, Mom has tapped her daughter's underlying academic worry: her concerns about achieving her goal—getting into the Bachelor of Science program at university—when she needs math in order to qualify.

CARL ROGERS AND THE "CLIENT-CENTERED" APPROACH TO COMMUNICATING

Using reflective statements as a way of opening up dialogue with another person is not an original idea of ours. Far from it. It is a widely used, very famous, tried-and-true method originally propounded by the late American psychologist Carl Rogers in his book, *Client-Centered Therapy*, published in the early '50s.

Rogers developed what he called "client-centered or non-directive therapy" in the late '40s and early '50s in his psychotherapy practice. Since then, it has been widely adopted by counselors and communicators in many fields. At the heart of client-centered therapy are reflective statements used by the therapist to mirror back the client's thoughts and feelings in a way that enables the client to feel comfortable and trusting enough to (eventually) divulge his or her innermost thoughts.

Rogers recognized this as an effective way for anyone to tap into another person's thoughts and emotions, not just professional counselors with their clients. The world has changed drastically over the last 40 years, but the essential ways people relate to one another have not, which is why Rogers's approach works as well now as it did then.

The professor who taught us this counseling method at graduate school in the mid-'60s used a very effective teaching method: the approach itself.

He asked two students to come to the front of the class. "One of you is the counselor," he said, "and the other is the client." He instructed the "counselor" to ask the "client" specific questions, and he instructed the "client" to answer in a straightforward manner. The conversation went something like this:

Q: "Why are you here?"
A: *"I don't know. I guess I'm worried."*
Q: "What are you worried about?"
A: *"I'm worried about school."*
Q: "What worries you about school?"
A: *"I don't like it."*
Q: "Why don't you like it?"
A: *"I don't know."* (Long pause.)

As you can see, the dialogue begins to lose energy after three or four questions. This is exactly what happened. The student counselor found himself running out of questions and, eventually, the "conversation" lost steam and came to a grinding halt.

At which point the professor intervened and said to the student counselor: "Okay. Now let's do it again. This time, I want you to say whatever you like to the client—so long as you don't ask any questions."

The student counselor was stymied, as were the rest of us in the class. We all looked at each other. How in heaven's name could you talk to someone and elicit conversation and discussion without asking any questions? Asking questions seemed like the only reasonable, natural way of interacting with a client and the only possible way a counselor could expect to open a discussion. Our entire class was very sympathetic to the student counselor, who had really been put on the spot. There were several awkward—silent—moments. The "counselor" could think of nothing to say. At last, mercifully, the professor intervened. He said, "All right. Here's how to get a conversation going without asking questions. You reflect back the feelings you think the client is experiencing. For example, if you look at the client and his brow is furrowed and his shoulders are hunched up, you might say, 'You look worried.' Or, if he's sitting back, knees crossed, head resting on the back of the chair, you might say, 'You look comfortable.' Or, 'I get the impression you're not sure quite what to say.' Or, 'You seem to be keeping things to yourself right now.' Or, 'I get the impression you're deep in thought.' "

All of these reflective statements indicate an initial attempt on the part of the counselor to put himself in the client's chair and see the world as he sees it. It's a first step toward building a relationship based on mutual trust, empathy, understanding and acceptance.

Using reflective statements to open up a dialogue with your Identity-Search Underachiever means giving up your cherished role as chief advice-giver, direction-maker and judge. This is not an easy thing to do as a parent—after a comfortable 16, 18 or 20 years in the commander's chair. So getting into it may take a little time.

But take our word for it, you have little choice in this matter.

Because if your child has embarked on a search for himself, then whether or not *you're* ready, *he's* ready for independence. He doesn't want—and, more importantly, he won't take—direction or advice. If you set yourself up as legislator or judge, you'll lose your chance to expand communication.

The only way you're going to maintain—or re-establish—contact with Identity-Search Underachievers is by reversing the roles you've grown accustomed to. It's your turn now to listen. It's your turn to put yourself in their shoes. To try to understand who and where *they* are. And reflective statements are the way to start this dialogue.

Here are some reflective statements that may help you open a dialogue with your child:

- "Tell me more about that."
- "Tell me about it."
- "I wonder what this means."
- "I wonder what you think about this."
- "It sounds as if you're upset."
- "You seem disappointed (angry, sad, depressed, uncomfortable, pleased . . .)."
- "I get the impression you're not sure what this means."
- "You seem unsure. I guess you're pulled in two directions."

Consider each one of these statements. None of them makes a demand on the other person to respond in a particular way. Each of them respects the other person's ability to make a choice about whether or not to respond. If she chooses to respond, *she* decides what the response will be. Each of the statements sends out a message of respect for how the other person feels. And each sends a message that you accept their independence in the relationship.

One caution: Although using reflective statements may be a very effective way to open up a dialogue with your Identity-Search kid, it is *not* as effective with all types of underachievers. For example, the Anxious Underachiever may find the absence of structure in reflective statements very upsetting. And this may raise his anxiety level. With other types of underachievers, using reflective statements may not be harmful, but it may not achieve much. But for the Identity-Search Underachiever, it is just the thing.

Make a concerted effort to listen empathically.
Real listening is listening with empathy—in this case, genuinely seeing problems and situations through the eyes of your son or daughter instead of through your own. This does not mean agreeing with everything your child says or feels or believes. What it does mean is suspending judgment.

Hold back the knee-jerk parental response in which you tell your child what *you* feel or think or what *he* should feel or think. Instead, try to identify what your child is feeling and thinking underneath the words, and mirror that back in your own words in the form of a reflective statement. Very often, this approach means you will be listening with empathy.

Here's an example of how you can use empathic listening:

Student: "I just don't know if school is for me. I take these courses that I don't care about. I don't like a lot of the teachers."

If you, the parent, decide that what your child is feeling or thinking underneath the words is that she's confused about what kind of career to pursue, then your reflective statement might be: "You're really not certain what you want to do."

If you conclude that your child is expressing anger at her teachers by turning off in class, you might say, "Those teachers really make you angry—angry enough to quit." Or, "Something about those teachers really bothers you."

In other words, there are many possible conclusions you may come to about what your child is feeling or thinking behind the words. When you try to mirror it back, you may be right and you may be wrong. Either way it doesn't matter, because you'll be listening with empathy and understanding. Your child will appreciate that and, if you're wrong, she'll tell you.

When you listen to another person with real empathy, the other person feels understood and accepted. (This is another of Carl Rogers's key concepts.)

Think about these words for a moment: *understand* and *accept*. When you tiptoe into the private spaces of your child's mind and heart and make the effort to understand where and how he is . . . and then go the extra distance required to *accept* where and how he is, you'll have gone a long way toward melting the barriers that separate you.

This can only happen when you as a parent temporarily give up your own agenda, your own needs, your own goals for your child and truly try to see what *his* are. If being authoritative or dogmatic is an entrenched habit for you, then surrendering your position may take an extraordinary effort of will. Try to see her dilemma, her successes, her failures, thoughts, feelings, reactions, ideas, hopes, confusions, perceptions, the way *she* sees them. Try to understand what she thinks it all means.

> "I guess it's not easy for you."
> "It's easier for you to say what you don't want than what you do want."
> "Sometimes it's tough to make decisions about things."

3. Guide your discussions with your Identity-Search Underachiever toward a fresh approach to achievement.
Let your child take the lead in these discussions.
As a parent, you probably are used to taking the lead and setting the tone in most discussions with your children. With an Identity-Searcher, especially one who is underachieving, you have to shift gears.

Not only do you have to learn to listen, but you also have to learn to *wait* and to *follow*.

Waiting literally means sitting there and saying nothing until the Identity-Search Underachiever decides to speak. For most of us, this is a new experience and often an uncomfortable one—especially with our own children. But it pays off. Just because there is silence does not mean that nothing is happening. Learn to trust that Identity-Search Underachievers will often appreciate that you are willing to sit there, silently, and give them the opportunity of taking things at their own pace.

Following means not directing the conversation in any particular way toward the points *you* want to get across. It means being willing to let your son or daughter take the lead, express whatever is on his or her mind and follow the discussion where he or she wants to take it. Remember, the greatest leaders in history are the ones who sense what people really want, and ally themselves with those underlying needs.

Be aware of Identity-Searchers' hopes and dreams. Do what you can to help them take shape and form and grow.

Remember our discussion in Chapter 1 about the four steps toward achievement? The first of the four steps was vision (followed by commitment, planning and follow-through). Identity-Searchers have hopes and dreams—they have a vision, although it isn't fully formed. But they're struggling to get it in focus. It's not quite clear as yet. And they're not sure how to jump with it—yet. But they're getting it. And if you'll only let it grow (without interference), and help them to let it grow (without blockages), it will make a real difference in their lives.

Try to tap into their indecision and help them find their way through it—without taking over.

Kids who are struggling with questions about their own identity are facing one of life's major issues. They're struggling with the crucial question of what their life means and who they are. They're deeply uncertain about this. They are examining their choices and actions and reactions in life, and they're hoping that each thing that happens to them will give them a clue that will help them define who they are.

The challenge here is to be with them as they address these questions—but to do this in a way that does not give them any definitive answers. Since *they* do not have answers to their questions, they will view any answers you offer as an indication that you don't understand what they're struggling with. In other words, you want to share the *questions* with them (Who am I? Where am I going? What does it all mean?), without providing the answers.

Don't talk down to kids struggling with this identity issue.

You may have been through all this before when you were a teenager. But your child hasn't. For her, this is the first time and it is terribly serious.

Identity-Searchers already feel the generation gap keenly. They're probably very critical of you—about how you run your life, about the kind of job you have, about the lifestyle you have chosen. "When I was your age . . . " will get you nowhere. In fact, it's likely to exacerbate the problems and widen the gap between you and your child. "Things have changed, Dad! This is the '90s. It's a different world out there."

Well, yes and no. As adults we realize that some things never change. But the world *has* changed in many seminal ways over the last generation, and in your child's eyes—which is what matters here—*everything* is different now. What's more, she's not the tiniest bit interested in how you felt at her age. Not right now. For the moment, she's interested in herself alone, and the only way you're going to get through to her is to approach her as an equal, not as an all-knowing authority figure ladling out wise advice.

Be prepared to go back to basic principles and wrestle with core questions about why achievement matters.
We tend to take for granted the values of education and of achievement: a general knowledge of the world we live in, enrichment of our lives through exposure to the world's collected culture, expansion of our minds through absorbing ideas, the knowledge acquired from the study of specific disciplines (science, poetry, sociology, psychology, physics, mathematics, drama and so on). And today especially, we realize the urgent necessity of having a substantial education as a preparation for a career.

We often *assume* these values and believe that others assume them also. They don't, necessarily. Especially Identity-Search Underachievers. They are right in the middle of questioning the value of education for the first time, and *they want to make up their own minds about it.*

So you have to be willing to re-examine those values with them. You have to be prepared to get into discussions, explanations, explorations of all of the pros and cons of formal education and its values. If you don't, your son or daughter will conclude (rightly) that you really don't understand. And they will be much less likely to take anything you· say seriously.

4. Support your Identity-Search child in making independent decisions about alternative academic structures or career choices.

Identity-Searchers are getting ready to strike out on their own. They don't want you beside them. But it's fine if you're behind them—encouraging, even making suggestions about possible alternative decisions.

"Have you checked into business? I don't want to lay anything on you, but I just wanted to know if you'd checked it out."

If your child does express an interest in business, support the idea and help her investigate various specific possibilities or alternative academic structures. So long as you don't jump in with both feet and take over.

If, for example, your daughter decides she'd like to restructure her school curriculum, give her some leeway and room to maneuver. It's entirely possible she'll do it in a very constructive way. In fact, she may blossom academically.

Going to university can be custom-made for the Identity-Search student. On campus, it's *normal* to discuss ad nauseam (and until sunrise) the Ultimate Significance of Life As We Know It. If your Identity-Search Underachiever is still in high school, however, it's possible his real problem is that he's a student ahead of his time—psychologically prepared for much more freedom than usually is allowed at the high-school level. So help him investigate variations in his curriculum—perhaps even an alternative school.

Let's look over our list of ways to help your Identity Search child begin to achieve again.

Summing Up: Helping the Identity-Search Underachiever

1. Take stock of your attitude toward your underachieving child.

2. Learn how to listen.

3. Guide your discussions with your Identity-Search Underachiever toward a fresh approach to achievement.

4. Support your Identity-Search child in making independent decisions about alternative academic structures or career choices.

What Changes Can You Expect Once You Start Working with Your Identity-Search Underachiever?

1. Expect sudden changes in feelings and ideas. "You're a different person from the one we met six months ago," we said (in a perfect reflective statement) to one Identity-Search Underachiever who came to us for help. His face clouded. "I'm a different person from the one I was yesterday," he replied.

He wasn't being funny or cute. He was serious. And he wasn't happy with his disruptive, internal shifts of mood and identity.

That's the way things go with Identity-Search Underachievers. It doesn't mean our efforts are useless. One minute your Identity-Searcher will be absolutely certain of his plan of action. The next he'll have forgotten he *had* a plan of action, let alone what it was.

Remember, change—real change—always takes time.

One day your struggling identity-seeker will be loving and cooperative and bursting with things to talk about with you. The next she'll tell you your generation can't seem to get its thick head around *anything*.

And of course, this invariably happens just when you expect it least—the morning after you've confided in a friend that you're making real progress with your child now that you've got smart and learned how to do the right thing.

2. Expect contradictions—and lots of them. In the confusion, introspective turmoil and painful changes they go through, Identity-Searchers lay themselves open to experiencing a wide range of feelings, attitudes and ideas. We're talking about real extremes: The tenderest sentiments can exist alongside the most callous cruelty. Crushing stupidity will follow hard upon blinding insights. The most childish behavior will occur seconds after flashes of awesome maturity.

These kids may seem pig-headed and opinionated, but the truth of the matter is they have mixed feelings about almost everything, especially the things that matter most. They haven't yet learned how to accept the inner contradictions and opposites that we all experience—let alone come to terms with these conflicting emotions and resolve them. All the empathic listening in the world isn't going to change this overnight. It's only going to ease the struggle from time to time.

3. Expect lots of openness . . . *if* you listen, are empathetic and don't try to lead.

4. Expect to see growth and maturity beginning to form, even if you can't predict when or how it will happen or what direction it will take.

5. Expect your relationship with your son or daughter to undergo a fundamental change: still parent-child, but also approaching (if never quite reaching) a respectful friendship between two equals.

6. As the Identity-Searcher reaches young adulthood, expect to be pleasantly surprised about how many of your values, attitudes and beliefs your child has internalized. You know the old joke: The 21-year-old remarks, "It's amazing how much my parents have learned in the past year."

The Identity-Search Underachiever as an Adult

Most Identity-Search Underachievers successfully emerge from their personal struggles and become productive young adults imbued with energy and focus. The intensity of the Identity-Searcher's quest plus the nature of the struggle are virtual guarantees that the search will not go on forever. The questions Identity-Search Underachievers immerse themselves in generate their own answers. And when Identity-Searchers find the answers they've been looking for, they often become intensely focused and motivated, almost overnight. They set goals with lightning speed. They make decisions rapidly. They just *do* it.

They've struggled long and hard to find their personal vision. Now they can go after their goals with tremendous energy.

Former Identity-Search Underachievers typically become involved in personally meaningful work. And their personal relationships are marked by honesty and commitment.

But what happens to Identity-Search Underachievers who don't change, you may be asking. The fact is, we see very few Identity-Search Underachievers who do not change. Virtually none, in fact. The nature of these kids' search means they are extremely open to change. So much so that there is a high probability they will resolve the issues they are struggling with. If they're open to finding out who they are at the age of 16, 18, 20 or 22, the likelihood that they'll be still looking when they're 32 is next to zero.

This means that in our experience, we do not see adolescent Identity-Search Underachievers growing into adult Identity-Search Underachievers. We do, however, from time to time see adult Identity-Search Underachievers who are unrelated to their younger counterparts. People find themselves immersed in questions about who they are at a critical point during their adult lives, for many reasons. A frequent trigger for a major identity crisis is a marital separation or divorce. The individuals involved find a core aspect of their adult identity suddenly pulled out from under them and are forced to face fundamental issues of identity: Who am I *now*? Who do I want to be now that I'm not half of this couple?

In a classic mid-life crisis, individuals confront disappointments, disillusionments, unrealistic expectations or unfulfilled dreams. They question whether they are happy with the direction their life is taking, whether their life has a sense of meaning, whether they need to make major changes and what the direction of those changes should be. Adults in mid-life crisis frequently behave very like adolescent Identity-Search Underachievers—uncertain, doubtful, moody, ambivalent, self-absorbed.

Whatever its genesis, a mid-life identity crisis can turn an achiever into an underachiever, at least temporarily. The person in crisis becomes so self-absorbed she loses the motivation to put forth her best efforts at work. And she will continue to underachieve until she sorts out new goals to pursue and a refurbished identity to don. What do former Identity-Search Underachievers look like as adults in the workplace? Identity-Searchers who have worked through their struggle, developed a vision and goals and, in the process, grown to adulthood often are identified by their colleagues as idealists and crap detectors. These are the people who expend a lot of energy at work questioning the values, goals and activities of the organizations they work for. People like this can be very valuable in an organization where the management is open to alternative points of view. But if the organization is not open to new ideas or change, or if it otherwise devalues these peoples' ideas, these former Identity-Search Underachievers may become disillusioned and unmotivated, and seek alternative employment.

CHAPTER 5

The Wheeler-Dealer Underachiever

As we mentioned earlier, when we test kids to see why they are under-achieving, we give them a series of cards with pictures on them and ask them to make up a story to go with each picture.

One of the cards we show them is blank. Nothing on it. And the message is: It's up to you. Make up whatever kind of story you want.

Here's a story a Wheeler-Dealer Underachiever concocted:

> "The title of this story is *Take Over*. All the kids have come to school on Monday and they have a plan. They throw the teachers out of school."

At this point in his story, the kid paused and thought for a moment. Then, with a wicked smile, he continued:

> "No . . . I've got something better: The kids place all the teachers under suspension. They round them up during the first period and make them sit in the auditorium all day long. The students take over and play rock and roll over the PA system into the auditorium and break all the rules—just for the hell of it!
>
> "At the end of the day, they escort the teachers to detentions. The homework they give them is—get this!—to copy

out the entire Bible 10 times. They stand over the teachers and tell them to start working on it *now*! Then the students fill the teachers' cars with whipped cream and lock their keys in the trunks. They pour booze into the staff room sink and take away the coffee pot.

"The police get wind of what's going on and surround the school. They let the teachers out at 5 p.m.—which is a *reasonable* hour. *(Presumably, this kid has often been detained until an* unreasonable *hour.)*

"The teachers are feeling broken-hearted. They go home and they resign. The school gets a whole new set of teachers with *fair rules*. And the school continues—but everyone's *much* happier."

This is *Apocalypse Now*—with a sense of humor. It's a story about a revolution. And the message is, "Get rid of the enemy and we'll all be a whole lot happier." And as for right and wrong: "Stuff it to the teachers who do nothing but moralize at us all day long. Make them copy out the Bible 10 times. That should give them a dose of their own medicine. See how *they* enjoy it!"

Wheeler-Dealer Underachievers want it all—and they want it *now*. They want action. Quiet, solitary hours reading a book, working on a project and watching it grow bit by bit just aren't on for Wheeler-Dealers. Wheeler-Dealers are impulsive. They're scattered. They want instant gratification. Wheeler-Dealer Underachievers are kids in a hurry, and their rush has nothing to do with school.

Wheeler-Dealers are always playing an angle. They can be charming and disarming when they want something and suddenly intimidating when things are not going their way. They are manipulative. Wheeler-Dealers use people.

Wheeler-Dealers see no percentage in achieving at school. "Excuse me, did you say good grades?" The message is, "Show me the payoff. School work is for people who are totally beneath anything I'm into thinking about. I mean, let's get a little action going around here."

The action that Wheeler-Dealers are interested in doesn't happen in the classroom. At school, *when* they're at school, they're behavior problems—lazy and unmotivated problem kids.

The truth is Wheeler-Dealer Underachievers *are* motivated. They're motivated to pursue goals a long way from the school yard. We'll get to their real motivation later in this chapter.

What's the Incidence of Wheeler-Dealer Underachievers?

Between 5 and 10 percent of underachieving kids are Wheeler-Dealer types.

Male/female ratio? This is the one kind of underachiever where males decidedly predominate. The ratio is about 4.5 males to one female. But the gap is diminishing. When we began our professional training 25 years ago, the ratio was 7:1.

What kind of families do Wheeler-Dealers come from? The specifics on the Wheeler-Dealer home front vary. But the bottom line is an unhappy situation. Let us explain:

In Wheeler-Dealer families:

- Parents often have strongly different views on their child's behavior and what needs to be done about it. For example, Father may be angry and think that his son needs to be punished, while Mother thinks that their son needs understanding and forgiveness. In this situation, Dad blames Junior for everything and Mom constantly bails him out of trouble.

- Wheeler-Dealer parents often do not present a united front to their children. And disagreements between parents are often expressed in front of the children.

- One parent (usually the father) may also have a history of being a Wheeler-Dealer student.

- Serious arguments, disagreements and open conflict are a typical component of everyday life in Wheeler-Dealer families. These confrontations go far beyond normal family ups-and-downs and spats.

Age of onset? We've seen Wheeler-Dealers in the making at six or seven years of age. But it's important here to distinguish between brief stages all kids go through—short periods of annoying or bad behavior that don't last—and genuine Wheeler-Dealers in the making. Many young children go through brief phases when they take to cheating, lying, blaming everything that goes wrong on somebody else or acting on their impulses whenever it strikes their fancy.

In general, if a parent confronts such behavior when it happens and deals with it firmly, it will pass quickly.

But the kids we are describing in this chapter are not just kids going through a stage. Wheeler-Dealer Underachievers are in it for the long haul. *The pattern is persistent and repetitive* and it quickly becomes apparent that they are *not* going to outgrow it.

Sometimes, when Wheeler-Dealer behavior suddenly appears in adolescence, parents wonder what's gone wrong. Everyone knows that teenagers tend to be heavily influenced by their peers and this is even more true when it comes to Wheeler-Dealer behavior. Adolescent Wheeler-Dealers who showed no sign of this kind of behavior as younger children frequently have fallen under the influence of like-minded peers.

*   *   *

Before we take a closer look at the Wheeler-Dealer Underachiever, it's important to make a distinction between Wheeler-Dealers and Wheeler-Dealer Underachievers.

Wheeler-Dealers are impulsive. Their main goal is to satisfy their *immediate* needs. And they are masters of manipulation. When they want something, they make sure they get it, and anyone standing in their way had better watch out. Wheeler-Dealers think nothing of trampling on a friend's feelings or violating the rights of others in order to get something they want. In fact, this basic lack of concern and respect for the dignity and rights of others is a defining characteristic of Wheeler-Dealers.

This impulsiveness and absence of respect can exist over a broad range of behavior, from mildly annoying to very serious.

On the serious side of the scale, Wheeler-Dealers get into so much disciplinary and legal trouble that lousy grades are no longer viewed as their major problem. These are the kids we used to call juvenile delinquents. They break and enter neighborhood homes, rob corner stores, set fires, join gangs, deal drugs, carry weapons. Wheeler-Dealer *Underachievers* weigh in on the less serious side of the scale. They're impulsive and manipulative, but they're not involved in serious antisocial behavior. These are the kids we will concentrate on in this chapter.

That having been said, the dividing line between the Wheeler-Dealer Underachiever and the Wheeler-Dealer lawbreaker is not always clearly defined. Like all human behavior, Wheeler-Dealer behavior exists on a continuum. Where a particular kid's behavior places him or her along this path is not always crystal clear. But our *intent* is to concentrate on kids for whom underachievement, not antisocial behavior, is the primary issue.

Anatomy of a Wheeler-Dealer Underachiever

1. They live for the moment.

Wheeler-Dealer Underachievers act on their feelings *right now.* Long-range consequences don't occur to them. They see something they want (for example, material goods that will provide immediate gratification) and they want it *at once.*

By the same token, if something unpleasant needs to be done in order to attain a long-term goal, they won't do it. Goals and achievements way on down the road are too remote to consider seriously. So if homework is a hassle, forget it. They just won't do it, no matter what the consequences to their grades.

Ditto for considering other people's rights or feelings. If they stand in the way of their immediate needs or desires, Wheeler-Dealers will disregard ordinary rules and the unwritten norms and niceties of day-to-day, civilized living.

2. They lie.

Many kids stretch the truth from time to time. But Wheeler-Dealers lie consistently and over a long period of time. Because they get lots of practice, many get good at it, and their lies can be effective and convincing. They lie to get what they want. They lie to get others to give them money. They lie to get out of doing their homework. They lie to get out of jams. And when they get into trouble, their lies often put the blame on others.

Parents who try to discuss things with a Wheeler-Dealer Underachiever often become frustrated, angry and distrustful. The Wheeler-Dealer often offers parents and teachers a highly selective version of the facts. Not a *lie* exactly, but not what happened either. In fact, if you'd been anywhere nearby when the alleged event occurred, chances are you wouldn't even recognize the place, let alone anything else based on the Wheeler-Dealer's story.

Wheeler-Dealers frequently are found out when other people, also present at the "scene of the crime," give a different version of what happened. Even then, when the Wheeler-Dealer is confronted with the discrepancy between the two stories, he'll doggedly defend his slant on what happened—if he thinks he can get away with it.

If not, he'll twist it as adroitly as possible to fit the new "facts." If he can possibly see a way, he'll deny and deny and deny. And if that doesn't work and he senses the game is up, he'll cavalierly shrug off the fact that he lied. Win a few, lose a few: That's the cost of doing business. The only "lesson" he learns when he's caught in a lie is what *not* to do if you want to lie and get away with it next time. Wheeler-Dealers aren't big on guilt or remorse.

3. They cheat.

He's playing Monopoly and he tries to get away with paying you one bill short of the agreed price. You catch him. He looks terribly surprised and says it was a mistake.

Cheating on tests, exams and assignments goes with the territory. If he can get away with it, he'll plagiarize, copy, sit close to the smart kid, even manipulate him into "helping."

Cheating serves three purposes:

- To avoid predictable failure—predictable because you haven't prepared (for example, cheating on tests because you didn't study at all).
- To beat the system (to succeed while flaunting the rules).
- To get something you want immediately, without exercising any self-discipline or self-control.

4. They steal.

Wheeler-Dealer Underachievers may not steal often and they may not steal big items (such as cars). But if they "need" something, if there is no other quick way to get it, and if opportunity knocks, they probably will avail themselves of the opportunity.

Stealing can happen at school, in the community or at home. When they're caught—and they are, especially early on when they're honing their techniques—they behave the same way they do when they're caught in a lie: They deny. *They're* innocent, of course. When they're feeling particularly cocky, they'll tell you who *really* did it.

The latter may be partially true—an example of a typical Wheeler-Dealer half-truth. Wheeler-Dealers frequently steal in collaboration with others. They plan the job—and get their lieutenants to do the dirty and dangerous work. As in the following:

Psychologist:	"So your younger brother was caught stealing at school. And you just happened to be with him?"
Matthew:	(15 years old) "Right! He stole some computer disks."
Psychologist:	"And he got caught."
Matthew:	"Right. A teacher saw him and he got caught. She said that I told him to—but that's not true!"
Psychologist:	"What gave her the idea that you had told him to?"
Matthew:	"She said she saw me pointing at the disks

	and telling him which ones to take. But that's a lie, like I told you."
Psychologist:	"Is that why you were suspended too?"
Matthew:	"Uh huh—because the teacher lied!"
Psychologist:	"So it wasn't your idea—and you didn't tell your brother what to do."
Matthew:	"Right."
Psychologist:	"Did your brother stick up for you and say that you didn't have anything to do with it?"
Matthew:	"Well, he never got a chance. The school called my parents."

A teacher had watched Matthew instructing his younger brother from a "safe" distance to steal specific computer disks from the school library. The third time it happened, the teacher moved in and caught the younger brother in the act.

This was not an isolated incident. Matthew's brother admitted later that they used the same modus operandi to steal from the corner grocery store. Matthew planned the operation and acted as lookout while his brother did the actual job. But Matthew continued to proclaim his innocence (which qualifies him as both a thief *and* a liar).

Wheeler-Dealers are just as likely to steal from other students (or from members of their own family) as they are to steal school or neighborhood property. *Wheeler-Dealers are out strictly for themselves.* Personal loyalties are not a concern unless it's a direct quid pro quo ("You don't squeal on me, I don't squeal on you").

At its extreme, stealing can escalate into breaking and entering. It can be a house, a public building (for example, the school) or a car. As in most Wheeler-Dealer activities, you don't discover what's going on until it's been happening for some time. And because the Wheeler-Dealer specializes in artful deception, you may be headed off at the pass the first time you get wind of it.

Fourteen-year-old David and a friend broke into a neighbor's house on a Saturday night while the people were away on vacation, and spent the evening in their living room polishing off the contents of their liquor cabinet. They got caught when another neighbor, who had been asked to keep an eye on the house, noticed a light on that had been off the previous evening.

Two months earlier, David had loudly proclaimed his innocence when he was questioned by the police about a group of teenagers who were suspected of a series of B&Es in the neighborhood. His mother had believed him—and defended him. When she thinks back on the incident now, she isn't so sure any more.

Little by little, as alibis get thinner and thinner, parents of Wheeler-Dealers begin to suspect the truth. But by the time they wise up, their kids probably have been involved in several "episodes."

5. They repeatedly skip school.

Many underachievers skip classes from time to time. But Wheeler-Dealer Underachievers turn playing hooky into a fine art. They may skip entire days or even weeks of school, often in the company of like-minded pals. When they return, they aren't the least bit concerned about what they've missed.

The following Grade 10 student was referred to the guidance counselor for truancy.

Counselor: "So what did you do while you were away last week?"

Teresa: "I went downtown with some of my friends. What's the big deal?"

Counselor: "I guess it isn't a big deal for you. But I was asked to check out whether you wanted—or needed—some help getting to class and staying in school."

Teresa: "No. Why would I? I'll come when I feel like it! Besides, I enjoy going downtown."

Counselor: "What did you do downtown?"

Teresa:	"Nothing heavy, really. Just wandered around, talked to some people I know."
Counselor:	"Like who?"
Teresa:	"Some friends. People who like to enjoy themselves."
Counselor:	"Enjoy themselves. Enjoy themselves how?"
Teresa:	"Oh, we have a few laughs."
Counselor:	"And a few drinks and smokes?"
Teresa:	"Yeah, sure. Why not? Look, all we did was smoke a little dope, have few drinks and a lotta laughs. Nothing wrong with that. And then I crashed at a friend's apartment downtown."

Teresa has no trouble being open about her need for immediate gratification and her disdain for school rules and values. But she's not really opening up—not by a long shot. Share confidences—with the school guidance counselor? Give me a break! This is *not* part of her game plan. And skipping school is not an isolated incident in Teresa's life. It's part of an evolving pattern in which she flouts rules and defies and confronts authority in more and more provocative ways. Teresa certainly is not going to meekly submit to counseling. She'll attend appointments sporadically, if at all, and when she's there, she'll carefully select and slant what she chooses to reveal.

6. They disappear from home overnight or for a few days at a time.

It's fairly normal for teenagers not to volunteer much information to their parents about their whereabouts. But it's not normal to disappear overnight, or longer, on a consistent basis.

Wheeler-Dealer Underachievers take off from home to spend nights with friends. And almost always, parents find out *after* it's happened. The kid goes out, supposedly for the evening, and that's the last you hear for a day or two. He doesn't phone home and when he returns, he tells you as little as he can get away with.

If you press him too much about exactly where he's been and what he's been doing, he gets angry. "What business is it of yours? Why should you give a damn? So, I was at Matt's, and we went out for a while . . . saw a few people, partied a little. I can't remember exactly where I was every minute! What does it matter, anyway? I had a good time—chill out, why don't you?"

7. They disrupt the constructive activities of others.

Wheeler-Dealer Underachievers are not content with screwing up their own achievement. Sometimes they go out of their way to screw up the achievements of others as well. In the following incident, Walter, a 13-year-old Grade 8 student, displays another typical Wheeler-Dealer characteristic: boastful tale-telling about exploits. Unlike Teresa, above, Walter is proud to let the psychologist in on his fun time. But the story he tells is highly slanted in his own favor, and he's oblivious to the potential seriousness of the events.

Psychologist: "Why did your teacher and mother want me to see you?"

Walter: "I think it's about the firecrackers."

Psychologist: "Firecrackers?"

Walter: "Uh huh."

Psychologist: "Meaning lighting and using them?"

Walter: "Uh huh."

Psychologist: "Scaring people with them?"

Walter: (immediate response) "No!"

Psychologist: "So . . . what? Just playing with them?"

Walter: "Yeah, that's it!"

Psychologist: "Okay. And the school and your Mom didn't think it was a great idea."

Walter: (smiles) "Right. But it wasn't during school hours."

Psychologist: "It wasn't during school hours?"

Walter: "No. It was in the school yard and it was at night. There was a play going on in our school almost every night last week. And during the intermission in the play, we went far away from the school and we lit a few firecrackers, and then we went back for the rest of the play. And it was then that the other kids got an idea to ruin the play the next night. Well, not really ruin it, but just bother it by lighting some firecrackers right next to the door of the auditorium."

Psychologist: "You mean while the play was actually going on?"

Walter: "Exactly. And then we all agreed to do that—but it wasn't my idea! Anyway, that night the other kids got sort of caught. But they didn't get caught that night because they ran away as soon as they did it. But then the next day, somebody knew who they were and a teacher overheard them talking about it. And the teacher asked where they got the firecrackers from—and my name got involved."

Psychologist: "Your name got involved?"

Walter: "Yeah, because they were my firecrackers, see?"

Psychologist: "You mean you were the supplier?"

Walter: "I wasn't the *supplier*."

Psychologist: "So what were you—the distributor?"

Walter: "Well, not really. I sold a few, sure. See, I know a guy who had a whole trunk full of firecrackers, and he lives just down the block from me. And I bought a few from him. And I brought them to school—but I didn't light any! And I didn't sell any!"

Psychologist: "Are you saying that you got nailed for things that you really didn't do?"

Walter: (face lights up) "*Exactly*. That's exactly what I told the principal and what I keep telling my parents. I always get in trouble for things I'm not really responsible for."

Psychologist: "So let me see if I understand what you're saying. You're in some kind of trouble with the school and with your parents because of what some other students did."

Walter: (enthusiastically) "Exactly! And I have a few more
              examples of that too."

Walter has disrupted a major school activity. And it's clear that he
enjoyed doing so and feels no guilt about it. Convinced he has a sympathetic (or at least a gullible) ear, Walter actually brags about his
"accomplishments."

8. They deliberately damage property.
It doesn't have to be something dramatic, like breaking a store window
or smashing a car windshield. It can be smaller, safer things. For instance:

> Tom is walking through the school parking lot with a set
> of keys in his hand, and it occurs to him that the snotty
> teacher who failed him in algebra arrived in a brand-new
> car this week. So he runs his key chain over the new paint
> job and, *man, it feels good.*
> Tom just happens to be in the area when Miz Algebra-
> Failer discovers her pride and joy all scratched to hell. And
> the expression on her face gives him a real rush. Luckily,
> she has no idea who did it! "Yeah," says Tom. "It was, how
> can I put it? It was . . . satisfying."

9. They choose other Wheeler-Dealers as friends.
Wheeler-Dealer Underachievers attract each other like magnets.
Many develop strong loyalties, albeit self-serving ones. They support
and abet each other's impulsive behavior. Parents of Wheeler-Dealers
worry (with good reason) about the negative influence their child's
buddies are exerting. As do teachers, school counselors and any
school personnel responsible for dealing with discipline problems.

10. They can be charming at times and intimidating at others.
Charming and intimidating may sound like contradictory characteristics, but Wheeler-Dealer Underachievers manage to incorporate both.

When they're being charming, they can be ingratiating, persuasive, friendly and appear considerate. They seem convincing and sincere, and they know how to make you feel good. Then comes the Mr. Hyde phase. Suddenly, anger and frustration erupt out of nowhere. Parents, teachers and classmates become fearful the Wheeler-Dealer may be unable to physically control his rage. The Wheeler-Dealer's manipulative "talents" can quickly turn into bullying tactics.

A Grade 11 Wheeler-Dealer boasts to classmates that he's got a key to the office and knows where one of the teachers keeps copies of an upcoming exam. He extracts promises from a couple of students to pay him for a copy of the exam. But before he gets his money, a "browner" squeals on him. The Wheeler-Dealer is furious. He goes after the browner and twists his arm. "Next time it'll be worse," he warns him. The story gets out, and the Wheeler-Dealer is suspended for a week. But he's unrepentant. "He needed to be taught a lesson," he says.

Anton, a tall, overweight 12-year-old, is suspended from school for extorting one dollar from Grades 5 and 6 boys every time they use the bathroom during recess and lunch period. He gets away with it for a full month before a distraught (broke!) youngster tells his parents. The upset—and furious—parents contact the school principal immediately. When the principal investigates, he discovers that Anton has two assistants completely under his control who do a lot of the lookout and collection work. She also discovers that Anton and his minions have punched and threatened several students who dared to challenge the fledgling extortion ring.

This kind of Wheeler-Dealer behavior can develop into the nightmare that parents and teachers fear most—violence. We're surrounded with many extreme examples of violence in the media, in movies, in books and, if we're unlucky, in our own neighborhoods and schools. For our purposes here, however, concerning Wheeler-Dealer *Underachievers,* the examples above are as extreme as we need discuss.

Summing Up: Anatomy of a Wheeler-Dealer Underachiever

1. They live for the moment.
2. They lie.
3. They cheat.
4. They steal.
5. They repeatedly skip school.
6. They disappear from home overnight or for a few days at a time.
7. They disrupt the constructive activities of others.
8. They deliberately damage property.
9. They choose other Wheeler-Dealers as friends.
10. They can be charming at times and intimidating at others.

Armed with our lengthy description over the preceding pages, it's time to pause now and see how similar your child's characteristics are to those of the Wheeler-Dealer Underachiever prototype. Remember, *the behavior must be consistent over at least six months.*

Parent Checklist

1. Does my child consistently act on the whims of the moment?	Yes___ No___ Don't Know___
2. Does my child lie regularly?	Yes___ No___ Don't Know___
3. Does my child regularly cheat (e.g., on tests)?	Yes___ No___ Don't Know___

4. Has my child regularly stolen?

Yes___ No___ Don't Know___

5. Does my child skip school repeatedly?

Yes___ No___ Don't Know___

6. Does my child repeatedly disappear for days or weeks at a time without informing me?

Yes___ No___ Don't Know___

7. Has my child deliberately damaged property often?

Yes___ No___ Don't Know___

8. Has my child regularly disrupted constructive activities of others?

Yes___ No___ Don't Know___

9. Does my child regularly associate with other Wheeler-Dealer Underachievers?

Yes___ No___ Don't Know___

10. Is my child charming at times and intimidating at others?

Yes___ No___ Don't Know___

If you answered "Yes" to five or more of the following questions, your child's characteristics may be similar to those of the Wheeler-Dealer Underachiever.

Where Do Wheeler-Dealer Underachievers Come From?

Now for the big question: *Why?* Why do Wheeler-Dealers behave the way they do? Where does this behavior come from? How does it start? What causes it?

The role of genetics: A possible contributor to Wheeler-Dealer behavior.

Researchers have found that genetic factors may contribute to the development of Wheeler-Dealer behavior. Let's take a brief look at some of these factors.

Recent research indicates that identical twins who were reared apart from each other are more likely to display similar antisocial behavior than are fraternal (non-identical) twins who were reared apart. If their genetic predisposition did not play a role, the probability should have been the same for both groups.

The same is true, of course, for other types of behavior. When identical twins are separated at birth and reared in entirely separate and different environments, there are remarkable similarities between them that can *only* be explained by the fact that they were born with identical genes or, to put another way, with exactly the same heredity.

But does this mean there's a gene for lying or stealing? Does it mean there's no hope for positive change?

No. It means nothing of the sort. Genetic predisposition does not mean that the pattern will show up for sure or that it can't be changed. It simply means that given the "right" environment, a genetic predisposition to behave in a certain way can blossom. A person's temperament does have genetic roots, and when this is combined with negative environmental factors, it may trigger hereditary patterns. We know, for example, that some people are more prone to alcohol addiction. But if a person with this genetic predisposition is raised in an environment where alcohol is seldom used, the chances of becoming an alcoholic dramatically decrease, despite the genetic tendency. So genetics is sometimes important—but it is never carved in stone.

Genetics also can contribute to a condition known as Attention Deficit Disorder or its more complicated cousin, Attention Deficit Hyperactivity Disorder, or ADHD for short. Some kids who have ADHD also exhibit Wheeler-Dealer behavior. Students with ADHD can't sit still or concentrate on *anything* for long. Whether or not school work interests them has nothing to do with it. They are physically unable to pay attention long enough to be successful in their school work. Children with severe ADHD may *develop* Wheeler-Dealer behavior because they are impulsive to begin with and do not have normal inner controls over their impulsiveness.

All things being equal, the more severe the Wheeler-Dealer behavior (when antisocial Wheeler-Dealer *behavior* gets far more attention than the underachievement at school), the more likely it is that genetics *as well as* environment play a part in the behavior's origins. But for less severe Wheeler-Dealers—those we are focusing on in this chapter—environment seems to play a more significant role in their behavior. Let's look at these environmental factors.

The role of environment: A major contributor to Wheeler-Dealer behavior.

In our experience, we have found that children with behavior problems frequently come from fractious families. These kids' parents often engage in intense arguments with each other. They do not present a united front when it comes to disciplining their problem child. Each parent relates to the child separately—and differently. One parent, most often the mother, falls into a pattern of spending time with the child and trying to sort out the behavior problems in positive ways such as praising or rewarding good behavior. The other parent, most often the father, falls into the role of disciplinarian. He takes on all the negatives—punishment, criticism, anger and rejection.

The mother falls into an endless rescue-and-excuse pattern—always rescuing her child from the consequences of his bad behavior, always making excuses for him to other people in authority. She allows herself to be manipulated by her child, pleading his case to teachers and vice-principals, forever begging them to give him "one more chance." The father tends to angrily reject his problem child, discount his wife's attempts at conciliation and sabotage her efforts to smooth things over.

Sometimes all this leads to one of the parents—most often the father—washing his hands of the entire unhappy situation and refusing to deal with the problem Wheeler-Dealer child ("You seem to have all the answers. Fine—go for it. He's your problem from now on!"). Sometimes the end result is even more drastic, with one parent walking out and leaving the family (once again, usually—but not always—the father. When it comes to complete marriage breakdown, of course, other factors doubtless will have contributed).

Where does this kind of family situation leave Wheeler-Dealer kids themselves?

Wheeler-Dealer Underachievers are fast studies. They learn young how to divide and conquer. At tender ages, they

- learn to blame others for their own problems;
- learn that the world is a hostile place in which their first task is to protect themselves;
- learn that many people can be manipulated and used;
- learn that some people must be watched and avoided;
- learn that their role in life is to defeat those in authority.

Adolescent Wheeler-Dealer Underachievers carry all the patterns they have learned at home to their outside environment—to their high school, to their teenage friends, to their neighborhood and community.

Like all teenagers, Wheeler-Dealers are heavily influenced by their peers. Initially, Wheeler-Dealers endure a lot of rejection among kids their own age because of their manipulative behavior and negative attitudes. But Wheeler-Dealers are survivors: Rebuffed by "brown nosers," they seek out—and quickly find—their own kind. Soon they're hanging out with a like-minded set, day and night. Wheeler-Dealers form tight groups that support, abet, incite and encourage one another's behavior.

One more point about environmental influences on Wheeler-Dealer behavior: Parents often ask us whether poverty and Wheeler-Dealer underachievement go together. We believe the answer is no—at least not poverty by itself. In today's urban world, poverty is usually at the center of the galaxy of problems associated with inner cities and urban decay. But despite media stereotyping, the fact remains that the majority of kids who live in poverty are not Wheeler-Dealers. However, if poverty is combined with drugs, family breakdown, gang influence, violence and abuse, and if predisposing genetic factors are present, then the chances rise dramatically. But they rise just as dramatically for middle- and upper-class families who are exposed to the same influences.

What's Really Going On with the Wheeler-Dealer Underachiever?

The obvious reason Wheeler-Dealers underachieve is because they are impatient and impulsive, they are obsessed with immediate gratification and they lack any respect for school structures and authority. What's more, they seem to embody The Underachievement Myth because they appear lazy and unmotivated at school.

The truth is, Wheeler-Dealer Underachievers *are* motivated. They're motivated to pursue other, very different goals. To find out where Wheeler-Dealers' *real* motivation lies, let's look at the Wheeler-Dealer Underachiever's inner life.

The Inner Life of the Wheeler-Dealer Underachiever

What you see is *not* what you get with Wheeler-Dealer Underachievers. Wheeler-Dealer Underachievers work hard at maintaining a facade—a thick, tough facade that can be as impenetrable as a suit of armor.

Let's look at the Wheeler-Dealer's suit of armor.

1. Wheeler-Dealer Underachievers live for the moment.

They always go for the immediate reward, no matter what negative consequences might result—or even if negative consequences are a sure thing. The Wheeler-Dealer doesn't worry about what might happen sometime later. He's addicted to instant gratification. The high he derives from getting what he wants immediately is worth all potential pain way on down the road.

2. Wheeler-Dealer Underachievers make the same mistakes and get into the same jams over and over again.

They don't learn from experience. Why don't they? Maybe one reason is because they never take any responsibility for their actions. Taking the blame means admitting fault. In their own minds, Wheeler-Dealers are never wrong: It's always someone else's fault. And since they're never wrong, why should they change? It's the rest of the universe that should change!

3. Although Wheeler-Dealer Underachievers talk about wanting to be rich and famous, these are not genuine goals.

Being rich and famous is just part of the Wheeler-Dealer's fantasy world. Wheeler-Dealers have no detailed plans, no internal discipline, no organization, no consistent follow-through to get them anywhere close to wealth or fame.

4. Wheeler-Dealers have friends, but not intimate friends.

"Real friendships take too much time and energy . . . and for what?" asks the Wheeler-Dealer. Wheeler-Dealer relationships are a series of episodes—sound bites, rather than an expanding process nurtured by openness, vulnerability and a desire for what is genuinely in the best interests of the other. Wheeler-Dealers often turn relationships into games—games they're playing to win.

5. Wheeler-Dealers separate people into three camps: the patsy camp, the enemy camp and the accomplice camp.

Patsies are people who can be manipulated. Enemies are people who can't be manipulated and may be in a position of power to stop the Wheeler-Dealer. A savvy school principal, a wise guidance counselor, a tough teacher who won't tolerate disruptive behavior and knows how to control her class all qualify as enemies. As for accomplices, usually they're peers with similar views and problem behavior. The ideal accomplice is someone the Wheeler-Dealer can control. This means that accomplices sometimes overlap with patsies. Matthew's younger brother, the one we described above who took the heat for stealing the computer disks, is a good example of an accomplice-cum-patsy.

6. Are Wheeler-Dealers ever vulnerable? Do they ever get sad or depressed?

Yes, they do—they could hardly be human if they did not—but they try to maintain their facade to the outside world at all costs. Underneath the Wheeler-Dealer's tough exterior lies an angry, sad, lonely person—someone who uses others to protect himself against the pain of being used himself. Wheeler-Dealers know how it feels to be used—and they want to make very sure they're the dealer, not the receiver.

Summing Up: The Inner Life of the Wheeler-Dealer Underachiever

1. Wheeler-Dealer Underachievers live for the moment.
2. Wheeler-Dealer Underachievers make the same mistakes and get into the same jams over and over again.
3. Although Wheeler-Dealer Underachievers talk about wanting to be rich and famous, these are not genuine goals.
4. Wheeler-Dealers have friends, but not intimate friends.
5. Wheeler-Dealers separate people into three camps: the patsy camp, the enemy camp and the accomplice camp.
6. Underneath the Wheeler-Dealer's tough exterior lies an angry, sad, lonely person—someone who uses others to protect himself against the pain of being used himself.

Helping the Wheeler-Dealer Underachiever: A Team Approach

Because most adolescent Wheeler-Dealer Underachievers are in trouble at home, at school and in the community, changing their behavior requires a team effort from start to finish. This is *not* a job to tackle on your own.

A lot of research and the work of many professionals have gone into the following plan. We realize that what we are suggesting takes energy, time and financial commitment. It will not be easy to implement, but it's the best chance we can offer for a positive outcome. Remember, the more serious the Wheeler-Dealer Underachiever's behavior problems, the greater the effort required to turn things around.

Step 1: Get a comprehensive professional assessment for your child and your family.

First, you need to know all the facts about your Wheeler-Dealer child's situation. If you haven't already done so, arrange for a *thorough* psychological assessment, either through the school or privately. The assessment should address the following questions:

1. Does my child exhibit the characteristics of a Wheeler-Dealer Underachiever?
2. Does my child have a specific learning disability?
3. Does my child have either an Attention Deficit Disorder or Attention Deficit Hyperactivity Disorder?
4. Does my child show any significant gaps in academic skills (such as a weak background in math or reading)?
5. If the answers to the above questions are "Yes," should I consider changing my child's academic program, class or school?
6. Does my child show significant signs of sadness or anger?
7. In what ways are our family interactions making the problem worse? In what ways are they making it better?
8. To what extent are negative peer influences a factor?

The results you receive from the assessment will form a guide to your next step. This next step usually means focusing on three major issues:

- Keeping tabs on your child.
- Disciplining your child.
- Changing the ways your family relates to one another at home.

Step 2: Work with a team to help your child.

You will need to enlist support from a number of people. As we said above, *you cannot do this on your own.* The members of your team will fall into place based on the results of your professional assessment. Keep in mind that the primary aim of the team is getting clear, up-to-date information about your Wheeler-Dealer Underachiever.

Usually the school member of the team will be a guidance counselor, a special-education teacher, a vice-principal or an attendance officer. A community member of the team could be a recreational club leader. You, the parents, are key team members.

And so is your child.

What? Are we serious?

Yes, we are. We are under no illusions that your Wheeler-Dealer Underachiever will participate wholeheartedly in this effort to turn around his behavior. But it is important for him to know how things will be co-ordinated. For example, if your son skips school, does he know how soon you will hear about it, and from whom? So when the vice-principal calls you and your son in for a meeting after only two missed school days instead of two *weeks*, no one will be surprised, least of all your son. *Wheeler-Dealer Underachievers thrive on secrecy and lack of communication among adults.* This information gap cannot be allowed to continue. They should know that this time, people will communicate with each other.

If, as a result of the assessment, counseling is recommended, the counselors must be active rather than passive in order to be effective with Wheeler-Dealer Underachievers. By this we mean they must be the kinds of people who do not hold back, who risk confronting issues, who concentrate on maintaining a tight focus on the problems at hand—and who don't get misled by the Wheeler Dealer's charm. *And: They must be willing to agree to share their concerns and information with parents or school officials if they think the student is heading for self-defeating or self-destructive behavior.* This means no secrets!

We have worked with two approaches to treatment that we find effective in changing Wheeler-Dealer behavior. They were developed by a team of psychologists at Yale University headed by Dr. Alan

Kazdin. They found that these approaches work best when used simultaneously. They are:

- Problem-Solving Skills Training (PSST)—for the child.
- Parent Management Training (PMT)—for the parents.

Most professionals who work with behavior-problem children and adolescents have developed their own versions of these two approaches. Two noteworthy examples are the research teams at the Oregon Social Learning Center (PSST) and Dr. Caroline Webster-Stratton's team at the University of Washington (PMT).

How PSST Works

Problem-Solving Skills Training is designed to help children with behavior problems focus on predictable, everyday situations that trigger automatic, negative reactions on their part. For example, PSST teaches Wheeler-Dealers less damaging ways to deal with teasing or a sneer from another child, rejection by another kid in the school yard or temptations to stray into forbidden activities such as stealing. Many Wheeler-Dealer Underachievers are intrigued when their thinking is analyzed for them and they realize for the first time in their lives how their automatic thought patterns get them into trouble.

Here's one example of how a group counselor worked with 13-year-old Gordon:

Gord: "I told you—he gave me a dirty look. I *had* to hit him!"
Counselor: "Okay, can we look more closely at what was going through your mind just before you hit him? What were you thinking about when he looked at you?"
Gord: (impatiently)"I don't know."
Counselor: "Gord, give it a shot—try to think about what you were thinking."
Gord: "I was thinking that he looked like he was going

	to haul off on me—so I decided I was going to get him first."
Counselor:	"Are you saying that you thought that he was going to attack you?"
Gord:	"Exactly."
Counselor:	"Where does that thought come from? What's it based on?"
Gord:	(looking somewhat puzzled) "What do you mean? *I* don't know."
Counselor:	"It sounds to me like you were acting automatically to protect yourself."
Gord:	"Yeah, I suppose so."
Counselor:	"So this other kid has you thinking that you're going to get attacked, even when all he does is give you dirty looks."
Gord:	"Yeah."
Counselor:	"Has he ever actually hit you?"
Gord:	(heatedly) "No—I've never given him the chance!"
Counselor:	"Hold on a minute. You're not even sure that he would hit you."
Gord:	(with a skeptical look) "Well . . ."
Counselor:	"Look, you're here today because you hit someone. And I've been told that there are other things that tick you off, too."
Gordon:	"For sure."
Counselor:	"And have some of those other things gotten you into trouble, too?"
Gordon:	"Sometimes."

The counselor and Gordon talked about some of the other incidents that landed Gordon in trouble. The counselor examined each incident to show Gordon how in each one, he automatically lapsed into knee-jerk reactions because he (automatically) assumed he was being threatened. In other words, the counselor showed Gordon how his automatic thoughts often led to his automatic actions.

Gordon was skeptical at first of this "psycho-babble" being thrown at him. But gradually he realized (and grudgingly admitted to the counselor) that the counselor really did understand where he was coming from. At this point, the counselor asked Gordon whether he was interested in learning more about his automatic thoughts and reactions. He explained that to do so, he would be asked to participate in group sessions with other students that included using videotapes of typical problematic situations. Gordon, along with the other kids in the group, would be expected to role-play in staged problem situations, watch how he performed on videotape, face the comments of the other kids participating and then choose from among a range of alternative reactions. Then he would be asked to try out some of these new behavioral methods in his own life. And at subsequent group sessions, he would be expected to report back to the group about how these new behaviors worked out.

The counselor made sure Gordon knew that all of this information was going to be shared with the team being put in place to help him (including the counselor, teachers, vice-principal and his parents).

Gordon agreed to participate because he wanted to be allowed back into school. His behavior was not going to miraculously change overnight. But a beachhead had been established.

Imagine exchanges like these and hundreds more over many sessions. And remember, none of this happens in a vacuum—the other members of the team are also doing their part.

How PMT Works

Parents enrolled in Parent Management Training (PMT) group sessions discuss behavioral problems they are having with their children and then view videotapes of good and bad ways of handling problems. Sometimes a group leader goes into participants' homes and videotapes family interactions (a typical family dinner, for example). These tapes are then viewed at the meetings by the other participating parents. The counselors guide the discussion to help the family in question learn more effective ways to relate to and interact with their children.

How do you find out about programs like PSST for your child or

PMT for you? Ask your family doctor, a guidance counselor at school, a minister or call the local mental-health association or child-guidance center for more information. Many social workers, psychologists, child and family therapists and other mental-health professionals are familiar with the major principles of PSST and PMT.

That's it then, the whole team—representatives from the school, the community, counselors, you and your child.

Step 3: Keep tabs on your Wheeler-Dealer child.

Out of sight—and into trouble. Wheeler-Dealers are notorious for getting into messes the moment you turn your back. No parent can keep a constant eye on their teenager. So let the team help you do this. The team can help you keep tabs until such time as your Wheeler-Dealer child improves.

When possible, share the burden with your spouse. Even if you don't agree about everything, you can increase your chances of success when both of you are clear about exactly what information is required. The sooner you begin this process, the better are your chances of positive change.

Maintain frequent contact with the school. And arrange periodic checks with all of the professionals involved, not only to get information but to pass information on. Make sure that if there are any changes in your child's behavior or situation—good or bad—you communicate these changes to other team members who ought to know.

You need to know where your child is—and who he's with. But be prepared for resistance, and lots of it, from your Wheeler-Dealer Underachiever. The first thing he'll do is accuse you of not trusting him. Here's how one mother was able to deal more effectively and honestly with her 13-year-old Wheeler-Dealer Underachiever:

| Kurt: | "Why do I have to tell you where I'll be? You don't trust me!" *(Note the attempt to make his mother feel guilty.)* |
| Mother: | "You're exactly right—I don't trust you. And I'm trying to build on something so I eventually can |

	return to trusting you. But whether that happens or not depends on you."
Kurt:	"Hell, I don't really care if you trust me or not."
Mother:	"Well, whether you like it or not, or whether you even care or not, it's still my job to help you develop enough self-discipline to keep out of trouble. And based on your behavior, I don't believe you have enough self-discipline—not yet. So, what's it going to be—information about your plans, or staying home?"

Step 4: Learn to discipline more effectively.

A crucial point about discipline: Discipline is *not* simply another word for punishment. Discipline encompasses everything you must do to help your Wheeler-Dealer Underachiever learn more self-control.

Appropriate disciplining of your child takes practice. Lots of practice. But it's worth the effort, because more effective discipline can break serious, negative cycles between parent and child.

Here are a few helpful hints:

Take the time to get the facts before you react. This builds in an automatic cooling-off period, and should allow you to determine appropriate disciplinary measures (a punishment to fit the "crime"). It will protect you from declaring a harsh punishment in the heat of anger, which you may later regret but cannot back out of enforcing.

If at all possible, co-ordinate disciplining with your spouse. Agree to consult each other whenever possible *before* disciplinary decisions are announced. This will allow for some discussion and may lead to greater agreement over what needs to be done and who needs to do it.

When you have reached a decision about the disciplinary measures you wish to impose, follow through. Often parents of Wheeler-Dealer Underachievers threaten to act, but don't do so consistently.

Put yourself in the following situation:

Assume you have received a phone call from the vice-principal informing you that your son, the Wheeler-Dealer Underachiever, has been suspended for stealing something valuable from another student. Let's say it was a silver ring inset with a birthstone. The vice-principal summons you and your son to an early-morning meeting. What's your reaction likely to be? Probably, "Not again!" Disappointment. Anger. Fear. Frustration. Annoyance.

Resist your immediate impulse to lash out and vent your frustration and anger. Instead, when you get together with your child, tell him in a straightforward, factual manner about the phone call and the upcoming meeting. Ask for his version of the story. In other words—listen. Don't jump to instant conclusions.

Let's also assume that, at the school meeting, solid evidence is presented that your son stole the ring. The vice-principal has decided that your son will have to either return or replace the ring before being allowed to go back to class.

Despite the evidence, your son maintains his innocence throughout the proceedings, which moves you to conclude that you need to take some additional action on the home front.

Here's how one couple effectively handled this situation:

Father:	"First, you're going to have to tell us how you plan to deal with this."
Marty:	"I told you—I didn't steal it!"
Father:	"You know, whether you did or not—and the evidence is pretty strong that you did—you've still got a big problem. The school won't let you back in until you return it or pay for it."
Marty:	"Yeah, yeah, I know. But it's a rip-off. I'm telling you, I have no idea where that ring is!"
Father:	"Okay. You don't know where the ring is. But if you want to get back into school you're going to have to pay for it."
Marty:	"Okay, okay! I'll figure out some way of digging up the money."
Father:	"I'd like to know exactly how you'll do it."

Marty:	"Well, I've saved up some from my summer job—I could use that money."
Father:	"Okay. The vice-principal said that $90 would cover it."
Marty:	"Are we done?"
Father:	"Not quite. Marty, I think we're going to have to do something more about this stealing than what the school has done. Mostly because this is not the first time it's happened. But I'm really not sure yet what that'll be. Your mother and I need to think about this for a while."
Mother:	"You're right. And one thing is clear. It's obvious you're having a lot of trouble controlling yourself. We're going to be discussing this—all of it—with your group counselor."
Marty:	(sarcastically) "Thanks a lot."
Father:	"Your Mom and I are going to talk about this in our parent group, too. Maybe there's something else we could be doing to help you stop getting into trouble. But right now, there's one thing you have to do: We want you home *right after school*."
Marty:	"What? *Why?*"
Father:	"Because that's when you get into trouble—*after* school."
Marty:	(angrily) "That's not fair."
Father:	"There are a lot of things that aren't fair. What's just happened isn't fair—to a lot of people. And I'm angry too—both at what you're doing to yourself and the position it's put your mother and me in."

These parents have learned several important points:

1. You can decide on *interim consequences* before deciding on

a final one. This has several advantages: It allows you to deal with the immediate situation in a natural reactive way. ("Come home right after school because that's when you get into trouble.") And it also gives you time to pull back and look at the big picture. When you give yourself the time and space to pull back, you will be able to fully explore alternatives with your spouse and the team.

2. *Discipline should be a corrective experience.* These parents are trying to help Marty learn from his impulsive behavior by pulling in the reins when he shows a lack of self-control.

3. *Expressing emotion*—displeasure, anger, frustration or fear—*is important.* It's honest and it's good feedback for any Wheeler-Dealer Underachiever.

4. *Shift the tension to its rightful owner—the Wheeler-Dealer Underachiever.* Marty now has to pay for the ring, stay closer to home and await future consequences.

Step 5: Learn to deal more effectively with your child's manipulative behavior.

Wheeler-Dealer Underachievers' manipulations take many forms. They charm, threaten, cajole and tell highly selective, self-serving stories. There are ways of learning how to detect and deal more effectively with these manipulations.

Here's one beleaguered Wheeler-Dealer's mother talking:

> "Sure, I promised to speak to the principal on his behalf, but only if what he was telling me was true. And of course he doesn't remember what he promised, only what I promised. Besides, he hadn't told me the whole truth. He had the gall to accuse *me* of breaking *my* promise."

Many Wheeler-Dealer Underachievers try to intimidate their parents by accusing them of not caring, of selling out or of breaking promises. And if they can raise the guilt level, their parents are more likely to give in to this manipulation.

Wheeler-Dealer Underachievers also try to exact promises from their parents to hide certain facts from teachers, guidance counselors, vice-principals or even the other parent. A rule of thumb: The more intense the pressure to keep secrets, the greater the reason to refuse secrecy. Often parents waver under such pressure. As in:

> "You know, I agreed to cover for his school absences for a while. He promised that he would straighten out. Now I know I made a big mistake—he never intended to change, just to get off the hook for a bit. And what really hurts is that I feel like an accomplice."

Don't let this happen. Train yourself simply to say that there will be *no* exceptions to the rule of open communication.

Step 6: Get out of the ruts you have fallen into.

Wheeler-Dealer Underachievers' parents often find themselves dealing with the same old problems in the same tired old ways. Here's how one father developed a new way of dealing with the issue of truth-telling—and avoided getting trapped as he had countless times before:

> "Through trial and error I arrived at a way to cut down on some of the arguments about what *really* happened, during those endless searches for The Truth According to Derek. I would simply confront him: 'You know, you may be right and you may be wrong. I haven't heard the teacher's side of the story, and in some ways I really don't need to. My question to you is this: Whatever the truth is, *you* were the one who got into trouble. And this isn't the first time. I don't understand how someone as bright as you can keep getting into trouble so often. Isn't there something you can do to protect yourself?' "

Step 7: Minimize the sermons.

Be firm about what's right and what's wrong—but don't get stuck harping on moral issues. Wheeler-Dealers already know right from wrong. They've just concluded that acting morally is a stupid way to live in general. You're wasting your breath if you dwell on these issues. It will only turn the Wheeler-Dealer off.

Step 8: Take a close look at how the members of your family relate to one another. Consider family counseling.

There are three issues you may need to look at. The way you and your spouse relate to each other, the way you and your child relate to each other and the ways your children relate to one another. You're going to need professional help with this.

As well, there are many self-help groups for parents of behavior-problem children. Seek them out in your community. Ask your family doctor, minister, school counselor or a trusted friend about these groups. Parent self-help groups can be enormously useful in helping parents recognize entrenched, unproductive parenting patterns.

Wheeler-Dealer Underachievers often have strained relationships with their brothers or sisters. They may bully their siblings or intimidate them in more subtle ways. Check out the extent to which this may be happening, and seek advice about how to stop it.

Summing Up: Helping Your Wheeler-Dealer Underachiever

Step 1: Get a comprehensive professional assessment for your child and your family.

Step 2: Work with a team to help your child.

Step 3: Keep tabs on your Wheeler-Dealer child.

Step 4: Learn to discipline more effectively.

Step 5: Learn to deal more effectively with your child's manipulative behavior.

Step 6: Get out of the ruts you have fallen into.

Step 7: Minimize the sermons.

Step 8: Take a close look at how the members of your family relate to one another. Consider family counseling.

What to Expect When You Help Your Wheeler-Dealer Underachiever

What might you expect after working your way through the steps above?

1. Well, for a start, expect the plan to drain you of energy.
But as the saying goes, "You can pay me now, or you can pay me later." If you do nothing and let the Wheeler-Dealer universe continue to unfold as it already is unfolding, the price you will be held to pay later will be much steeper. Plus you'll have less control over the outcome.

2. Expect to be tested by your child immediately after the recommendations are implemented.
For example, Wheeler-Dealers may skip school shortly after the new regime is put in place. Take heart: This is *not* a bad sign. What they're doing is seeing if they can still get away with it. This is a good sign— even though parents don't think so at the time. It means that the child has acknowledged the new structures and is probing to find out where the weak spots are.

3. Expect to get really fed up from time to time.
When you initiated this new program to improve your child's behavior and achievement level, you began with a certain amount of optimism. But as the team of professionals does its best to improve the situation, you will experience many ups and downs.

At times, you will believe and rescue your Wheeler-Dealer Under-achiever. At other times, you will feel used and betrayed by your child. When he wants or needs something from you, you'll be the center of attention. When he concludes that you won't give in, he'll move on without a backward glance. At times like this, you'll feel manipulated and rejected. A mother accurately captured this when she said: "I feel like there's an enemy in my own house, the one place I expected to feel safe."

So, as the process lurches along, expect to find yourself longing to be free of all the problems your child has created. At times like these, parents often wish their child would just disappear until he grows up. But these feelings generally don't last long.

4. Expect that each time you receive a message to call the school, scenes of disaster will race through your mind.

As in: "I feel as if I'm always on guard, or on duty. My heart jumped into my throat when my secretary told me that the school principal had called. And guess what, it wasn't about Scott at all—this time!"

The professional term for this is *hypervigilance*. People who are under constant stress and who fear that a disaster could happen at any moment tend to keep constant vigil. And the energy drain is enormous. So we usually caution parents to pace themselves, and make sure they give themselves regular breaks from the stress of the situation.

5a. Expect to be mesmerized—and fooled—at times by the stories your Wheeler-Dealer Underachiever tells you.

One father said to us: "I can't believe it—I actually sat there and listened to all the details of this latest scam Brian has got himself into."

Remember, your child has had a lot of practice in the use of selective information. You have been had by an expert! Learn from it and move on.

5b. Expect at times to be overly skeptical and wary about the yarns your child spins.

This is wise in light of the Wheeler-Dealer's history of lying. Many parents of Wheeler-Dealers do this to protect themselves from getting misled. One parent developed the following philosophy: "I now follow two principles: (1) Say 'No' to almost every request, at least to start with. And (2) Don't believe what she's said until her story can be corroborated by someone I trust. These simple rules give me time to think about how I'm being set up."

5c. Expect that sometimes your skepticism will be unwarranted.
Wheeler-Dealers don't lie about everything. When that happens, expect to feel guilty for not having had more faith. And expect to be accused by your child of overreacting and not trusting him. Remember, this is all part of the game—your Wheeler-Dealer may be softening you up for the next scam.

6. If your child's behavior deteriorates, expect that you will have to consider changing his environment (putting him in a new school or a residential treatment center).
This is especially true if the Wheeler-Dealer is older and is getting into more serious trouble. And expect these decisions to be heart-wrenching for you.

7. Expect that in spite of the best efforts of many professionals, your Wheeler-Dealer Underachiever may act in a way that takes all decisions out of your hands.
For example, it's possible that the school may decide to expel your child because of his or her problem behavior, and that there may be nothing you can do about it.

8. Expect that change will occur very slowly.
With Wheeler-Dealers, successful intervention has very high ups and very low downs. Expect to react with joy when you see the beginnings of change—and to be disappointed when backsliding occurs.

The Wheeler-Dealer as an Adult

Wheeler-Dealers—to distinguish them from Wheeler-Dealer Under-achievers for a moment—are a well-defined personality type. And Wheeler-Dealers who take advantage of their positive characteristics, and learn how to hold in check their socially damaging and self-destructive qualities, can become very successful adults.

We all know successful Wheeler-Dealers. These are the people with a lot of street-smarts and a gift of the gab, who have a high energy level, a drive to win and buckets full of charm. Successful Wheeler-Dealers are experts at operating within a pragmatic ethic focused on winning. Successful Wheeler-Dealers can be scrupulously honest in their business dealings.

For example: A successful Wheeler-Dealer salesman we know *never* indulges in unscrupulous tactics (such as the used-car salesman who turns back the odometer or concocts stories about the old lady who owned the car and only drove it to church). Why not? In his eyes, it's strictly a matter of expediency: If he wants to stay in business, he knows he has to rely heavily on word-of-mouth referrals and repeat business. He can't *afford* to be dishonest.

Wheeler-Dealers who hone their skills of charming and influencing others can become successful in any career: salespersons or managers—or lawyers or politicians. The adolescent whose impulsiveness got her into a lot of trouble may, as an adult, channel her impatience into a readiness to take risks and assume initiative in a legitimate job.

A high-risk, high-stress entrepreneurial activity such as starting a small business requires a driven, self-seeking, dominating personality focused on getting what he or she wants. This is precisely the Wheeler-Dealer's behavior pattern and Wheeler-Dealers can be very successful in fields such as this.

*   *   *

But what about Wheeler-Dealers who continue to underachieve?

Well, Wheeler-Dealers' most destructive characteristic probably is their disrespect and disregard for other people's dignity and rights. By the same token, the key to success in adult life for Wheeler-Dealer Underachievers is learning to hold this in check. And Wheeler-Dealer Underachievers who never develop moderate amounts of empathy for others, along with self-discipline (to counter their impulsiveness and need for immediate self-gratification), will continue to manipulate as adults.

These are the people who are always on the verge of making it big—and, sadly, never do. They're constantly trying to put together deals that they never quite bring off because they don't have the patience to build a solid foundation or a good team. Wheeler-Dealers are impatient people who sometimes never learn how to work and build toward a long-term goal. Many lead adult lives fraught with personal and career problems, some of which can escalate into legal, ethical and moral problems.

But Wheeler-Dealers who overcome their impulsiveness and their tendency to run roughshod over others can lead successful adult lives. They can become very direct and honest in their personal relationships, and attract others who value this quality. And their energy and willingness to risk enables them to seek the most that life has to offer.

And when Wheeler-Dealers do learn from their mistakes, they can literally bank on their failures—using classic Wheeler-Dealer skills. An individual we know spent time behind bars for embezzling money when he was a young man. His academic and personal history, as he told it to us, was that of a classic Wheeler-Dealer Underachiever. Yet today, he is a successful counselor whose ability to cut through the manipulations of his Wheeler-Dealer clients makes him highly effective. The key to this individual's success was developing a great deal of self-knowledge. And he clearly recognizes that his success is due in no small part to his insight into his own history. Maybe it really does take one to know one!

CHAPTER 6

The Sad or Depressed Underachiever

Depressed Underachievers are custom-made for The Underachievement Myth. It's easy to label Sad Underachievers lazy and unmotivated because that's the way they seem to behave. Depression often masquerades as apathy. And sadness slows you down and makes you look lazy. This is what Depressed Underachievers often look like to teachers and parents.

When we put the kids we see through a battery of tests to sift out erroneous impressions such as this, we hope to learn *why* they're underachieving and what is really motivating them.

One of the most telling tests we have used is this: we show the student a blank card and ask him to make up a story for the card. Here is the story a Sad Underachiever made up to fit the blank card:

> "I don't see anything. It just looks like nothingness to me. (Pause) It looks like a snowstorm that's wiped everything out. I can't see anything. I guess everyone's lost."

This certainly isn't the kind of story a lazy and unmotivated couch

Note: This chapter describes the ordinary sadness and depression that can be experienced by anybody at certain times or in certain situations. We wish to make a distinction between this and the medical and psychiatric syndrome of clinical depression. When we discuss the psychiatric syndrome, we will use the term "clinical depression."

potato would offer. It can't even be called a story. It's a non-story—a fumbling attempt to comply with the counselor's request made by a lonely, hopeless, lost person. It's an uncertain stab at making sense offered by a Sad Underachiever.

We all experience changes in mood, and teenagers are among the worst offenders in the ups and downs department. Fickle, overactive hormones are the culprit most of us blame when we try to explain why one day our darling daughter is the apple of our eye and the next we're sharing living space with Jezebel.

All of which is just part and parcel of life unfolding as it has through the ages. Adolescence is a time of major change and transition. Teenagers anguish about their physical appearance, their sexuality, how well accepted they are by their peers, their grades at school, their changing relationships with their parents, the uncertain future looming before them. It's little wonder that temporary mood fluctuations are common.

The key here is *temporary*. Most kids' shifts in mood are transient. They last several hours or days or, on rare occasions, a few weeks before the clouds lift for mysterious reasons of their own and life resumes its time-honored rhythms.

Length of time and degree are important here. *The longer the sadness persists and the deeper it becomes, the less likely it is that spontaneous change will occur.*

If your child's "down" mood has lasted the better part of a year, you may have a genuinely sad or depressed child on your hands. As for his or her underachievement: Poor marks are a byproduct of the energy drain caused by continued unhappiness. Sometimes the sadness causes or precedes the underachievement, and sometimes the underachievement causes or precedes the sadness.

How Often Do We See Sad or Depressed Underachievers?

About 7 percent of underachievers fit the Sad Underachiever prototype (clinical depression is much less common—less than 2 percent of all children before puberty). *We see Sad Underachievers at all ages, but the male/female ratio changes as kids get older.* Before puberty, the ratio of boys to girls is 1:1. But beginning in the teens and continuing through life, twice as many women report sadness and depression as men.

Why the shift? Two factors may be playing a role here. First, it may be more acceptable for female teens to admit they are sad. And second, males may express their sadness in other ways. For example, some male teens take out their sadness in the form of aggression or irritability instead of obvious, down-at-the-mouth gloom.

What kind of families do Sad Underachievers come from? A wide range of types. But we see a higher proportion of Sad Underachievers who come from disorganized, broken, or rejecting homes and we also see a disproportionate number who come from newly arrived immigrant families.

The Sad Underachiever pattern has chameleon-like qualities that the other five underachieving prototypes do not have. For example:

- The pattern can transform itself, either in whole or in part, into any of the other types.
- Conversely, any of the other five types can become depressed to a degree that they resemble the "pure" Sad type.

The Sad Underachiever, then, is the most likely of the six types to be a "Combination Underachiever." The combination we see most often is the Sad Anxious Underachiever. *Most Sad Underachievers share characteristics of the Anxious Underachiever (worried, tense, perfectionist).* And, as we mentioned in the chapter on Anxious Underachievers, a full 50 percent of Anxious Underachievers are also sad. What happens is this: Their heroic efforts to do well are stymied by their overwhelming inner tension. And when they fail despite their efforts, the inner tension that possesses them is replaced by an overwhelming sense of hopelessness.

Other "combination types" we often see are Sad Wheeler-Dealer Underachievers and Sad Identity-Search Underachievers. A Wheeler-Dealer Underachiever's tough exterior may hide sadness. The

Wheeler-Dealer has developed manipulative skills to protect himself. And an Identity-Search Underachiever's struggle with questions about her inner self can quickly spiral into depression if the answers she is searching for seem elusive.

*   *   *

Before we probe deeper into the Sad Underachiever, please note:

Parents of a seriously depressed child under, say, the age of 12 rarely shrug it off as a normal stage in the business of growing up. They view deep sadness in a young child with alarm—and rightly so. Depression in children of this age is usually the result of more central and serious problems that need attention—psychological problems that take priority over underachievement at school.

So the sad kids *we* see in our practice usually are in their teens. By then, parental alarm bells have reversed their priorities: Parents of teenagers are more likely to be upset about their child's underachievement than they are about their sadness (many, in fact, do not even realize that their child is suffering from depression). So the Depressed Underachievers we talk about in this chapter are primarily adolescents. They're the ones we have had a lot of experience dealing with.

Let's look at the seven most readily identifiable characteristics that set the Sad Underachiever apart from other kids who underachieve.

Anatomy of a Sad or Depressed Underachiever

1. They are depressed or irritable.

How do you know when you're sad? People experience sadness as a change in their normal, day-to-day mood. We feel down, cheerless, dejected. Our normal level of optimism plummets. Or, if we're naturally pessimistic, we lose all sense of balance and perspective. Everything looks bleak, including the color of the kitchen walls.

Sad Underachievers experience a prolonged depressed or irritable mood. Their sadness doesn't last just for a day or a week. It lasts months and even years at a time. They appear apathetic. They accomplish very little. They seem to go about every task at an unconscionably slow pace. They may sleep a lot. They don't seem interested in anything. "Shape up!" many parents say. "Get off your behind and *do* something!" Often, parents have no idea that their child is depressed. They assume the obvious—that he's bone lazy. Lazy and unmotivated. A sleepwalking, barely sentient example of The Underachievement Myth.

From the outside looking in, it's very easy to interpret the Sad Underachiever as a student who just doesn't care. But for the Sad or Depressed Underachiever, nothing could be further from the truth. Listen to this 13-year-old, who was referred to a school psychologist for assessment:

Psychologist:	"Barbara, your parents and teacher have been worried about you. They asked me to see you. They said that you seem to have changed over the last while. Could you tell me about it?"
Barbara:	(sighs, pauses, and slowly answers) "I can't believe it. I used to be a good student. Not a genius, but a solid B average."
Psychologist:	"And now?"
Barbara:	(looks away) "I'm embarrassed to even say. My average is around a D now."
Psychologist:	"So you've slipped a bit."
Barbara:	"Not a bit—a lot! I did quite well up until about two years ago."
Psychologist:	"What do you think happened?"
Barbara:	"I really don't know. I just seemed to lose interest."
Psychologist:	"So, this has happened over about a two-year period?"
Barbara:	(pauses) "I guess that's right. Yes. And I can't seem to shake this feeling. I just feel down, even though I'd like to get back to the way I was. Sometimes I've wondered if I have mono or something like that."

Psychologist:	"Actually, that's important. When was the last time you had a complete medical exam?"
Barbara:	"I've had two checkups in the last year. And I'm perfectly okay physically. That's not the reason. (Pauses.) I wish it was. At least it would explain things. My parents think I'm lazy. (Dejectedly.) I suppose they're right."
Psychologist:	"You know, Barbara, you seem concerned about what's going on. Most people who are concerned about themselves are *not* lazy. Confused maybe, but not lazy."
Barbara:	"Yeah, I guess that's true. And I didn't mean to criticize my parents. They're really good to me."
Psychologist:	"I didn't take your comments that way at all."
Barbara:	(looking and sounding relieved) "Good."

Barbara's depressed mood has lasted for about two years. She knows she's unhappy but she's unable to identify the cause or get out of the rut she's in. This is common of many Sad Underachievers. They clearly don't like how it feels, but they are often unsure what the roots of the problem are or what solutions to pursue.

Some Sad Underachievers also report feeling irritable—overly sensitive to certain issues. They seem to have lost their even-keeled, good-natured temperament.

A cautionary note: Mood shifts can be due to biochemical changes in the body such as a hormonal imbalance, poor nutrition, infection or other physiological causes. If you suspect any of these physical reasons may be behind your child's sadness, be sure to have a thorough medical checkup.

2. They have poor appetites or overeat.

If your child has *unintentionally* gained or lost more than 10 percent of normal body weight, the underlying cause may be depression. Most people who experience prolonged sadness show changes in eating habits—either they undereat or they overeat.

Keep in mind "unintentionally." Many teenagers lose or gain weight intentionally, and as long as these planned changes are not extreme, they generally are not considered a sign of sadness.

3. They sleep too much or have trouble sleeping.

Sleeping patterns are vulnerable to mood the same way eating patterns are. Some of us sleep for inordinate lengths of time when we are sad. And when we wake up, we still seem to feel tired. One way of interpreting this is that our body needs rest in order to recover from whatever trauma we have experienced, or to cope with whatever we are going through. Another interpretation is avoidance: At least while we are asleep, we don't have to experience our sadness.

Some Sad Underachievers report sleeping as much as 14 hours a day. They come home from school and lie down for a two-hour nap. They eat supper, struggle through some homework and go back to sleep. Can you see how easy it would be to interpret this excessive sleep as laziness or lack of motivation? Another consideration if your teenager seems to sleep much more than seems normal to you: In the middle-teen years (14-16), a time when adolescents are growing quickly and undergoing many physiological changes, many normal kids need a lot more sleep than the average. So if your child is sleeping a lot, but does not exhibit other characteristics of the Sad Underachiever, do not jump to conclusions.

The flip side is not being able to sleep because we can't stop thinking about the hopelessness of our life or because we can't get our minds off the unhappy circumstances that have caused our sadness. Sad Underachieving teenagers who suffer from sleeplessness toss and turn, continually thinking about their problems. Not getting enough sleep exacerbates the Sad Underachiever's problems, decreasing the ability to concentrate or make decisions, lowering energy levels and increasing irritability.

4. They experience low energy and feel tired all the time.

Fatigue can be caused by a wide range of physical conditions, and most fatigue should *not* automatically be considered a sign of sadness. Conversely, most depressed people do experience fatigue.

The symptoms of depression-based fatigue are much the same as those of fatigue with a medical basis. Everything slows down, including walking, talking and thinking. Sometimes just moving the body from one place to another becomes a chore.

The Sad Underachiever may start drastically curtailing activities because of energy depletion, which produces its own side effect—a less active social life. Sad Underachievers may find their teenage friends starting to ignore them simply because they haven't exerted enough energy to maintain friendships.

5. They experience low self-esteem.

Low self-esteem often underlies depression. The Sad Underachiever feels worthless, dumb and very often unattractive—a dull, boring, ugly person who just can't accomplish anything and whom no one else would want to be with. As the cycle deepens and feeds on itself, self-doubt can segue into self-pity.

Sometimes the beginnings of this downward spiral can be traced to a specific event. This event is usually the loss or feared loss of a significant relationship. In the following example, 17-year-old Ron discusses the breakup of a year-long relationship with his girlfriend.

> Psychologist: "Ron, you mentioned that you've been like this ever since you and Cindy broke up. That's about a year now, right?"
>
> Ron: "Yes."
>
> Psychologist: "Okay, tell me about the breakup."
>
> Ron: "What's there to tell? We'd been going out for about a year when she met this other guy. He's a little older than me, a senior. Out of the clear blue she said she wanted to date other guys just to see whether we were meant to be. I suppose

she was right. I'm not the most exciting guy in the world."

Psychologist: "What do you mean?"

Ron: "Well, I'm just pretty steady, but nothing more than that. I guess she decided she wanted something different. I sort of knew it was coming. She seemed bored a bit with our relationship after a while. He plays for the school basketball team. I guess I just wasn't good enough for her."

Psychologist: "Did you feel this way about yourself only when the relationship with Cindy was about to end, or earlier than that?"

Ron: "You mean not being good enough?"

Psychologist: "Yes."

Ron: "I guess I've always felt a bit insecure about myself, but this relationship was the first longer relationship I've ever had. I really felt good about it. (Sighs.) And now it's gone for good."

Ron's self-esteem is at an all-time low. It was never extremely high, but the loss of the relationship has thrown it into a downward spiral, and his grades have dropped in several courses.

6. They have trouble concentrating.

Like fatigue, difficulty concentrating can have many causes. Sad Underachievers, however, have difficulty concentrating only when they're depressed. And the deeper the sadness, the poorer their powers of concentration. Before the onset of the sadness, these students demonstrated a normal ability to concentrate.

So if your child has always had a problem concentrating, the source of the difficulty is probably something else. But if this is something new that has emerged during a troublesome period, it may be a result of depression.

7. They feel hopeless.

One of the most pervasive feelings experienced by Sad Underachievers is a sense that no matter what they do, it won't make any difference. Some of these students have stopped trying precisely for that reason. So it's become a self-fulfilling prophecy.

Sally is a 14-year-old student whose mother is terminally ill with cancer. She daydreams a lot in class and has begun to miss handing in assignments and preparing for tests. The quality of her homework has also slipped. A concerned teacher arranges to meet with her after school.

Teacher:	"Sally, you didn't hand in your project today."
Sally:	"I'm sorry. I guess I just didn't think I could do it. It seemed very hard."
Teacher:	(somewhat frustrated) "You mentioned that the last time too. I wish you had told me that's how you felt. I announced in class that anyone who was having difficulty with the assignment should come and talk with me."
Sally:	"I know, but I guess I felt embarrassed. I've really not been very with it lately."
Teacher:	"Well, if you want, maybe we can talk about it now. I could give you an extension 'til the end of next week?"
Sally:	"Actually, I don't know. (Pauses.) I don't think I can do it. It won't work out. Forget it."
Teacher:	"Sally, I've been worried about you ever since you found out that your mother has cancer. Have you talked with anyone about it?"
Sally:	(sighs) "No, not really. It's hard to, and besides, what good would it do? It won't change my mother's situation."

Sally is lucky to have a teacher who is concerned enough to try to get her some help. But it won't be easy to get Sally to agree, because she genuinely believes that nothing will make a difference. She has been taken over by a sense of hopelessness.

Summing Up: Anatomy of a Sad or Depressed Underachiever

1. They are depressed or irritable.
2. They have poor appetites or overeat.
3. They sleep too much or have trouble sleeping.
4. They experience low energy and feel tired all the time.
5. They experience low self-esteem.
6. They have trouble concentrating.
7. They feel hopeless.

Armed with our lengthy description over the preceding pages, it's time now to pause and see how similar your child's characteristics are to those of the Sad Underachiever.

Parent Checklist

1. Has my child been in a depressed or irritable mood for most of the past year?

   Yes___ No___ Don't Know___

2. Has my child shown poor appetite or serious overeating for long periods of time during the last year?

   Yes___ No___ Don't Know___

3. Has my child shown major changes in sleeping patterns, either sleeping much more or having trouble sleeping during the last year?

   Yes___ No___ Don't Know___

4. Has my child shown low energy or fatigue frequently during the past year?

Yes___ No___ Don't Know___

5. Has my child shown signs of low self-esteem frequently during the past year?

Yes___ No___ Don't Know___

6. Has my child found it hard to concentrate frequently or to make decisions during the past year?

Yes___ No___ Don't Know___

7. Does my child seem to give up easily and complain that things are "hopeless" frequently during the past year?

Yes___ No___ Don't Know___

If you answered "Yes" to Question 1, and "Yes" to *at least two* of the remaining questions, your child's characteristics may be similar to those of the Sad Underachiever. However, even if your child exhibits only one of these characteristics, don't discount it. It may reflect the beginning of a problem.

What's Bothering Your Sad Underachiever?

It's pretty clear to all that the Sad Underachiever is not playacting. What you see on the outside mirrors what's going on inside. The low energy, pessimism and lack of pleasure in daily activities are a reflection of the Depressed Underachiever's inner feelings. He may go through the motions of going to class, handing in some assignments and trying to study for exams but overall, life is a real struggle. As one father commented: "Jack's spark or juice just seemed to disappear slowly over time. It's not like it suddenly evaporated. I can't tell you definitely that on such and such a day, he suddenly changed. It was more gradual. But at some point, my wife and I noticed the difference. And I guess we really took notice when his school effort and his marks started to tumble."

How do Sad Underachievers think and what do they think about? Let's get inside the mind of the Depressed Underachiever.

The Inner Life of a Sad or Depressed Underachiever

Most Sad Underachievers truly want to do better. But inside they're convinced that they won't be successful even if they try. They are preoccupied with these thoughts of inadequacy almost all of their waking hours.

Notice the kind of thinking that the following 16-year-old Sad Underachiever uses:

Counselor: "You were saying that you didn't do well on the math test. Tell me more about it."

Peter: "You know, I thought I really could do the math, but I guess I was fooling myself. Everyone else in the class is better at it than I am. And everything that I do just isn't good enough."

Counselor: "I'm not sure exactly what you're saying. Are you saying that you aren't capable of doing the work? That it's too hard—that you're not bright enough?"

Peter: "Well, it feels that way."

Counselor: "What evidence do you have that you don't have the ability?"

Peter: "Well, I guess now that you mention it, it probably isn't ability. I just don't seem to have the energy to get through the work. I can't seem to concentrate either. I suppose that if I had the energy, I'd understand most of it. I have before, you know."

Counselor: "So you're struggling to concentrate and your energy level is low too."

Peter: "Exactly. Is there anything you can do to help
              me?"

Let's get inside Peter's mind.

First, he *selected* a single "fact"—that everyone else in the class
outperformed him on the math test. This probably isn't true, but Peter
genuinely believes it is. (Did he check everyone's mark? Probably
not.) Even if he did get the lowest mark on *one* test, it's not at all clear
why that happened.

But Peter has no trouble clarifying the reasons. He *generalizes*
from his first thought that he is incapable of doing well.

*Sad Underachievers tend to select one fact and generalize negatively
about themselves.* Often they exaggerate their weaknesses and magnify
the strengths of others. Peter thought that the other students were better than he was in math. And some of them may be. It's even possible—
but not probable—that all of them are. But this is precisely the type of
thinking that fuels Peter's pessimism and results in greater hopelessness.

Is this abnormal thinking? Don't we all downplay our abilities at
times and think that others have more going for them? Doesn't everybody select facts to bolster beliefs? Yes, we do. But most people don't
think this way *most of the time*. And such thoughts don't paralyze us
from performing adequately.

Sad Underachievers freeze up when faced with making decisions.

They feel paralyzed and overwhelmed, and tend to withdraw from
others. Isolated and feeling very much alone, they feel guilty about
their indecision.

Instead of sizing up each situation and then making a considered,
rational decision, Sad Underachievers tend to jump rapidly—almost
automatically—to negative conclusions. As a result, they never get
any practice going through the small steps, each one leading to the
next, that are the normal process of making a change in one's life.

For example, in the normal course of life, people struggle daily with
a range of issues. A typical teenager's menu of issues might include

curfew, house chores, choice of clothes, amount and use of allowance, drug use, selection of friends, dating, privacy. Sad Underachievers approach this collection of problems by concluding that an immediate solution to *all* of them is impossible and, therefore, they're failures. So they address none of the problems separately—and none of the issues is resolved.

As Sad Underachievers fall into an abyss of pessimism, they begin to believe that their problems will never get better. So they stop trying. A sense of helplessness can set in, which sometimes leads to thoughts of suicide. Incidentally, it is not unusual for adolescents to think about the meaning of life—and about suicide—in the same breath. However, for most teens these thoughts are only fleeting. In the case of the Sad Underachiever (indeed, of *any* child or adolescent), *any* longer ruminations about suicide should be taken seriously and evaluated by a professional.

Sad Underachievers feel no joy in their daily life. They describe their lives as "boring."

Boring is a favorite word adolescents use to describe their parents or teachers. Sad Underachievers, however, use "boring" in a much more incisive way. For them, "boring" connotes a sense of inner emptiness and complete absence of pleasure. For typical adolescents, parents or school may be boring, but their personal lives are seldom boring.

Sad Underachievers report difficulty in getting themselves "up" for almost anything. One student called this "moving in slow motion."

Parents and teachers often view this lack of effort as a sign of apathy, and are quick to label the student as lazy and unmotivated. This is unfortunate, because what looks like a lack of care may mask the deeper problem—pervasive sadness.

To sum up: Sad Underachievers perceive the world as an unhelpful place and the future as grim. They blame themselves for many of their difficulties. Guilt, thoughts of incompetence, difficulty in making decisions, pessimism and a lack of energy are all part of their every-day experience.

What's at the Root of the Depressed Underachiever's Sadness?

Most mental-health experts believe that the psychological basis of depression is anger: unexpressed anger—anger turned inward. Sad Underachievers are angry at themselves for not being good enough or at someone else for causing their deficiencies. And instead of acting out the anger against others, they turn it inward against themselves. Denied a chance to vent or express itself and run its course, the anger festers inside, causing its owner deep sadness and unhappiness.

Research has uncovered several things about depressed under-achievers. Any of the following may have contributed to pervasive sadness in an underachiever:

1. There's another depressed person in the family.

If someone else in the family has been diagnosed as clinically depressed, there is a greater chance that one or more of the children will be affected by sadness. The statistics are quite dramatic: The offspring of depressed parents are eight to 10 times as likely to develop depression. Whether this is due to heredity (a genetic predisposition to mood prob-lems) or to the family environment doesn't change the statistic.

2. There's a lot of conflict in the family.

Studies have shown that more conflict exists in families of depressed adolescents than in families of non-depressed teens, and that depressed teens have a more negative view of their parents. In other words, one of the sources of adolescent sadness may be embedded in the family.

3. The Depressed Underachiever has suffered a loss.

Loss may also be at the root of sadness. The loss may be due to a death, someone's departure or a debilitating injury. Sad Underachievers may be reacting to an actual loss or to a perceived loss (one that they believe they have suffered or are about to suffer). And the loss need not be catastrophic: The extent of the loss very often lies in the eyes of the beholder. But this does not detract in any way from the devastating nature of that loss to the child involved. The following example illustrates what a youngster felt as a major loss, although not all of us would have experienced it as significant.

Twelve-year-old Randy's academic performance had begun to deteriorate two years earlier at the beginning of Grade 5, but no one in his family could figure out why. Even Randy couldn't explain the reasons for his poor marks. His parents were comfortably married, and he got along well with his older brother and younger sister. The family had experienced no unusual crises, and was very stable.

Randy had been a quiet but happy youngster. In talking about his favorite activities, he finally got around to talking about his love of animals. He often used to visit his grandfather's farm and especially enjoyed caring for the animals. As he spoke warmly about those times, tears came to his eyes. Unfortunately, due to increasing frailty, his grandfather had been forced to sell the farm. And although Randy continued to visit his grandfather regularly in the new senior center close to his home, he clearly missed his close relationship with the farm animals.

Once the intensity of his feelings were visible, and once the connection was made between his loss and his poor academic performance, everyone realized the depth of Randy's feelings about the loss. Randy experienced the relief of finding out what had been the cause of his sadness, and his family responded with understanding and ideas for dealing with the situation.

Unfortunately, not all Depressed Underachievers are as straightforward to deal with. *The loss of a parent* through death, separation or divorce, or *the loss of another close family member* such as a brother or sister or grandparent can cause severe, long-lasting trauma. Both the loss itself and, in the case of a long, terminal illness, the uncertainty and tension that come with an approaching loss are very likely to cause an academic downturn for an extended period of time.

Loss of a friendship or relationship can also trigger deep and continuing sadness, as we saw earlier with Ron who lost his girlfriend. Likewise the *loss of health* that can result from a severe accident in which the child (or another family member) loses a limb or the ability to walk or is disfigured.

Another loss which is quite common these days is *job loss*. We often see young underachievers who come from homes where at least one parent has lost a job. Unemployment can precipitate enormous change and upheaval in a family's life. It places great pressure on the marital relationship and may result in loss of the family home, severe cutbacks in family income and spending or a move to a different neighborhood or city, with the loss of friendships and roots that entails. Some marriages survive extended periods of unemployment, others don't, and during prolonged periods of unemployment, all family members feel a sense of loss. Children and teenagers are especially vulnerable to these changes.

In all loss, things change, and change in itself is the source of a lot of the stress in life. Loss also can entail betrayal, isolation or rejection, which complicate and exacerbate the trauma of the loss.

4. There are marital problems in the family.

Marital discord can also precipitate deep sadness, fear, anger and a dramatic drop in school performance in some children and teenagers. Kids usually react in one of the following ways to their parents' unhappiness:

- They try to persevere with their own lives, vowing never to make the same mistakes as their parents. (*"A plague on both your houses."*)

- They turn inward, blaming themselves. (*"I'm the cause of it all. If only I weren't here, my parents would be okay."*)

- They take their frustration out on others. (*"I don't care who's at fault. I'm angry and someone is going to pay."*)

- They side with one parent against the other. They enter the battle in an attempt to protect one parent from the other and to get back at the "bad" parent. (*"It's all Dad's fault. How could he have left Mom for her?"*)

The second reaction—turning inward and blaming oneself—is perhaps the most likely to cause sadness. But any of the above reactions can cause guilt and depression.

Which one of these roads a child takes depends on the child's age, sex and temperament, as well as on the personalities of the parents and the route the marital problems take. In general, the more disruptive the marital conflict and the longer it lasts, the greater the chances are that a child will show signs of sadness and underachievement. The school itself also has an influence on how severe the sadness or underachievement of a child of divorce becomes. Many children lean on caring teachers and supportive school friends to counterbalance their unstable home environment.

And if both parents maintain meaningful and regular contact with their children after a divorce—and if they don't use their children to get back at each other—many children are able to maintain their school grades.

For some, divorce can be a convenient scapegoat for a drop in a child's performance at school. It's important not to fall into this trap. Remember, not all children react to separation or divorce with plummeting grades. Many maintain their performance level.

The following case illustrates a few of the different ways children react to their parents' marital problems.

> Carol and Carl were 12-year-old twins. Their parents had been able to hide their most intense arguments from the children. But the parents concluded that their differences were irreconcilable, and decided to inform their children that they were planning to separate.
>
> Carol continued doing well in school for a while. She seemed to be handling the impending separation reasonably, continuing with her chores, school work and friendships.

She admitted to being somewhat sad about her parents' breakup, but said that two of her friends also had divorced parents and talked freely about the breakup of their families.

Carl, however, began to have behavior problems at school shortly after he learned about his parents' separation. First, he got into shoving matches with friends in the school yard. Then he began to defy teachers, who reported that Carl had suddenly become very angry. He wanted to spend all of his time with his father, and began making sarcastic remarks to his mother. At the advice of the school, Carl's parents contacted a mental-health professional to deal with their son's worsening behavior.

A year after the separation, Carol began to experience difficulties at school as well. She complained of having trouble concentrating. She was not disruptive; on the contrary, she seemed to be "fading into the woodwork," in the words of one teacher. As her marks dropped, she appeared to take less pride in both her work and her appearance. These changes coincided with two events. The first was Carol's father's announcement that he was leaving town to pursue business opportunities elsewhere. The second was that one of Carol's close girlfriends was also leaving, because her family was moving to Europe.

The twins' losses affected them in different ways and at different times. Although Carl was hesitant to express his sadness, his irritability was unmistakable. He took out his frustration, anger and undeclared sadness on teachers, friends and parents. His academic performance suffered almost immediately.

Carol held it together until she was hit with two losses that were too great for her to bear. She, too, had denied the impact of her parents' impending separation, but her denial took a different form. She plowed on, hoping that she could just ignore it and everything would be okay. And for a while, everything seemed to be.

Summing Up: What's at the Root of the Depressed Underachiever's Sadness?

1. There's another depressed person in the family.
2. There's a lot of conflict in the family.
3. The Depressed Underachiever has suffered a loss.
4. There are marital problems in the family.

Helping Your Sad or Depressed Underachiever

1. Try to find out what's bothering your child.

The sorrow that Sad Underachievers experience can come from many sources. To find out where your child's sadness began, you can start with the obvious: by simply asking your child what's wrong and how he or she thinks it developed. Or you may ask the question indirectly by making an observation. Such as, "I've been noticing you spend an awful lot of time alone these days," or, "You seem to need so much sleep these days," or, "You don't go out with your friends any more. That worries me."

Then it is important to be quiet and listen. Use reflective statements (as described in Chapter 4 for the Identity-Search Underachiever) to try to understand what is bothering your child.

Your child may be able to identify a specific cause, such as peer problems at school or course material that is too hard. If you can pinpoint the problem source, you can then generate a plan of action.

But it's probably not going to be so easy. First, your child probably won't be aware of the source of the problem. He'll say something like, "I can't explain it, Mom. I just feel down, that's all." Or he may blame his mood on something other than sadness. Such as, "I guess I'm just tired."

And your child probably will find it difficult to talk about being sad, especially to a parent. One of the most common symptoms of depression is a tendency not to express yourself—or, to put it another way, a tendency to have trouble expressing yourself. And if you and your child have trouble communicating, and if you have contributed (even unknowingly) to the sadness, then helping your child to open up may be very difficult. If this is the case, consider involving someone else in the family—or a friend—whom your child seems to be able to talk to more easily.

Most Sad Underachievers (and often their families) need professional assistance from a psychologist, psychiatrist or counselor. If you enlist professional help, look for the following feedback:

- Does the psychologist, psychiatrist or counselor convey the findings to your child in a way that makes sense to both your child and to you?
- Has the assessment let you know to what extent *you* are a source of the sadness?
- Do the assessment findings point to a need for school involvement?
- How about family or couple therapy?
- Has the professional recommended individual or group counseling for your child? If so, why?

If a professional assessment concludes that sadness is a major contributor to the child's problem, the professional should be able to identify the source of the sadness and recommend a treatment plan. For many Sad Underachievers, just seeing that another adult understands what has been going on can be an enormous relief.

2. Practical suggestions to help your Sad Underachiever.

Once you determine what's bothering your child, there are practical things you can do to help your Sad Underachiever. Choose what's appropriate for your situation from among this list.

Increase physical activity.

Around 400 BC, Hippocrates, author of the famous doctor's oath, suggested that moderate exercise would be helpful in treating melancholia, the word then used for depression. The buzz word now is endorphins, which are released in the body through exercise and help the physically active person see the world through more positive eyes.

Sad Underachievers are prime candidates for the release of a few endorphins. These kids tend to slow down physically. They move more slowly, participate less in physical activities and generally are less active. Sluggish body, sluggish mind. Exercise may help get more positive emotions coursing through your child's body. So encourage your Sad Underachiever to get involved in some kind of physical activity. But be prepared for some resistance. When you're down, just the idea of exerting yourself may seem overwhelming. Don't just say, "You need to get out there and exercise." Be more specific. You know your own child and what kinds of activities she enjoys. Suggest something you know she likes *and* that she's likely to stick with. A social activity that requires a partner—tennis or squash, for example—might kill two birds with one stone. That is, it would both get your child exercising and help maintain, re-establish or create friendships.

Encourage relaxation exercises.
Why relaxation exercises? Aren't Sad Underachievers relaxed already? Well, they may look immobile, but they're far from relaxed. Their tension can take many forms, including the tension of having self-defeating thoughts constantly racing through their minds. Relaxation exercises are an effective way to counteract these negative thoughts. The relaxation exercises we outline in Chapter 3 for the Anxious Underachiever are equally appropriate for the Sad Underachiever.

Encourage your child to do the simple breathing exercises described in Chapter 3 before starting any activity that triggers automatic negative thoughts. For example, if your child begins to think negatively while doing homework, writing an essay or preparing for a test, suggest going through a relaxation exercise. Negative thoughts tend to disappear during these exercises and their impact is diminished.

Identify—and counter—false assumptions in your child's thinking.
Most situations, viewed realistically, have pluses and minuses. But Sad Underachievers always look on the bleak side. Their glasses are

always half empty. They think in ways that increase their sadness and deepen their sense of hopelessness.

Learning how to decipher the false assumptions embedded in a Sad Underachiever's thinking is a skill that can be practiced. And getting the gist of doing this can go a long way toward stopping your child's downward spiral.

Here is an example of what we mean:

Lisa, a frustrated 13-year-old, is doing her homework at the kitchen table. She pushes her books away, and declares:

Lisa:	"I guess it's no use any more. Math is a curse." *(The false assumption: Just because Lisa is having trouble in this subject, she concludes that she won't be able to understand it and has no reason to hope any more.)*
Mother:	"What do you mean 'no use'? You sound like you're giving up."
Lisa:	"I must be stupid. I'm no good at math, and I never will be."
Mother:	"Hold on. What's the problem?"
Lisa:	*"Everything's* the problem!" *(Another false assumption: Lisa has been able to get at least average marks in math up until this school year. So everything in math is not a problem, although Lisa may feel this way.)*
Mother:	"Come on, you did okay in math last year! What's going on now that looks so impossible?"
Lisa:	"But you don't understand. It *is* impossible!"
Mother:	"Okay, that's how you feel about it. But let's get specific. What's giving you trouble?"
Lisa :	(pointing) "These stupid problems."
Mother:	"Right, let's see what you don't understand."
Lisa:	"Like *this* one." *(Don't dwell on feelings. Show your child that you understand the frustration,*

but move quickly to tackling her problem. In this case, Lisa and her mother worked on the problem and, with a little help from her older sister, Lisa was able to understand something that had really given her trouble.)

Mother: "That's great. You got it!"

Lisa: "Yeah, but you guys helped me." *(Here's another aspect of Lisa's thinking: She's minimized her contribution and maximized those of her mother and sister.)*

Mother: "Yes, we pointed out something that you weren't looking at, but who did the work?"

Lisa: "Okay, I guess I did."

Mother: "And there are another nine problems like the one in your homework assignment. Try them. Let's see how many you get right."

Lisa: "Probably none."

Mother: "Sounds like you've already decided that you won't be able to do them. That's what got you in trouble before—your negative thinking. But you just solved one of these! Try the others." *(Lisa's mother challenged her daughter's eroded self-confidence and encouraged her to act. Lisa worked on her homework and was somewhat pleased that she was able to solve seven of the remaining 10 problems.)*

Lisa: "Well, I knew I couldn't figure them *all* out."

Mother: "You got seven out of 10. That's seven more than when you started tonight. You know, that's terrific! But you only seem to focus on what's wrong, not on what's right. How fair do you think that is to you?"

This is a good example of countering negative beliefs with positive beliefs. Because of her sad mood, Lisa viewed herself and her accomplishments in a negative light and stopped trying. Her mother offered Lisa another perspective by questioning the automatic false assumptions behind Lisa's thinking. In this way, Lisa's view of herself and the future was not automatically allowed to be negative.

Encourage your child to question false assumptions.
Encourage your Sad Underachiever to examine his own faulty assumptions. When you hear your child saying something with a false assumption embedded in it, ask him point-blank whether he's able to detect where the defect in thinking lies. This can be extended to much more than school work. For example, "I'll never be asked out on a date" is no different in its thought structure than "I'll never be able to get this math."

Over time, these kids are better able to use skills of thought detection to stop themselves from reaching automatic and unfair assumptions about themselves. And when they generalize this skill to areas that have nothing to do with school, they'll be helping end the negative spiral that has overtaken their lives.

An important caution: Being able to help a child question negative automatic thoughts requires a positive relationship between parent and child. If the relationship is *not* positive or open, probing for false assumptions may spark angry retorts. If this describes your situation, as with any approach that appears to make things worse, you probably should cease and desist.

Offer a balance of praise and criticism.
Sad Underachievers are already thinking negatively. They don't need additional ammunition from parents. So give praise where praise is due. But be careful: Depressed kids have overactive sensitivity antennae and they'll pick up false praise at once. And you'll lose all credibility.

The reason they're shy of praise is because they're actively looking for reasons to doubt themselves. If they sense that you're not realistic in your praise, they'll immediately conclude that you too have seen their shortcomings and are just trying to make them feel better. In other words, false praise adds to Sad Underachievers' sense of inadequacy and worthlessness.

On the other hand, Sad Underachievers will always exaggerate criticism. Remember, they're constantly waiting for proof that they're losers and that things will never improve. So be careful when you criticize them. Be sure it's balanced and fair. Sad Underachievers are likely to dwell on criticism and blow it out of proportion.

Incidentally, when providing feedback to your Sad Underachiever, ask what she heard you say and how she feels about it. Don't be surprised if she heard a different message from the one you intended. For example:

Father:	"You really look nice tonight."
Teenager:	(depressed) "Thanks a lot."
Father:	"What is it you think I just said?"
Teenager:	"I know you were just saying that to make me feel better—not because it's true!"

This child has automatically inserted a false assumption: that her parent is just trying to make her feel good. This is a good opportunity to help a Sad Underachiever learn to question assumptions. As:

Father:	"Is there something I've said or done to make you think that?"
Teenager:	"Well . . . no."
Father:	"Then maybe I really am complimenting you on something that's true."
Or:	

Father:	"Is there something I've said or done to make you think that?"
Teenager:	"Yeah, you're always trying to cheer me up."
Father:	"Always? You mean every minute of the day? Every day of the *week*?"
Teenager:	(smiles) "Well, not really."

Father: "Then maybe I really am complimenting you on
               something that's true."

Suggest small, attainable goals.
Many Sad Underachievers perceive their problems as insurmountable
and overwhelming. You can help by suggesting that larger tasks be
divided into smaller ones. And working out a reasonable schedule for
dealing with the smaller tasks also makes sense.

The key word here is *reasonable.* If you're the parent of a Sad
Underachiever, don't let your child promise too much, especially initially. Because when they aren't able to come through, they'll blame
themselves. They won't recognize unrealistic expectations as just
that—unrealistic. They'll conclude instead that they're inadequate
and incompetent.

Successfully reaching small, attainable goals increases a sense of
personal control. And that will counteract the sense of lack of control
that Sad Underachievers almost always have regarding their lives.

How do you know when a goal is attainable? Here's a general rule:
Realistic goals take into account a person's present skill, and the time
and effort required to attain an added skill. And someone who is
depressed may not have the energy, even though they have the skill.
So shrink the goal. That will increase the chances of attaining it. And
creating a realistic goal should lead to specific, realistic steps for
reaching the goal.

Target these goals to the specific issues that trigger the sadness.
These may be individual school subjects, a problem with writing essays,
family conflicts or problems with your child's social life. Perhaps your
Sad Underachiever has trouble making or keeping friends. Maybe he's
painfully shy and afraid to risk reaching out in social situations.

Anticipate problems and discuss potential solutions.
One way to decrease Sad Underachievers' pessimism is to discuss problems they think might arise, along with potential solutions. For example:

Parent: "Suppose you have trouble understanding the

	math assignment. What do you think you might do then?"
Teenager:	"I don't know."
Parent:	"Well, maybe there's something you can think of so that if you do run into trouble understanding it, you'll be prepared with something you can do about it."
Teenager:	(slowly) "Well . . . I suppose I could call Suzanne. She's really good at math."
Parent:	"Good idea. I'm sure Suzanne would be more than happy to help you—*if* you feel it's necessary."

Now, if this student does have trouble understanding the math assignment, the parent can remind her of the Suzanne contingency plan. This should help her avoid more frustration and sadness.

Encourage activities that your child truly enjoys.
What has your child delighted in? Going to the movies? Riding the most terrifying ride at your local theme park? Going to the zoo? Playing a game of catch with you? Fooling around with his Frisbee or on his skateboard? Think back to earlier years and the things your child just plain had fun doing—before he started analyzing his activities and feeling he had to compete.

As a parent, the idea of your child's long-ago youth may seem ludicrous or farcical. But your child's timeline is different. Last *year* may seem to him like his distant, carefree childhood before overwhelming responsibilities and problems arose.

Parents of Sad Underachievers need to adopt this approach, perhaps by suggesting one of these things again "just for fun" or "for nostalgia's sake." It's crucial that your child experience some pleasure, if for no other reason than to help her realize that she still can have some fun. If you identify activities that make a positive difference to your child's mood and schedule these periodically, you can counteract the lack of pleasure your Sad Underachiever often experiences.

Use (but don't overuse) humor.
Humor in this situation is a double-edged sword. It might lighten some of the burden and give your child a bit of a lift. It can send a message that problems are not *that* terrible and don't have to be experienced as overwhelming.

On the other hand, your child may feel that your attempts at humor indicate that you're not interested in, don't take seriously or even are frightened by their unhappiness. The reaction to humor is a very individual matter, and there are no firm guidelines as to when it will be helpful and when it won't. You have to rely on your own intuition.

3. Explore your own attitudes and reactions to sadness.

Many people have a great deal of difficulty facing sadness or coping with it. This is especially true for parents, who are often frightened by sadness in their children. They often worry, and with some justification, about how low their child will sink and how long it will take for the sadness to disappear.

We have found that many parents of Sad Underachievers don't cope well with their own sorrow. We encourage parents to spend some time exploring their own attitudes and beliefs about sorrow and depressed feelings. How do you cope with your own sadness? Do you run from it? Are you more comfortable expressing anger than sadness? Have you been sad for long periods in your life? How has your child reacted to this?

Summing Up: Helping Your Sad or Depressed Underachiever

1. Try to find out what's bothering your child.

2. Practical suggestions to help your Sad Underachiever:

   - Increase physical activity
   - Encourage relaxation exercises

- Identify—and counter—false assumptions in your child's thinking
- Encourage your child to question false assumptions
- Offer a balance of praise and criticism
- Suggest small, attainable goals
- Anticipate problems and discuss potential solutions
- Encourage activities that your child truly enjoys
- Use (but don't overuse) humor

3. Explore your own attitudes and reactions to sadness.

What to Expect When You Help Your Sad Underachiever

1. Expect positive change.

Let's begin on a note of optimism. Sadness or depression in children and adolescents is treatable, and with a fair degree of success. Overall success rates run at about 80 percent, and even for the other 20 percent, some improvement is possible. Some Sad Underachievers even get over their sadness without professional assistance. A caring parent, an involved teacher, a sensitive friend may make the difference. And new developments in the counseling field have increased success for the Sad Underachiever too.

2. Expect resistance to your suggestions.

Most Sad Underachievers are quick to point out why well-meaning suggestions won't work. That's the nature of their thinking—don't worry about it. They're also good at continuing to generate new faulty reasoning. We caution parents of Sad Underachievers to expect their son or daughter to resist change. But it's critical to keep in mind that these children are doing so almost automatically.

3. Expect to have to repeatedly point out false assumptions.

False assumptions permeate the thinking of Sad Underachievers. Be prepared to have to expose them often, and expect to get tired of doing this.

4. Expect your child's inertia to be contagious at times.

We don't mean medically contagious. But when someone is feeling down and "doesn't feel like" doing much of anything, the inertia may spread like the flu. At times you may feel pulled down by the dead weight and also feel like doing nothing. Well, to look on the bright side, there's nothing wrong with vegging out once in a while. Maybe it will make your child feel better understood!

5. Expect your child to get increasingly frustrated.

As you mobilize to deal with your Sad Underachiever, you must be prepared for your child to accuse you of making him or her more frustrated. This is not simply a way of trying to get you to stop. It's a genuine reflection of your child's increased internal frustration.

6. Expect to feel frustrated and angry at times.

Being with someone who seems committed to viewing the world in negative terms, and who constantly makes it clear that he or she believes that nothing will ever change, can be extremely frustrating. Be prepared to react with anger at times. This is natural—don't waste energy feeling guilty.

A father told us that after his Sad Underachieving son rejected many suggestions for physical activities, he felt "so incompetent, so impotent. Then I got mad. I felt like hitting him. I actually had to hold myself back from taking it out on him."

Remember, your child is not doing this *to* you. He's suffering too, even if it doesn't look that way. At times like this, when it gets the better of you, it's best to pull back rather than continue to plug away, trying to help. Parents need a break too!

7. Expect gradual improvement.

Although, as we said, the prognosis is good over the long term, sadness usually does not disappear rapidly. Be prepared to see the sadness diminish very gradually and, concomitantly, to see your child's energy increase in dribs and drabs. Look for small signs of change. Perhaps your child is able to stick with her homework longer. Perhaps he begins to take an interest in spending more time with friends. Perhaps she smiles more often, even cracks the odd joke.

The Sad Underachiever as an Adult

The Sad Underachiever pattern rarely continues into adulthood.

Let us explain: Sad Underachievers are unique among our six types of underachievers. They're different because they are not three-dimensional personality types with a particular kind of motivation, as are the other five prototypes. In contrast, the Sad Underachiever is defined by a single emotional state. Therefore, if the symptom—that is, the sadness—disappears, then so does the type. This is *not* true for other underachieving types, where the absence of one or more characteristics still leaves a particular personality type with a central motivation.

When sadness does persist into adulthood, we have seen it follow one of the following patterns:

1. The clinically depressed person.

Clinical depression rarely goes undiagnosed these days. A person who is diagnosed with clinical depression almost always is prescribed anti-depressant medication by a professional. The medication effectively controls the depression, and the clinically depressed person's sadness is not permitted to significantly affect job performance. Many of these individuals lead normal lives and achieve.

2. The Sad "Combination" Underachiever.

As we said near the beginning of this chapter, the Sad Underachiever pattern has a chameleon-like capacity to combine with other under-achieving types. This is because sadness is a single emotional state rather than a personality type.

When sadness combines with another personality type, the person may live with a complex of problems that limits achievement in the workplace. In our experience, we have seen adults with a history of depression who struggle to function adequately in the workplace but who simply do not have the internal resources (energy, attention span, self-confidence, ability to concentrate) to realize their potential.

3. Half-empty-glass people.

Some people who may not appear clinically depressed still live their lives on a perpetual down. These are chronic pessimists. They are unhappy about the weather. They are dejected about the town or city they live in. They're miserable about their job, their family, their health, the state of the world.

There are a multitude of reasons for this kind of mind set. A deep sense of personal insecurity and worthlessness is high among the reasons. These people often underachieve if for no other reason than that nobody wants to work alongside them.

4. People whose sadness is caused by a specific life event.

Anyone can suffer a personal setback causing sadness that affects their performance at work—at least temporarily. Losing your job, an illness or accident affecting someone close, marital problems, a death in the family—any trauma or disruptive event can cause depression for a time. And this can affect a person's achievement, sometimes significantly.

This has nothing to do with enduring personality characteristics or a history of adolescent depression. It can happen to anyone as a result of any number of changes or problems or upheavals in their life: organizational restructuring, an itch for a career change, imminent retirement. Sadness caused by specific problems usually ebbs once the problems are resolved or the person adjusts to the change of circumstance in their life.

CHAPTER 7

The Defiant Underachiever

One of the tests we often give kids to see why they are underachieving (and where their *real* motivation lies) is a sentence-completion exercise. We provide the beginning of the sentence and ask the underachieving student to complete it.

Here are some typical sentence completions made by the underachieving kids we call Defiant Underachievers:

- *He often wished that he could* . . . do things his way.
- *She felt proud* . . . when she didn't cave in.
- *If I had my way* . . . I would never ever have to take orders.
- *If I can't get my own way* . . . I go on strike.
- *I wish that school* . . . didn't have any rules.
- *When they told him what to do* . . . he didn't cooperate.

These kids turn everything into a power struggle. And they're bound and determined *they* won't be the ones to blink first.

Let's rewind the tape for a moment and take a look at a classic parent-child power struggle when the child is very young. It's guaranteed to make every parent nod knowingly.

A 2-1/2-year-old is happily seated in a grocery cart being pushed by his parents from aisle to aisle in a supermarket. He's enjoying the ride immensely. They round a corner and *voilà!* He's in heaven—Cereal Land. He points at a colorful box with dinosaurs on it just out of his reach. "I want that one, Mommy!" he chirps. "I saw it on TV!"

"No," Dad says firmly, reaching for another box, minus dinosaurs. "*This* one is your favorite, remember?" Under his breath he adds, "And it doesn't have nearly as much sugar as Dinosaur Brand."

Junior appears stunned by his father's calm refusal. He reaches for Dinosaur-Minus Brand, now in the bottom of the grocery cart. He picks it up and hurls it down the aisle, knocking over a row of canned vegetables in the process. Two young women dressed in business clothes turn around and glare at the happy family. When *they* have children, you can be sure nothing like this will ever happen!

Meanwhile back in Cereal Land, Junior is digging in for the duration. "I want Dinosaur cereal!" he announces loudly. "*Now*, Mommy!" he adds, upping the whine ante and turning an imploring smile on Mom, the well-known softy.

Junior is standing up in the cart now, hurling his arms in as many directions as he can find. The tears have started to flow, and they're not gentle sobs. They're piercing screams, enough to make the two young women consider pulling their cellular phones out of their briefcases and calling Children's Services.

The end of this story is simple and clean:

Dad picks up Junior, hoists him over his shoulder (holding down his legs and arms as best he can to protect himself from the resounding kicks and thumps), and heads for the exit. Mom pays for the groceries while Dad, stony-faced, carries Junior out to the car and straps him into his car seat. He turns on the radio loud and waits for Mom to arrive with the groceries. They start toward home, a 20-minute drive. By the time they get there Junior, swollen-eyed and puffy-faced, is slumped in his chair, fast asleep. He's screamed himself to exhaustion.

The next morning Junior happily eats a large bowl of Dinosaur-Minus Brand. As he does every morning.

Now fast-forward the tape. You're the parent of a pre-teen. And he's barely an inch shorter than you are. Plus his grasp of debating skills is so advanced you'd think he'd been to law school. And he just *loves* to argue. In fact, he never lets up. He contradicts everything you say—or if not everything, almost everything. It certainly *feels* like everything. And despite his ability to wear you down with sophisticated argument, he is doing very poorly at school. His teachers mouth The Underachievement Myth, calling him lazy and unmotivated—and possessed of an unpleasant and decidedly uncooperative attitude. You pine for the long-ago days when you could hoist him over your shoulder, strap him into his car seat and let him cry whatever it is that's eating him out of his system. But you know—and he knows—those days are gone forever.

What do you do now?

That's what this chapter is about.

Who Are Defiant Underachievers?

Isn't defiant behavior the hallmark of all adolescents? Isn't it what they live and breathe for?

Yes, but within limits, and not for every teen. It's true that most adolescents will defy their parents at some point. But the type of underachiever we are going to describe in this chapter goes one step beyond what is typical of most teenagers. *The angry, confrontational behavior of Defiant Underachievers is at the extreme end of typical adolescent rebelliousness.*

Defiant Underachievers save the bulk of their rebelliousness for the home front. They may *talk* about how much they dislike teachers and school in general, but they do not act out as much at school. And interestingly, outside the home this argumentativeness tends to surface mostly with people they know well. With adult strangers, the defiant behavior may never appear. It's as if Defiant Underachievers are testing their limits within boundaries they know and understand. They may not be confident enough (or angry enough) to strike out against the world in general.

Even at home, the defiance is not always present (although when it's there, it feels like 24 hours a day to parents!). But on days when defiance is absent, Defiant Underachievers can be very pleasant. They may even *volunteer* to help with household chores.

What triggers the defiance—and when it appears—is impossible to predict. An issue that provoked defiance on Monday may not produce the same intense reaction by Friday. But rest assured that the defiance will settle on another issue—and soon.

Wait a minute, you may be thinking. Is this not the same pattern as Wheeler-Dealer Underachievers?

No, it is not. There are some big, big differences.

First, unlike Wheeler-Dealer Underachievers, Defiant Underachievers do not generally violate the rights of others. Nor do they bend the rules just to bend the rules. In fact, values and a high sense of moral purpose are often very important to Defiant Underachievers.

Second, the conflicts they get into with parents, teachers and others are problems of *attitude*. Whereas the conflicts that Wheeler-Dealer Underachievers are embroiled in are problems of *behavior*.

How Often Do We Find This Pattern?

Only 5 percent of the underachievers we see fit this pattern. But we feel certain that what we see is only a small sample of who's out there. You see, Defiant Underachievers are notoriously uncooperative and resist any kind of professional help. We don't call them defiant for nothing! We've been stood up more than a few times by kids who probably fit the Defiant Underachiever profile. Their parents arrange the interview or professional assessment, and the student fails to materialize in our office. Sometimes they refuse outright to keep the appointment. Other times they say they will go, but don't turn up.

A second reason we believe that our 5-percent estimate is low is because Defiant Underachievers are easy to confuse with other underachievers with rebellious characteristics. Wheeler-Dealers in particular are easy to mistake for Defiant Underachievers. But Identity-Search Underachievers and even Anxious Underachievers can be angry in ways that may be confused with the Defiant prototype.

Age of onset? This kind of behavior typically peaks in early to mid-adolescence (roughly between 11 and 16 years of age), when kids start struggling with issues of autonomy and independence.

Male/female ratio? More male students exhibit this pattern prior to puberty than female students, but once puberty arrives, the ratio is about even.

What kinds of families produce Defiant Underachievers? In our experience, there is no "typical" family that spawns Defiant Underachievers. But the way parents deal with this kind of adolescent rebelliousness can influence how it develops and whether or not the kid settles into an extended Defiant Underachiever pattern of behavior. We'll look at the ways families influence Defiant Underachiever behavior in more detail later in this chapter.

Let's look at the specific characteristics of Defiant Underachievers.

Anatomy of a Defiant Underachiever

1. They lose their temper easily.

It's normal for two-year-olds to have temper tantrums when they don't get their way. It's normal for young adolescents to have occasional temper flare-ups too. But Defiant Underachievers go beyond the pale. They lose their temper very quickly. The most common flash point is some limit or expectation imposed by parents.

They use the threat of anger in the same way that young children use temper tantrums—to try to get what they want. And their anger is real: They're irritated by any attempt that they perceive will restrict their independence.

Here's how one quick-tempered Defiant Underachiever explained her behavior:

Counselor:	"Do you *like* to study?"
Cindy:	"No, not really. (Pauses.) Let me put it this way: When I'm *told* to study, I don't like doing it. But I don't mind doing it on my own. I study whenever I need to—if *I* want to."
Counselor:	"I get the impression that you don't exactly like to do what you're told to do."
Cindy:	(in an animated tone) "Right! I mean, I do things *sometimes* when I'm told to, but mostly I don't."
Counselor:	"Have you always felt that way and acted that way?"
Cindy:	"No. My dad says that I've changed in the last two years."
Counselor:	"How so?"
Cindy:	(laughs) "He always used to be able to get me to do school work. Now he says it's harder. He says I have a temper problem."
Counselor:	"Temper problem?"
Cindy:	"Oh yeah. I get mad, start to yell when I disagree with what he says. And I won't do school work just because he tells me to do it! And his idea of curfew is from 1000 years ago."

2. They argue with authority.

Defiant Underachievers tend to argue when they perceive that their parents are making "unreasonable" demands and/or placing "unfair" restrictions on them. They respond to these statements by arguing hard and long, often focusing on one dimension only and accusing the parent of not understanding the main point.

Defiant Underachievers are stubborn arguers. They dig in their heels and maintain their position even, at times, in the face of reasonableness. The message is: "Don't tell me what to do, even if it's good for me!"

Here's a typical exchange:

Parent:	"Sam, you really should read this book. It's right up your alley."
Sam:	"Don't tell me what to do!"

Or:

Parent:	"You've done really well in math this term."
Debbie:	(scowling) "Don't try and butter me up."

The following is a classic example of Defiant Underachiever behavior. Rita is 16 years old.

Rita:	(intensely) "You're *never* going to let me drive the car now that I've failed the driver's test."
Father:	"The driving examiner failed you because you drove too erratically, not smoothly enough. I've told you before: You need to take more driving lessons, go and take the test again, pass it—and then we'll talk."
Rita:	"See, you're not going to promise me that I can have your car when I get my driver's license."
Father:	"That's right."
Rita:	"So I'm right! You'll never trust me."
Father:	"You're not listening. I didn't say I would or wouldn't. I just think you need a lot more practice before you even take the test again."
Rita:	(haughtily) "And I suppose that I'll have to pay for the lessons!"
Father:	"Mom and I agreed to pay for the lessons you took originally. But you quit and took the test

too soon. (Resignedly.) But we're *still* willing to pay for the lessons."

Rita: "Okay, and then I can drive your car?"

Father: "I won't promise that. We'll talk about it when you've got your license."

Rita: "Well, can I at least take the driver's test on your car?"

Father: "No, I want you to take the test using the driving school's car. I don't want you to touch our car until after you're fully licensed to drive. We have to change the insurance. We can even get a discount on the rates if you complete the course."

Rita: (indignantly) "Right, and then you'll set up some new rules to stop me from getting the car. Well, forget it. I won't take any more lessons." (Rita stomps out of the room.)

Most teenagers are desperate to begin driving and would do almost anything in order to be allowed to do so. But Rita was willing to give up what she really wanted because she perceived her parents' demands as unreasonable and too restrictive. She believed that they were treating her like a baby.

We'll come back to Rita in the next section.

3. They defy authority.

Defiant Underachievers frequently refuse or defy adult requests. These confrontations go beyond typical adolescent lack of cooperation and tend to escalate into complex, emotionally charged exchanges that build and persist over time.

And to liven up this situation further, be advised that there are two types of Defiant Underachievers:

Active Defiant Underachievers prefer to defy in direct and open ways. They'll tell you straight what they don't like and what *you* need to do to set matters right. Their motto is "I will not do what *you* want me to do!"

Passive Defiant Underachievers are more indirect and less open in their resistance. They avoid telling you straight what they don't like or what they won't do. They may even grudgingly indicate that they will comply at some later time. Their motto is: "In a minute, in an hour, soon, sometime this week—when I can get to it." Parents of this Passive type report that arguments erupt only after many unheeded reminders, when the parents have finally lost faith and patience.

Both the Active and the Passive type appear to fulfill The Underachievement Myth. The Active Defiant Underachiever is usually labeled unmotivated and the Passive Defiant Underachiever is usually labeled lazy. But the end result is the same: Both avoid school work and both underachieve, as a conscious act of rebellion.

To continue with Rita's story: Rita's parents went out of town for a weekend a few months later. While they were gone, Rita invited several friends over and decided to take them for a drive in her father's car. And wouldn't you know it: A neighbor saw her drive by and reported it to her parents when they returned.

Rita:	"Okay, so I took the car. You said I needed more lessons—but I drove well! All my friends think that I drive better than they do, and they have their licenses already."
Father:	"You took the car without permission and without a driver's license."
Rita:	"That's not true. I have my learner's permit. And George has his driver's license. So I was legal! Besides, nothing happened."
Father:	"The point is that you took the car without permission. I could have you charged with theft."
Rita:	"You probably would. That's how you think!"
Father:	"It's a question of trust."
Rita:	"I *knew* you didn't trust me. You hardly let me use the phone, I can't go out late on the weekends, I can't go camping with my friends. Let's just forget it."

Notice how Rita focuses exclusively on her father's reactions. That's her way of trying to shift the focus away from the critical issue—her lack of personal responsibility. Rita wants the focus to be on her parents' unfair restrictions and lack of trust in her. She deeply believes she is being deprived of her rights to independent action. She feels that her father is treating her like a baby. Her father, on the other hand, believes that she is acting like one.

Rita's battles are not restricted to her father. She wants to go away for a few days on a camping trip with her friends, and her mother wants to know who plans to go, where they will be going and what adult will supervise.

Mother:	"All I'm saying is that I'd like to know more before I give permission. I'd like to speak to Sandra's mother, if that's who'll be there."
Rita:	"Why? I don't believe you! Nobody else's mother has to know. My friends can just go! I'm embarrassed to ask all these questions. (Pauses, looks unjustly done by and defiantly announces:) Okay, I won't go. You don't want me to have a good time, so I won't go!"

Rita's words and actions convey a subtle threat: "If you don't let me go, I'll make sure that you'll be sorry."

* * *

Another example: Victor is a bright 16-year-old who did well academically until Grade 10 when he received an F in math—his first failing mark. Victor's parents requested a psychological assessment because they were concerned about their son's stubborn refusal to do school work and baffled about how to change his behavior. Here's an excerpt from that initial interview:

Psychologist: "So you say your marks just seemed to take a nose dive. Any ideas about why?"

Victor: "I don't know. I guess I just didn't care about doing the work."

Psychologist: "So you think it's because you really don't care?"

Victor: (smiles, and hesitates) "Well, I think also . . . I was also a bit mad at my parents. I got a job, but I got it in April, and I found a better job at the beginning of September."

Psychologist: "Part-time?"

Victor: "Yeah, both were part-time. And when I found the better job my parents said, 'No, you can't work there!' "

Psychologist: "Tell me a bit about each job."

Victor: "Well, the first job was at a fast-food place, because all my friends worked there. And then the second job I found was at a restaurant that paid more. I worked a few week nights at the new job and my parents said I'd have to give it up because I seemed too tired."

Psychologist: "How come the difference? Was the fast-food place on the weekends?"

Victor: "No, they were both on week nights, but the boss doesn't allow high-school students to work more than two- to three-hour shifts. The other restaurant allowed me to do five-hour shifts and get paid more per hour. And you know what really burns me up?"

Psychologist: "What?"

Victor: "I told my parents I wanted a better-paying job and they said I could change. But when they found out it was longer hours they changed their minds."

Psychologist: "So you were ticked off about how they seemed to change their stand about the new job?"

Victor: (irritated) "They *did* change their stand!"
Psychologist: "So you sort of went on strike?"
Victor: (laughs heartily) "No, not really. (Pauses.) Well,
                        I guess so."
Psychologist: "You felt that they were not fair. What do you
                        think would have been fair?"
Victor: "What do I think? I think I could have handled
                        it myself. And if it didn't work out, I might have
                        quit anyway at some point."

Victor's defiance is indirect. He could not bring himself to defy his parents directly by keeping the "better" job he wanted. So he shifted to indirect defiance—poor academic performance, something he knew would trouble his parents a great deal. He "goes on strike" at school—and looks like another lazy and unmotivated example of The Underachievement Myth.

Notice the self-defeating quality to this Defiant Underachiever's behavior. He enters battles over what appear to be questions of independence. But the choices he makes during the battles do not lead to greater independence. In fact, they lead to continued dependence, because of his *choice* to underachieve. Yet he still feels vindicated because he refused to let them "win."

In the following example, 15-year-old Cindy is adamant about not giving in to what her father wants. The issue is not what *she* wants, but that she will not do something *because others have suggested it.*

Counselor: "About how much education do you see your-
                      self wanting to get in the future? How far do
                      you want to go in school?"
Cindy: "I don't want to go to college. Whatever college
                      my dad wants me to go to, I don't want to go to.
                      And whatever college I might want to go to, he
                      doesn't want to talk about. So, I just won't go."
                      (Cindy folds her arms, and sits back in her
                      chair.)

Counselor:	"Do you think that you two could talk more about it? You still have lots of time before you have to make a decision about college."
Cindy:	"Only if he will let me go where I want to go."
Counselor:	"Okay, let's talk about another aspect of the future. What do you want to be or do when you get older?"
Cindy:	"I am older already!"
Counselor:	"Okay, I meant when you are an adult."
Cindy:	"Well, I used to want to be a teacher. Now I don't want to be a teacher any more."
Counselor:	"Any particular reason?"
Cindy:	"No, not really. I just don't like what they force me to do, like homework."
Counselor:	"Okay, any other ideas about the future?"
Cindy:	"Other than that, I really don't know."
Counselor:	"So you're sure what you *don't* want to be—a teacher."
Cindy:	"Exactly!"

Cindy was adamant about what she would *not* do. But she was very unclear about what she was willing to commit herself to. In other words, she knew what she was against. But she had no idea what she was for.

*   *   *

Most teenagers will test parental limits. The crucial difference for Defiant Underachievers is that they are willing to give up what they really want rather than let parents "win" on issues such as what responsibilities should accompany increasing privileges. These youngsters genuinely believe that giving in to their parents' demands constitutes a defeat of monumental proportions. They cut off their nose to spite their face.

And it's impossible to predict when a comment will trigger an intense argument. The same comment, word for word, that set off a wild argument on Monday may produce no reaction at all on Friday.

But Defiant Underachievers always deliberately provoke the arguments and focus them squarely on the parents.

4. They deliberately annoy.

Young children honing their skills in the deliberate antagonism department call people names, tease relentlessly and the like.

Defiant Underachievers use the same approach to antagonize, with more sophisticated methods. One irritating technique is *deliberate inefficiency*. For example:

You ask your Passive Defiant Underachieving son to clean up the yard before the family goes out for a Saturday evening dinner. After a number of reminders, he finally moves to the garage to get the garden tools. But he moves in slow motion. You and he both know that if he were going out to one of his friend's parties, he would be moving through that yard like greased lightning. As you open the back-porch door to remind him about the passage of time, he gives you an innocent look you know too well and says: "I'm doing it the way it should be done." This situation spells heaven for the Passive Defiant Underachiever. He's finally doing what you asked, but he's doing it in a way guaranteed to annoy you. He basks in your frustration with his work-to-rule tactics.

Passive Defiant Underachievers have another deliberately annoying technique up their sleeve. In response to a question from parents or teachers—when it's clear the kid being questioned either knows the answer or has an opinion about the subject—they respond with an elaborately casual shrug of the shoulders or the answer "I don't know."

In other words, they *withhold* a response that they know you are looking for—and then wallow triumphantly in watching you get upset because once again they've thwarted your attempts to tell them what to do. Does the following exchange sound familiar?

Parent: "Tell me why your math grade dropped."
Teenager: (No answer.)
Parent: (getting angry) "Are you going to tell me about math?"

Teenager:	(Sneers and shrugs shoulders.)
Parent:	"I'm your parent. I have a right to know why your math grade has gone down."
Teenager:	(another shrug) "I don't know." (Glares at parent.)

If you redouble your efforts—tripping yourself up with your good intentions, unsuccessfully trying to get the Defiant One to cooperate and open up—you are left feeling tired, frustrated and abused. This plays right into these Defiant kids' laps. They are sure they've won—and have proven how independent they are.

We facetiously call this passive resistance to authority the Mahatma Gandhi Approach. But it's not really an equivalent: Gandhi was engaged in a genuinely idealistic struggle, trying to get others to confront their values. The aim of Defiant Underachievers' "lofty" struggle is to demonstrate to the world that *no one* can tell them what to do.

5. They are spiteful or vindictive.

We mentioned earlier that Defiant Underachievers are willing to give up what they really want rather than let parents "win." Defiant Underachievers can behave spitefully and vindictively, and when they do, this same self-defeating quality rears its head. They are quite willing to suffer some negative side effects, provided the target of their spite suffers more. As in:

Counselor:	"So, tell me if I understand you. You don't like the rules your parents have laid down, and you've decided—"
Maurice:	(interrupts) "Right, not to give in!"
Counselor:	"Even if it hurts you?"
Maurice:	"I don't see how it hurts me at all. I just let go of my school work, that's all."
Counselor:	"I thought you said that they grounded you after this last report card."

Maurice:	"That's true."
Counselor:	"And you don't see how that hurts you?"
Maurice:	"Well, a little, but it hurts them a whole lot more."
Counselor:	"How so?"
Maurice:	"Now at least one of them has to stay home to watch me."
Counselor:	"And I suppose that's what counts the most?"
Maurice:	"That's right."

6. They blame others for their own actions or mistakes.

Defiant Underachievers often blame others for the consequences of their own actions. In the following exchange, a 13-year-old Defiant Underachiever describes to his guidance counselor why he is doing poorly in Spanish this year.

Counselor:	"You said you didn't want to take another Spanish course. How come you did?"
Henry:	"Guess."
Counselor:	"No, you tell me."
Henry:	"My *mother* wanted me to. I got a B in the first Spanish course I took, so she figured I could continue to do well. I said, 'Mom, you're wrong.' And she said, 'Too bad. Take it.' "
Counselor:	"Are you saying that she's the reason you're not doing well this term in Spanish?"
Henry:	"Right!"
Counselor:	"So you're not going to do better?"
Henry:	"No. Why should I? If my mother would only get off my back, maybe I'd consider it."

Henry blamed his mother for his poor performance in Spanish. Why? Because she had forced him to take another Spanish course. Henry thinks that pure logic is dictating his response—consciously failing in order to teach his mother a lesson.

7. They are touchy or easily annoyed.

Defiant Underachievers go out of their way to deliberately annoy others. But they too are easily annoyed. And they can be moody as well. In other words, they can dish it out but they're not very good at taking it. Listen to what 17-year-old Kurt had to say about how he has rendered his parents "impotent."

Counselor:	"Do *you* want to do better in school?"
Kurt:	"Yeah, I guess so. It's got to be done eventually."
Counselor:	"Well, what that means is that *you'll* have to do it eventually. Do you want to?"
Kurt:	"Like now? (Pauses.) Not really. I guess so. I don't know. (Impatiently.) I don't want to talk about this any more."
Counselor:	"Okay, let me ask you a different type of question. If you lived on your own, without your parents on your back, would you be satisfied with your present grades?"
Kurt:	"No, because I know these grades won't get me anywhere. But I don't think I'd be pushing myself either."
Counselor:	"So you're saying that you need somebody to push you."
Kurt:	"That's it!"
Counselor:	"But when they do?"
Kurt:	(smiles) "Yeah, I know, I don't work."
Counselor:	"I guess nothing your parents do these days seems to get you to achieve in school."
Kurt:	(proudly) "That's right! And when they try, it really bugs me."

Kurt became very uncomfortable when confronted with his choice to do poorly, and he knew that the conversation could get more difficult. His ambivalence about achievement and increased personal responsibility was about to be exposed, and he wanted no part of it. The only reason this exchange didn't heat up rapidly was because the counselor decided to shift the focus slightly.

8. They are resentful.

Notice the energy and intensity in the following exchange between 15-year-old Sheila and her father.

Father:	"No, I'm not expecting her to go to university if she doesn't want to. But I want her to have sufficient grades to get into a field of her choice in any university if she decides some day to go. In other words, to keep the doors open."
Counselor:	"What are your goals, Sheila?"
Sheila:	(sullen) "I don't know yet."
Counselor:	"Well, do you agree or disagree with what your father has just said?"
Sheila:	(pauses, and with resentment in her voice) "I can't believe what he's just said. *That* sounded good, but that's not how it is at home! It's totally different. (Turns to her father.) You expect too much. Always, no matter how good my grades have been, you've always pushed for higher grades. And don't tell me about how well I did in Grade 6. I remember bringing home my report card then and you said, 'You could get so much higher, you could do so much better.' I got the same story back then as you give me now."
Father:	"Okay, but then you tried harder than you do now."
Sheila:	"Right. No more! You're not going to make me study any more!"

Sheila had always resented her father's pressure to achieve. But it's only recently that her resentment has led to a self-defeating decision to underachieve. Her father may indeed need to lay off a bit and try to foster a little give-and-take, but instead of negotiating a solution, father and daughter are locked in a battle.

And it wasn't until the above exchange occurred, in the counselor's office, that Sheila directly expressed her resentment about the pressure. She had always remained relatively quiet and outwardly compliant. Her father was amazed at his daughter's intensity.

That completes our list of characteristics. Let's look over them again.

Summing Up: Anatomy of a Defiant Underachiever

1. They lose their temper easily.
2. They argue with authority.
3. They defy authority.
4. They deliberately annoy.
5. They are spiteful or vindictive.
6. They blame others for their own actions or mistakes.
7. They are touchy or easily annoyed.
8. They are resentful.

Parent Checklist

Armed with our description over the preceding pages, it's time to pause now and decide how similar your child's characteristics are to the Defiant Underachiever prototype.

1. Does my child lose his/her temper easily? | Yes___ No___ Don't Know___

2. Does my child argue regularly with adult authority figures whom he/she knows well? | Yes___ No___ Don't Know___

3. Does my child regularly defy authority?　Yes___ No___ Don't Know___

4. Does my child deliberately annoy others (teachers, siblings, friends, classmates)?　Yes___ No___ Don't Know___

5. Does my child regularly act in spiteful or vindictive ways?　Yes___ No___ Don't Know___

6. Does my child usually blame others for things he/she is responsible for?　Yes___ No___ Don't Know___

7. Is my child touchy, irritable and easily annoyed?　Yes___ No___ Don't Know___

8. Is my child resentful of the actions and attitudes of authority figures?　Yes___ No___ Don't Know___

If you answered "Yes" to five or more of the above questions, your child's characteristics may be similar to those of the Defiant Underachiever type.

What's Really Going On with the Defiant Underachiever?

Why are Defiant Underachievers constantly on the offensive?

Remember the kid in the grocery cart? Behind the tumult and the shouting—and the dinosaurs—what do you suppose *really* was going on?

Well, as dozens of books on child development will tell you, striving for autonomy and learning self-control are part of the normal breaking-away and growing-up process between the ages of 18 months and three years. During this period, children learn to say "No" with irritating frequency and ferocity.

This is a necessary and normal part of child development. Every child has to seek his own separateness and independence from adult authority and protectiveness. And when children are frustrated in these attempts to control their own lives, temper tantrums result.

Fast-forward to the teenage Defiant Underachiever. He too lashes out at authority, especially parental authority. His favorite word is "No," too. But he has (at least!) progressed to more sophisticated methods—arguing, non-compliance, deliberate attempts to annoy, spiteful and vindictive behavior.

And unlike the two-year-old, whose tantrums rise and fall over things he sees and wants *now*—this minute!—the Defiant Underachiever is working on a long-term issue, the issue of independence.

Defiant Underachievers redefine the meaning of independence, and use this redefinition as a reason for refusing to cooperate.
Defiant Underachievers want to become more independent, to prove themselves. They want to test out that independence, to get out in the world, to enter a process that eventually will lead to adulthood and maturity.

But Defiant Underachievers (especially in their early teen years) have a problem. As young adolescents, they are in no position to embrace genuine independence. They are not ready yet to step out into the world—and they know it. They're awash with dependency needs— emotional, financial, physical, intellectual. They need to develop dozens of skills before they're ready to venture out on their own.

They're caught in a dilemma: It's intolerable to them to continue to see themselves, and to continue to be seen by others, as dependent, not-yet-grown-up persons—in other words, as children. They can't go back to being children, and they can't move ahead and really be independent. They're stuck in the middle. And they're hurting.

So what do they do?

They redefine the meaning of independence.

Let's backtrack for a moment and consider what independence really means. True independence means taking responsibility for your own decisions—full, open-ended responsibility. To do this, you must first figure out who you are. And then you have to stand by that self-awareness, stand for the person you are. You must make decisions—and take both the credit and the blame for the consequences.

But what do Defiant Underachievers do? They redefine the meaning of independence. *Their* definition goes like this:

> "Independence means doing the opposite of what is expected of me. As long as I'm doing the opposite of what people expect me to do—not cooperating—then I'm being independent. And if I do what they expect me to do, then I'm not being independent."

Defiant Underachievers can now salvage their pride. They can be independent—as *they* define it—without having to deal with the frightening aspects of genuine freedom and responsibility. All they have to do is have something to fight against.

They have a clear, straightforward battle plan: Whenever someone else tells them what to do, they conclude they're being robbed of their independence. So . . . they must strike back.

And since these inner feelings are always present, Defiant Underachievers constantly need to rebel (which, of course, is exactly what they do).

WHY THIS REDEFINITION OF INDEPENDENCE DOESN'T WASH

The Defiant Underachiever chooses to ignore two fundamental truths.

Number one: *No one is utterly free of direction and constraint from the outside.* We all face situations daily in which other people tell us—explicitly or implicitly—what to do. As independent adults, it is our responsibility to make choices but only within the range of possibilities available to us and the constraints already in place. Defiant Underachievers think that they can and should be completely free of *any* such restraints. This is both unrealistic and ultimately self-defeating.

Number two: *Defiant Underachieving teenagers choose to ignore the self-evident truth that they are hugely dependent on their parents.*

They choose not to recognize *any* dependency needs. And as long as they ignore this, they are freed up to feel affronted, angry and upset whenever they're not treated as independent persons—which is why they drive their parents stir-crazy.

Every time a parent bugs them, they get angry: "Stop telling me what to do!" And when the parent stops bugging them, it's: "I knew it, you don't really care!" Defiant Underachievers put parents in an impossible bind.

The bottom line of Defiant Underachievers' brave recasting of the definition of independence is that they avoid defining who they really are. What they in fact are doing is forcefully declaring who they are *not*.

If there were nobody around to tell them what to do, they would have to look inside themselves for direction. And this they wish to avoid at all costs. Therefore, to remain safe from uncomfortable self-analysis, they need an "enemy" to continually pit themselves against. They have to keep generating opportunities from the outside world against which to rebel. As long as they have someone in the outside world, some authority figure to rebel against, they don't have to really confront themselves.

This is the reason they only feel good about their independence when they're rebelling. So they're always on the lookout for people and things to rebel against.

When Defiant Underachievers confront authority, they convince themselves they are fighting for some principle or cause.
Defiant Underachievers present a discipline problem—but only within clearly defined boundaries. They defy and confront, but they don't actively encroach on other people's rights and they don't bend the rules or manipulate other people the way Wheeler-Dealer Underachievers do.

In fact, they would find this kind of behavior reprehensible. They would consider such behavior repugnant because when *they* confront authority, they believe they are fighting for some principle or cause. When they decide they won't cooperate with a teacher, for example, they do so because they're standing up for the other "abused" kids in the class, the other "victims": "I'm not going to produce in that class!

The teacher runs things like a dictator." They're worried about the way the teacher treats the entire class, not just themselves. They identify with the underdog.

Like Identity-Search Underachievers, they feel strongly about values. But Identity-Searchers and Defiant Underachievers act upon their strong feelings about values in very different ways. The Identity-Searcher's concern with values has to do with defining the self. Defiant Underachievers use values as a weapon in their rebellion, regardless of how deeply they feel about the values.

And they carry this "noble" cause to extremes. If necessary, they will not hesitate to sacrifice their own interests to prove a point. They'll go as far as to say, "I'm willing to *fail*, rather than let someone else tell me what to do." It becomes a point of principle to go the distance for their "beliefs" and be willing to fail, rather than give in to ignorant people who tell them what to do.

Defiant Underachievers perceive their parents and many adults as people who don't understand, who have no sensitivity, who don't care and who get others to do what they don't want to do. Defiant Underachievers are hypercritical of the adult world in general and of parents and teachers in particular.

Their antennae are on red alert, scanning for offensive comments from adults such as, "This is what I think you ought to do." "Aha!" Defiant Underachievers pounce. "Wouldn't you just *love* to tell me what to do!" They're hypersensitive to anything said that appears to compromise their sense of independence.

For the Active Defiant Underachiever, this sensitivity results in open rebellion characterized by verbal defiance and "lippiness." For the Passive Defiant Underachiever, the rebellion is much more subtle. An impassive stubbornness is the characteristic demeanor: They don't say anything directly, but they're immovable. They refuse to budge.

Defiant Underachievers often mix these two stances, reserving the bulk of their open anger for their parents and displaying a more passive, sullen sort of rebellion at school. But savvy teachers sense what's going on. They know that this type of student is sending the message,

"Go ahead and tell me what to do, if you like. But I'm *not* going to do it for you." "This kid is not only lazy and unmotivated," the teacher may sigh. "This kid has an *attitude*."

Why is the Defiant Underachiever doing poorly in school?

Many types of underachievers appear to oppose authority. So it's important to understand the difference between the way—and the reasons—other underachievers thumb their noses at authority and how and why the Defiant Underachiever does it.

For Wheeler-Dealer Underachievers, defiance is part of a much larger picture, one in which they can manipulate others to get what they want. For Identity-Search Underachievers, defiance is part of a genuine attempt to try out different values and ways of being. For Coasting Underachievers, the defiance is passive and is not part of a push for independence. On the contrary, the poor grades are designed to maintain dependence.

But for the Defiant Underachiever, underachieving in itself is an act of rebellion. For Defiant Underachievers, refusing to do the work that will lead to good grades is a weapon in a power struggle. For them, exemplifying The Underachievement Myth is a declaration of war: "You wanna see lazy and unmotivated? Let me *show* you lazy and unmotivated—in a way you're not going to forget!" They're well aware of what they are doing. It's their way of expressing their independence.

Summing Up: What's Really Going On with the Defiant Underachiever?

Why are Defiant Underachievers constantly on the offensive?

- Defiant Underachievers redefine the meaning of independence, and use this redefinition as a reason for refusing to cooperate.
- When they confront authority, Defiant Underachievers convince themselves they are fighting for some principle or cause.

- Defiant Underachievers perceive their parents and many adults as people who don't understand, who have no sensitivity, who don't care, and who get others to do what they don't want to do.

Why is the Defiant Underachiever doing poorly in school?

- For the Defiant Underachiever, underachievement is an act of rebellion.

Helping Your Defiant Underachiever

As you read our suggestions about working with Defiant Underachievers, keep in mind that the reason they're rebelling is because they're struggling to be independent, but don't know how to bring it off.

Keep in mind, too, the following: Contrary to what you might expect, Active Defiant Underachievers are sometimes easier to work with than Passive Defiant Underachievers because their rebellion is focused and out in the open. Passive Defiant Underachievers often are more difficult to deal with because they initially may appear willing to cooperate ("Yeah, sure, I'll do it soon"). It's only later you discover they never really intended to follow through—so your efforts have been fruitless.

We have found the following suggestions useful.

1. Avoid focusing on attitude.

Most of the battles you get into with Defiant Underachievers are confrontations over *attitudes*: their anger over yours or your anger over theirs. Usually, these attitudes are expressed in non-verbal ways (such as angry facial expressions or shoulder shrugs), rather than in words. They convey the Defiant Underachievers' rejection of whatever it is that the adult wants, and their unwillingness to cooperate in any way.

When a parent asks a Defiant Underachiever to help wash the dishes, and the Defiant Underachiever says "okay" with an obvious and hostile sneer, the parent is sorely tempted to respond to the sneer rather than the "okay." The parent is drawn into an argument that begins over the kid's uncooperative attitude about doing the dishes—and escalates into an angry shouting match about everything, including the kitchen sink!

The parent finds him or herself in the unhappy position of acting as angrily and uncontrollably as the child, without getting through to the child. Defiant Underachievers consistently provoke confrontations like these.

The key to confrontations like the ones above is this: These kids are experts at stirring you up. They know exactly where your Achilles heel is. Defiant Underachievers *want* to tangle with you about these issues. They *want* the battle to be focused on issues of attitude. They thrive on confrontations. For them, confrontation is an opportunity to experience and confirm their growing sense of independence.

So don't let yourself get lured in. If you focus on negative attitudes, you'll be confronting them head-on. And they will be delighted. Remember, they have committed a great deal of energy to fighting adults who challenge their attitudes.

So your object is to shift the battle away from a struggle over attitude. What *should* you focus on?

2. Focus on behavior.

Stay away from challenging attitudes and focus on their behavior. As in:

Mother:	"How about helping with the dishes?"
Jane:	(angrily and with a hostile sneer) "Okay."
Mother:	(cheerfully, ignoring the attitude and tone of voice) "Thank you, I appreciate it."

By ignoring her daughter's foul mood, this mother wins the battle without ever declaring war. She robs her daughter of the satisfaction she was looking for: making her mother angry—possibly so angry she would order her out of the kitchen and the daughter would get out of doing the dishes. Jane finds herself both performing a chore she finds distasteful *and* unable to manipulate her mother's even temper. By focusing on Jane's *behavior* instead of her *attitude*, her mother has taken the teeth out of the fight that Jane was so looking forward to.

Here's another slant on the same situation:

Mother:	"How about helping with the dishes?"
Jane:	(angrily and with a sneer) "No, I don't like doing the dishes."
Mother:	(cheerfully) "You don't have to like it. In fact, I don't like it either, but it *is* your turn, and we all have to pitch in."
Jane:	(petulantly) "Why should I?"
Mother:	(slowly and evenly) "You're a member of this family and it's your turn. Get on with it."

By confining her attention to behavior and ignoring attitude, the mother is able to stand her ground.

3. By focusing on behavior, show the Defiant Underachiever who really is winning and losing.

Like all combatants, Defiant Underachievers fight to win. But their perceptions of who wins and who loses are skewed. One solution is to point out their fallacies in logic. In the following conversation with Steven, a 15-year-old Defiant Underachiever who had exasperated his parents and teachers by refusing to do any school work, the school psychologist does a masterful job of pointing out Steven's self-defeating reasoning.

Steven:	"You ask me what the problem is with this class? I'll tell you: The problem is, I absolutely *despise* the teacher! There's no way I'm going to do any work in that class! I'm *not* going to give him the satisfaction."

Psychologist: "So who wins in that situation?"

Steven: (broad smile) "It's obvious—*I'm* going to win. The teacher's not going to win. He's got no control over me."

Psychologist: "Okay. Let's talk about 20 years from now. That teacher is going to be applauded for the way he handled you. Because he was tough. *You* are going to help him in his career. And 20 years from now he may be retired, or in another position. He'll have had a successful career—and he won't even remember your name."

Steven: (somewhat at a loss for words) "Yeah. So what?"

Psychologist: "Well, now let's look at you. You, by flunking this course, may cut yourself out of a possible direction or career in which you can be successful. This might change the course of your life. It may, or it may not—*but you don't know.* You might really be affected at some future date—you may have to take it again in order to get into something you might want. Now tell me again who's winning. I don't understand what it is you have won."

Steven: (with a self-righteous edge to his voice) "But the teacher doesn't like me—and I don't like him!"

Psychologist: "Right. And that's why you're going to let him screw you in this course?"

Steven: "But you don't understand."

Psychologist: "*He's* such a loser that you are going to allow *him* to control how you react in his course."

Steven: "But I'm not. I just won't work for him!"

Psychologist: "Right. Let me see if I've got this: One, you won't work for him. Two, he doesn't care about you at all. So, three, you've decided to get even with him by doing something that is going to hurt you, not him. So now he's got you reacting totally to

him, and he doesn't even care. You might even
want to get a credit in this course, but there's no
way you'll let yourself do it, because you think
he's in this to defeat you. He doesn't even care
about you—that's what you said about him
before. So, you know what I think?"

Steven: "No, what?"

Psychologist: "I think he's already won, and won big. You
have lost, and lost big."

Steven: "I don't think so."

Psychologist: "Of course you don't. You are so intent on
defeating him, you don't care whether you sacrifice yourself at the same time. You're letting a
guy you think is an idiot determine your future."

Steven: "Well, maybe."

Instead of saying something like, "Why don't you like this teacher?
Are you sure he's as bad as you say he is? Prove to me that he can't
teach," the psychologist bypasses Steven's negative attitude to his
teacher entirely. Instead, he zeros in on the *effects* of Steven's negative attitude. "At what cost are you behaving this way?" he asks
Steven. In other words, he points out Steven's self-defeating behavior.

Step by step, he leads Steven through the self-defeating consequences of his behavior. He re-frames Steven's battle and shows him
that his so-called victory is self-destructive. And he shows Steven a
way to win for himself.

4. Acknowledge genuine areas of independence.

It is important to remember that Defiant Underachievers are striving
for independence in many significant and *healthy* ways. These areas
of their behavior (and, indeed, attitude) are often ignored in the mael-
strom of conflict. Make sure you look for and acknowledge signs of
healthy independence when they occur. Remember, not every action
of a Defiant Underachiever is negative.

5. Pick and choose the behaviors you confront.

When there's a Defiant Underachiever in the family, *everything* seems to flare into an argument. Whether the arguments start over trivial or over important issues, they all seem to flow into one central drain and end up the same—a struggle over attitude. There is no differentiation between important issues and trivial pursuits. Arguments go on all the time with little or no resolution.

The subjects of the arguments are wildly diverse: "You didn't make your bed again!" "You're late! You've slept in!" "No, we will *not* pay for your car insurance!" "Another lousy report card!"

You need to judiciously choose which behaviors you confront. And let the other things go. Don't sweat the small stuff! Don't allow arguments about household chores to unfold with exactly the same intensity as the decision about whether or not your child should go to college.

6. When you've stood your ground, move on.

Once you've focused on behavior and stood your ground, do *not* continue to argue the point. If you continue to argue, as the Defiant Underachiever dearly wants you to, you'll probably weaken under the continuing barrage. As one weary mother admitted, when asked why she gave in to her daughter's demands "I was plum tuckered out!"

There are various ways you can move on. You can change the subject. You can say you don't want to talk about the issue any more. You can leave the room after announcing the discussion is now over. When your Defiant Underachiever child raises the issue again (usually within minutes), you can reaffirm your intention to refuse to discuss the topic further.

You can even use humor, as Sally's mother does in the following exchange.

Sally:	"So when are you going to be ready to talk about this?"
Mother:	"We've already talked about it."
Sally:	"But we haven't decided it yet."
Mother:	"You know, you always say that when we haven't agreed to do what you want."

Sally:	(smiles) "So, when are we going to talk?"
Mother:	"I'd rather fight than talk. You wanna fight?"
Sally:	(Laughs.)

Sally's mother was able to lighten the discussion, while at the same time highlighting the unspoken battle that was lurking just below the calm. Her humor lends just the right touch: It is *not* sarcastic.

7. Do not take attacks personally.

Listen to these comments thrown at parents in the middle of a heated argument: "You're so pathetic! *How* can you believe that? You're *just* like my teacher! All my friends have better parents than you. You're absolutely hopeless! My friends aren't treated like children! Their parents *respect* them!"

Parents are human too and sometimes it's hard to rise above what's being said to you. Defiant Underachievers make it hard at times not to take things personally.

But when parents of a Defiant Underachiever succumb to taking personal offense, the argument quickly escalates and becomes more painful. If you find you do this, you may need to learn ways to deal with your child's anger or with your own.

Try to take comments like the ones above in the spirit in which they're thrown at you: with no underlying thought or plot. Take them at face value. They're not the cutting slurs they may sound like. Your child is not in an objective position to judge your entire worth as a parent. All he's doing is trying to put you on the defensive.

8. From time to time, try agreeing with what your Defiant Underachiever says.

This can stop the Defiant Underachiever in his tracks. An example:

| Teenager: | "You're the most rotten parent who ever lived." |
| Parent: | (calmly) "You're probably right. But I'm your parent, and I care about you, and I'm doing the best I can. I'm afraid you're stuck with me!" |

Summing Up: Helping Your Defiant Underachiever

1. Avoid focusing on attitude.
2. Focus on behavior.
3. By focusing on behavior, show the Defiant Underachiever who really is winning and losing.
4. Acknowledge genuine areas of independence.
5. Pick and choose the behaviors you confront.
6. When you've stood your ground, move on.
7. Do not take attacks personally.
8. From time to time, try agreeing with what your Defiant Underachiever says.

What to Expect When You Help Your Defiant Underachiever

1. Expect at times to feel inadequate as a parent because you can't "control" your child's attitude.
2. Expect to feel misunderstood, unappreciated, and rejected by your Defiant Underachiever, especially when you first implement our suggestions.
3. Expect, at times, to continue to get lured into arguments over attitude.
4. Expect to hope that when your new approach works for the first time, that it will work forever. And expect to find out that it won't.
5. Expect to become increasingly adept at avoiding arguments over attitude.
6. Expect to gain personal satisfaction from your increasing effectiveness in dealing with your Defiant Underachiever—especially because you see how much it is helping your child.

The Defiant Underachiever as an Adult

Fortunately, Defiant Underachievement does not often carry over into adulthood. Usually kids *do* grow out of it. They grow out of it because as adults, they attain independence whether they like it or not. They no longer can create a private definition of independence, complete with its own parameters and realities—and reasons for defiance. These persons may, however, retain their fundamentally argumentative natures. They may continue to be quick to state an opinion or pick a quarrel.

Defiant Underachievers who do not grow out of their defiance and combativeness carry their negativism into the workplace. They are people who are self-righteous, one-sided, lacking in self-awareness or humor and, in our experience, thoroughly unpleasant to be around.

And although the world cuts a rebellious teenager a lot of slack, *nobody* suffers an antagonistic adult gladly.

Adult Defiant Underachievers can be Active Defiant or Passive Defiant, just like their teenage counterparts. Passive Defiant employees typically behave sullenly, especially when asked to do something by management. They constantly criticize the attitudes and decisions of supervisors or managers—behind their backs, of course. They express their anger indirectly by doing less than their best on the job—their way of "showing" a superior that they cannot be coerced or pushed around. And like their adolescent forebears, they cut off their noses to spite their faces: They rationalize that they are doing their superiors harm rather than themselves ("If they don't treat me right, there's *no way* I'll do a good job for them!"). They are more than willing to sacrifice their own work record as a form of defiance.

The Active Defiant employee is openly argumentative and often finds ready excuses to antagonize other workers. They interpret useful suggestions by others for improving their productivity as criticism of *their* method—which is the best, of course. They pick arguments with co-workers and complain that other workers are always getting favored treatment or "fairer" duties or work schedules.

But even Defiant Underachievers can mellow. And if the fires of rebellion have cooled, the defiance is integrated into a more mature personality. They still have an argumentative streak, but it is better channeled and can even be interpreted as a positive contribution. Some adults with defiant characteristics function well in the workplace. They are viewed by colleagues as bringing an independent perspective to the job. They may identify problem areas overlooked by others. And because they say what they think when they think it, they can make valuable contributions to an organization's competitiveness, efficiency and vitality.

CHAPTER 8

Loose Ends and Your Underachieving Child

Underachievement is a complex problem. We've worked with underachievers far too long ever to make the mistake of oversimplifying. And we know from long experience that the problem of underachievement has loose ends. In this chapter, we gather up some of these loose ends and show how they relate to your underachieving child.

"What Ifs" and Your Underachieving Child

1. What if our suggestions don't work?

What if you try some of our suggestions to help your underachieving child—and the suggestions don't work? *Then* what?

Well, remember that our six underachieving types are just that—prototypes. They're "pure" types of underachievers we have known and worked with. It's unlikely that all of our suggested techniques and practical approaches will *always* work all of the time. So even if your underachiever's characteristics *seem* to fit the prototype like a glove, you may have overlooked or failed to recognize aspects, idiosyncrasies or even obvious characteristics of your child that are different from the prototype. We human beings are complex, unpredictable creatures, and many of us don't fit so neatly into defined categories.

It's because of all this that we have included cautionary notes within each chapter. The What To Expect section at the end of each chapter also addresses this issue. In What To Expect, we have gone out of our way to advise you about what *not* to expect—as well as not expecting too much too soon.

And here's another reason you may be frustrated in your attempts to help your underachieving child.

2. What if you wrongly identify your underachieving child with one of the six underachieving prototypes?

In Chapter 1, we discussed the problem of wrongly identifying the type of underachiever your child may be. You are probably too close to your child to be objective about what's going on. You may need to seek confirmation of your conclusions with a qualified professional.

How do we know in our professional practice if an underachiever has been wrongly typecast? We discover this by looking at the effectiveness of treatment—the same way physicians often use a patient's reaction to a certain medication to test whether their initial diagnosis was accurate.

So let's say that we systematically test our suggestions and they just don't seem to be working with a particular underachiever. We then need to consider whether we may have wrongly identified the type that this student most resembles.

For example, we may honestly believe a student we are working with is a Coaster when, in fact, she's an Identity-Search Underachiever. And since some of the types do indeed have characteristics in common, this *can* happen. For example, Anxious Underachievers can get depressed, Identity-Search underachievers can become anxious, Wheeler-Dealer Underachievers can be defiant. And *any* underachiever can offer excuses or procrastinate.

The important thing to remember here is that no judgment about a particular underachiever should be carved in stone. The labels we use to describe the six types of underachievers are meant to be used as working, tentative guidelines.

As the parent of an underachiever, do *not* assume that your child perfectly fits any of the types described in this book. Especially if you have not had an appropriate professional assessment or if your experience of your child is inconsistent with the description of the prototype.

And don't be discouraged if you find it hard to decide which underachieving type fits your child. Parents often see characteristics from many types in their child. *In fact, in our professional practice, we agree only 40 percent of the time with parents' judgments about the type of underachiever that best describes their child.*

Surprising? Yes and no.

First, remember The Underachievement Myth. It's very easy for a parent to attribute poor performance to laziness and lack of motivation when, in truth, it may reflect sadness, anxiety or a rock-hard motivation to maintain mediocre grades.

Second, it's always easier to make accurate judgments when you are not a player in the scene. Other psychologists have asked us to assess their own underachieving teenagers because they sensed, quite rightly, that as parents, they were tied in to the overall problem. If you're a dentist, you can't drill your own teeth.

Third, you may not have all the information you need to make an accurate judgment. Children, especially underachieving children, often are hesitant to share key facts with their parents—facts they may be willing to share with someone else.

So be careful about reaching definitive conclusions about your underachieving child. The different types of underachievers we describe should provide you with a useful overview. But seek professional opinions.

3. What if your child is a "Combination Underachiever"?
The six types of underachieving kids we have identified are prototypes. Very useful prototypes, we might add—but prototypes nevertheless.

So if your underachieving child is similar to one of our six types, and you try some of our suggestions and your efforts seem to be going nowhere—or they're only partially successful—consider the possibility that your child is a Combination Underachiever. In other words, he or she has characteristics from more than one type.

In the section in each chapter entitled Anatomy of an Under-achiever, we list characteristics that interact to produce each type of underachiever. The number, range and variety of these characteristics illustrate both the diversity within each prototype and their relationships to other prototypes.

Different types can—and do—blend, because many characteristics of children at various stages of development are similar to the types we have been describing. For example, at some point most adolescents resist or defy parental authority. And many pre-adolescent and early adolescent children go through periods of underachievement in which they seem to have excuses for everything. With underachievers, however, these problems last longer and have a greater impact on academic performance.

The prototype we most often see in combination with other types is the Sad Underachiever. For example:

- An Anxious Underachiever who has been struggling unsuccessfully to achieve may exhibit many characteristics of the Sad Underachiever.

- Identity-Searchers may experience many of the characteristics of the Sad Underachiever, although these moods tend not to be as pervasive or as long-lasting as those of the Sad Underachiever.

But almost any combination is possible.

If your underachiever seems to be a mixture of more than one type, review the relevant chapters. Ask yourself which set of characteristics predominates. Perhaps neither set predominates, or perhaps one set predominates in some situations and the other set predominates in other situations. Once again, don't assume that reading this book makes you a diagnostician. Seek professional confirmation of your perceptions.

Learning Disabilities and Your Underachieving Child

We are not going to launch into an exhaustive treatise on learning disabilities. What we *do* want to sort out is their relationship to underachievement.

What exactly are learning disabilities?

Think of a learning disability as a broken link in a chain. Apart from this dysfunctional link, the chain is sound. In other words, the child with the learning disability is not *mentally* disabled (or mentally challenged as often is said today). *The child with a learning disability is fully capable of learning.* The problem lies in a specific neurological weakness in one or more of the processes necessary for learning. The typical example is the bright child who reverses letters as he reads and is labeled dyslexic. This does not mean this child has any problem *understanding* what he reads.

One of the signs of a learning disability a parent can look for is *early* academic difficulty in *specific* subjects, in a child who is otherwise intellectually average or above average.

Learning disabilities were once considered something of an affliction, but now carry little stigma. Quite the contrary. Some parents even fight to have their children labeled "learning disabled" because it entitles them to special services within the school system—smaller classrooms, more individual attention, specially trained teachers and educational materials.

In the 1940s and '50s, many students with bona fide learning disabilities were identified as underachievers. Today, the trend is reversed. Now, many underachieving students are identified as learning disabled. Because, you see, being learning disabled is now much more socially acceptable than falling under the spell of The Underachievement Myth—and being one of those lazy and unmotivated couch-potato underachievers!

The directors of Canada's first university-based Learning Disabilities Centre at Toronto's York University (set up during the 1980s) have found over the years that a significant proportion of their incoming learning-disabled students do not qualify as learning disabled when they are assessed during their first year at university. It has been found that many children who were genuinely learning disabled in fact outgrew their disability in adolescence, and thus don't test out as such in university. However, it's also true that when the directors of the Learning Disabilities Centre query the parents of these students, many of the parents admit that they worked to have their children identified as learning disabled in high school, because the LD diagnosis qualified their children for LD programming—which they saw as superior to normal programming.

Tremendous strides have been taken over the last two decades in identifying and helping learning disabled students. During the 1970s and '80s, a great deal of research was done on learning disabilities and significant advances were made. Meanwhile, the issue of underachievement has been relatively ignored.

Underachievement, after all, is a much more fuzzy concept—not easy to diagnose scientifically—more confusing and more difficult to treat. We now know a great deal about learning-disabled students, and we have many specialized programs for diagnosing and helping them. But there are few programs that work primarily with underachievers.

For our purposes here, we simply want to sort out the tangle of learning disabilities and underachievement. We want to make sure every child is identified correctly and treated appropriately.

Is it possible to be both learning disabled and an underachiever?

Yes. And it's important to determine whether the underachievement is entirely due to the learning disability—or whether other factors are contributing.

We certainly see learning disabilities among our six underachieving prototypes. At the high-school level, two of our prototypes predominate: the Learning-Disabled Anxious Underachiever and the Learning-Disabled Wheeler-Dealer Underachiever.

Anxious Underachievers respond to their learning disability with tension, a sense of inadequacy and reduced self-esteem. We have found they often can be helped by following the steps we outline in our earlier chapter on the Anxious Underachiever—in addition, of course, to specialized tutoring for their learning disability.

Wheeler-Dealer Underachievers respond to their learning disability the way they do to any frustration in their lives—by taking it out on the people around them. The result? Their behavior problems often mask the learning disability—the same way they mask their underachievement.

We see learning disabilities among our other types of underachievers too. Not all of them greet the news of a learning disability with sadness, shock or worry. Coasting Underachievers generally are only too pleased to learn that they have a learning disability. How convenient! Now they can blame their underachievement on their LD. They have another excuse for giving up. They can ride their learning disability into the sunset. (But don't expect them to gallop. An easygoing canter will do.)

So, is it possible that your underachiever also has a learning disability? Yes! And is it possible that she *only* has a learning disability? In other words, is it possible that she is underachieving because and only because of her learning disability—and, therefore, that she does not match any of our underachieving prototypes? Yes, again.

Any suspicion of learning problems requires a specialized assessment. The longer a child with a moderate to severe learning disability has to struggle without help, the more likely it is that additional problems will develop.

What additional problems you may ask?

Self-esteem tops the list. If a kid in grade school internalizes early on that he's "dumb," it can cause lasting damage to his overall self-image. Even relatively mild learning disabilities among young kids can trigger self-esteem problems, confidence problems and motivational problems. It doesn't take much to torpedo one's self-concept. Sometimes these problems persist even when these kids achieve despite their learning disabilities. Their academic success notwithstanding, and in spite of the fact that everyone else thinks they're very smart, deep down they continue to suffer from low self-esteem.

Self-Esteem and Your Underachieving Child

In recent years, there has been an intense discussion in education about the role of self-esteem in academic achievement. One group of educators believes that self-esteem is necessary *in order* to achieve, while another group believes that self-esteem results *from* achievement, and the accomplishments and mastery of skills that achievement entails.

We don't belong to either camp. Where, then, *do* we stand on the subject of self-esteem and achievement?

First, it is true that some students with low self-esteem achieve, while others underachieve. Second, we have observed that achievement does not always result in increased self-esteem. And third, we know that increased self-esteem in some underachievers does not necessarily lead them to higher achievement.

In other words, while self-esteem may affect achievement, we do *not* consider self-esteem and achievement to be inextricably linked.

Regarding our first observation, that achievement is possible even if your self-esteem is low: History is rife with examples of famous high achievers who had low self-esteem. And today, as gossip chroniclers and paparazzi and biographers expose the private lives of the rich and famous, we are titillated daily with the self-esteem problems of movie stars, musicians, sports heroes, political leaders, artists, scientists and celebrities. Talent and hard work and good luck aren't the only reasons many of these people are achievers. Some may be highly motivated as a way of compensating for their low self-esteem. But, alas, alack, their considerable accomplishments have not necessarily rewarded them with high self-esteem. Self-esteem is *not* an automatic reward of achievement.

Now let's look at self-esteem and the *under*achiever. Are there underachievers with reasonably high self-esteem who continue to underachieve? Yes, there are—plenty of them. Many research studies on self-esteem demonstrate that increased self-esteem in underachievers does *not* automatically lead to increased achievement.

Think about our six prototypes. The most obvious example of underachievers who have no problem with self-esteem is Coasters, who have enough positive vibes about themselves to coast along comfortably. Likewise, Defiant Underachievers can feel good about themselves, especially following a "victory" over their parents. And although the self-esteem of Identity-Searchers often fluctuates, in general it is strong.

And then there are people who underachieve in school but achieve elsewhere. The student who starts his own business, for example, or the single-minded dancer or athlete who has no time for school work. These kids may be defined *academically* as underachievers, but they may have high self-esteem and be working toward meaningful goals outside school.

However, low self-esteem often *contributes* to underachievement. Low self-esteem can lower a student's motivation and the result will be underachievement. *The critical point is this: Poor self-esteem alone has not caused the poor achievement.* The poor achievement reflects other problems that need to be addressed too.

ADHD, ADD and Your Underachieving Child

Attention Deficit Hyperactivity Disorder (ADHD), hyperactivity combined with an inability to concentrate, can contribute to a child's underachievement. (We discussed ADHD and Wheeler-Dealer Underachievers in Chapter 5.) Kids suffering from ADHD have trouble concentrating and are filled with unholy amounts of energy. Both at home and at school, they flit from activity to activity with a speed that can be very disruptive.

Children who have trouble concentrating and focusing, but are not hyperactive, may be suffering from Attention Deficit Disorder (ADD).

Much more is known these days about both these disorders and a parent who suspects their child suffers from either of these problems should ask for a medical assessment.

Giftedness and Your Underachieving Child

Unfortunately, the gifted child is not guaranteed academic success. Remember what we said in Chapter 1 about intelligence being only one of many factors contributing to achievement? This applies—big-time—to gifted children.

Gifted students who underachieve usually do so for a number of reasons. For example, female students may experience enormous peer pressure to underachieve to be more "popular." Other reasons include:

1. The school may not challenge them enough and they may become bored.

Gifted children are exceptional. That is, they exhibit unique character-istics. For example, when they begin a task, they may not pay as much attention to the details as do other children. They tend to spend more time analyzing the "big picture," devising strategies and really getting into (even reveling in) the theoretical complexity of it all. But they then spend *less* time than average students actually *doing* the project.

One of the problems this poses for any school system is the constant challenge of making the school environment creative and stimulating enough to keep the gifted child interested. When gifted students underachieve, they frequently complain that their classes are boring and simple-minded.

If you are the parent of a Gifted Underachiever, you probably already know how hard it is for you and the school to design a curriculum and a series of challenging academic tasks geared to your child's unique talents. After all, it is very difficult for any school system to come up with individualized curricula and educational strategies to fit the different needs of each and every student.

2. Their maturity may not match their IQ.

Gifted children in general, and particularly Gifted Underachievers, have highly developed verbal skills. They are so intelligent that they can be very convincing and snow their parents when discussing less than satisfactory grades. Parents may become so spellbound by these explanations, and so awed by their child's intellectual ability, that they lose sight of the child's emotional immaturity.

Many parents assume that the ability to use verbal logic is a sign of emotional maturity. But just because gifted children have a large and impressive vocabulary and are able to use it appropriately does *not* mean that they are handling their lives with the wisdom that can only come from time and experience.

3. Although they are very bright, they may lack basic academic skills.

Many Gifted Underachievers resist finishing tasks, claiming that they've already figured out what needed to be done. They don't see any value in doing a task they already understand. As a result, they do not practice basic written-language or numerical skills. Parents and teachers often assume that, because these students are so verbally fluent and so obviously intelligent, their math and written-language skills must also be equally well developed.

This is not so. On the contrary, we have found significant academic-skill gaps in many Gifted Underachievers. Even gifted students have to go through the basic slogging required to master academic skills and knowledge. By the same token, many Gifted Underachievers lack solid study skills and the academic self-discipline any student needs to achieve at school. And compounding this problem, many Gifted Underachievers with academic-skill deficiencies don't want to admit to or face their deficiencies.

So, if your child is a Gifted Underachiever, it may be a good idea to have his or her academic skills tested. You may be surprised by what you find.

4. Some Gifted Underachievers may be getting good grades, but have poor work habits.

The parents of some *achieving* gifted students come to our clinic because they have noticed that, although their child attains good grades effortlessly, he does so without any substantial effort or self-discipline. These parents worry—and rightly so—that no matter how good their child's grades are, his work habits will lead to failure as he goes on in school, and certainly in the adult world. The person who does not know *how* to work is in for a difficult future. With this type of gifted student, we have always made sure we discuss work habits and their relation to future performance and the attainment of goals.

5. Gifted Underachievers may fit one of the six under-achieving prototypes.

We have seen many gifted students who fit into our six underachieving prototypes. When they do, it adds a special challenge to our work. For example, consider the challenge of changing the behavior of a brilliant Wheeler-Dealer Underachiever. He's a specialist in the con game and may run circles of deceit around you. Or a gifted Coaster may construct excuses so clever they are utterly convincing.

Parents, teachers and counselors often have to be exceptionally alert in order to keep on top of what's going on.

Study Skills and Your Underachieving Child

The longer a child underachieves, the more baggage she will accumulate—that is, the more deficient in work habits, self-discipline and study skills she will become.

One of the first pieces of luggage that will weigh her down and make the cycle of underachievement harder to reverse is not knowing how to study. Any student who has been underachieving for a number of years because she hasn't worked hard in school—especially if the pattern began early in elementary school—will not have learned how to study. She won't know how to read a textbook or how to take effective notes or how to review for a test. And as time goes by, the gap will widen between her work habits and those of her contemporaries.

When parents recognize their underachiever's problem to be a lack of study skills, they often pack their child off to a study-skills course. This is fine, as far as it goes. But each of our six under-achieving prototypes will bring a unique perspective to a study-skills course.

For example, Anxious Underachievers may really benefit from the pointers, especially if the course helps them structure their time more effectively. Wheeler-Dealer Underachievers may not even show up for the classes. Coasters may show up, but they won't listen, take notes or remember what they've learned.

So don't assume that merely addressing the issue of study skills will fix the problem. You have to tailor your approach and the structure of the program to the type of underachiever you have.

Learning Styles and Your Underachieving Child

A lot has been written over the past 20 years about differences in learning styles. Some people learn best visually, others need both sight and sound to maximize retention. Still others need hands-on experience and learn almost entirely by doing. Some students learn best in groups, others individually.

Coasters usually thrive in groups: The momentum of the others carries them in its wake. Anxious students, on the other hand, prefer to toil alone because they're nervous about exposing their inadequacies to others. Some kids can concentrate no matter how much noise and activity surrounds them; others need library quiet or complete solitude. Some students find it very difficult to learn from a written page but can develop and sharpen ideas during verbal debate. Some blossom in a conventional classroom with a teacher, a blackboard and uniformed students sitting in orderly rows of desks. Others like the intimacy and give-and-take of tutorials or small seminar groups. Some students retain information better by writing things down, others best absorb information visually and mentally from a television screen or monitor. And today, as kids grow up in a computer-driven world, more and more students are attuned to learning on-line.

Good students tune into the learning style that works best for them and, over time, develop and build on it. Achievers learn what works for them and use it. Underachievers, on the other hand, do not tune into their natural learning style and, as a result, fail to develop or use it. So any program to help your underachieving child should include a focus on learning style.

Gaps in Basic Academic Knowledge and Your Underachieving Child

No matter which type of underachiever your child resembles, if he has missed a lot of classes or hasn't paid much attention over a considerable period of time, he almost certainly will not acquire core knowledge of specific subjects. So working on study skills and improving motivation, important as they are, may not be enough to turn an underachiever around.

The best way to determine if such gaps in your child's essential knowledge exist is to request an academic-skills assessment from the school. Find out how strong or weak your underachiever's basic knowledge is in math, languages and science.

Tutoring and Your Underachieving Child

"Get thee to a tutor!" is one of the knee-jerk responses of frustrated parents of underachievers. If the underachiever is similar to one of our six types, the results of tutoring alone are often much the same as in a study-skills course: Each of the six underachieving types will approach tutoring with a different set of lenses. Each will have her own kind of mind-set and motivation (or lack thereof).

- Wheeler-Dealer Underachievers may skip appointments with the tutor.

- Defiant Underachievers will relish the sessions because it gives them an opportunity to get into power struggles with an "expert."

- Coasters will generally get along well with the tutor and perform well. The tutor will predict wonderful results in the classroom. And their grades *may* improve slightly—as long as they continue with the tutor. But once the tutoring sessions end, classroom progress will cease.

- By now you probably can predict what happens with an Identity-Search Underachiever. He and the tutor spend the entire session discussing the value of life and learning, and may never even get to the math lesson!

All of which does not mean that tutoring will fail to make a difference. But it will be much more effective if the tutor recognizes how different underachieving students are and modifies the teaching approach for each type of underachiever.

Because tutoring will only make a difference when the student is genuinely motivated to improve. And to motivate your underachiever, we suggest you go back to the How to Help section of whichever chapter best describes your underachieving child.

The School and Your Underachieving Child

Many parents of underachievers agonize about whether changing classes, teachers or schools will make a significant difference.

"What about enrolling her in a private high school?"
"Might boarding school make a difference?"
"Should I send him to military school?"
"My sister lives in a school district where the schools are supposed to be better. Should we use their home address and transfer our daughter?"

Of course, the characteristics of a school *do* make a difference. Which school a child attends can have a major impact on his or her academic performance.

In our practice, if we conclude that a change in classes, teachers or schools is warranted, we often suggest that parents talk to their school's guidance counselor for information about educational alternatives, and then explore what makes sense for their child.

Remember, some solutions work better for particular types of underachievers than for others. For example, a school in which freedom of behavior and choice are emphasized probably is a questionable choice for a Wheeler-Dealer Underachiever. A more structured environment such as a good boarding school or a military school may be better, provided the parents try other, less radical solutions first.

An Identity-Search Underachiever, on the other hand, who is placed in a rigidly structured school environment is likely to continue to underachieve because the school offers little freedom to explore and choose.

Of course, practical concerns (such as your financial means and commuting distances) must be considered. If you cannot afford what appears to be the ideal solution for your child, you may have to choose a more realistic alternative that takes into account your family's circumstances.

Separation and Divorce and Your Underachieving Child

Studies consistently show that behavior problems and deteriorating performance at school frequently follow a parental breakup.

But do not despair. This is not universally true.

The achievement levels of many children of divorce return to previous levels after a period of adjustment, usually two years. And some reports show that when the parental relationship was ravaged by acrimonious or violent arguments, separation and divorce may actually lead to improved academic performance. In other words, exposing a child to serious marital conflict may be worse than the results of separation or divorce.

However, some studies report continuing underachievement among children of divorce. And the reasons for this are many. We know, for example, that divorce frequently leads to considerably lowered financial status. Less money puts additional strain on an already stressful situation, and makes adaptation more difficult.

So, what makes for a positive or a negative adjustment? As much stability and continuity as possible in an otherwise changing environment is what every divorced parent should strive for. The more stable and continuous your child's life, the more minimal the long-term impact of the breakup on her academic achievement is likely to be.

Parents who use their children to get back at their former spouse are asking for trouble at school. On the other hand, divorced parents who work together for the sake of their child can reasonably expect favorable results.

So if a child is doing poorly following the breakup of a marriage, we often advise parents not to rush into a change of school. Marital separation often means a move, so this may not be practical. But generally, if the bonds a child has formed with teachers and schoolmates seem strong, parents should do what they can to maintain these. We usually urge parents to consider the impact of additional change before they rush to move as far as they can from the painful memories.

Gender and Underachievement

Are there differences between male and female underachievers?

Until the 1980s, most research on underachievement was done using male students. Over the last 15 years, a greater effort has been made by researchers to include female underachievers.

In general, twice as many male students are identified as underachievers as female students. But this 2:1 ratio is not reflected in the number of male and female high-school underachievers who are brought to us for professional assistance. Here the ratio is approximately 5:1. Why is this so?

Perhaps parents of male underachievers feel greater societal pressure than parents of female underachievers. Perhaps they are more likely to embrace The Underachievement Myth when they think they have a lazy and unmotivated son than when they have a lazy and unmotivated daughter.

In an effort to find out more about this, the Institute on Achievement and Motivation at York University in Toronto has embarked on an intensive research project focused on female underachievers.

Regardless of what the research eventually will tell us about the similarities and differences between male and female underachievers, so far in our experience, the issues of personality style or type far outweigh male/female differences in determining how to best help these students.

Seeking a Professional Assessment

Each chapter in this book contains a parent checklist to help you determine whether or not your child is similar to a particular underachiever profile. The following list contains a more complete range of factors that, ideally, should be part of any comprehensive professional assessment:

1. Medical or physical problems.
2. Specific academic-skill deficiencies.
3. Attention or concentration problems.
4. Learning disabilities.
5. Personality and motivational characteristics.
6. Family problems.
7. Peer-group problems.
8. School-based problems.
9. Community-based problems.

CHAPTER 9

The '90s and Beyond:
Transcending Underachievement

We've met a lot of underachievers—but we have yet to meet a lazy and unmotivated underachiever. The underachievers we have known are all motivated. And they're motivated in very different directions. To remember exactly how each type of underachiever is motivated, imagine a glass of water that is half full—and half empty.

- The Coasting Underachiever will look at the glass of water and say, "No question about it. It's half full or half empty. I'll get back to it tomorrow."

- The Anxious Underachiever will give it a worried look and say, "Would you like me to fill it up for you?"

- The Identity-Search Underachiever will look the glass up and down carefully and say, "I don't think I like the shape of that glass."

- The Wheeler-Dealer Underachiever will say, "How much do you want for the glass?"

- The Sad Underachiever will say, "It's clearly half empty. And there'll probably be less tomorrow."

- And the Defiant Underachiever will look at the glass and say, "I didn't order water!"

Each of these kids has taken a different journey to arrive at the same destination—but *none* of them is lazy and unmotivated. Each has a different view of the world. And whichever of the above best describes your kid will determine how you use the suggestions we make in this book.

But someday, not so long from now, this too shall pass. Your child's underachieving years at school will be over and he or she will go on to the next stage of life. What can you realistically expect then? As the parent of an underachiever, how much should you worry about the future?

Underachievement and Your Child's Future

There is recent evidence that underachievement that is not reversed by the end of high school frequently does have long-term consequences—the very kinds of long-term consequences parents fear.

In 1993, Dr. Robert McCall, a professor of psychology at the University of Pittsburgh, published the results of a wide-ranging comparative study of 5,000 achievers and underachievers 13 years after high-school graduation.

The findings reached by Dr. McCall and his colleagues were telling. The researchers found that underachievers with the same mental ability as achievers completed fewer years of post-secondary education: Underachievers had one chance in five of completing college, compared with one chance in two for achieving students. Underachievers frequently got off to a poor start in the job market, progressed less rapidly, changed jobs more often and ended up in lower-status, lower-earning jobs. Underachievers also were 50 percent more likely to divorce during the 13 years following high school.

And which underachievers have the best chance of catching up to achievers, according to the McCall researchers?

Both the expectations of the kids themselves and the educational levels of their parents made a difference to which kids got second chances. In McCall's words:

" . . . underachieving high-school students *who expected to go to college and to graduate* [our italics], who believed they were sufficiently competent to complete college, who displayed relatively more interest in academic school work, who participated in school and non-school activities, *who had relatively more self-esteem and self-confidence, and who had parents who were relatively more educated* [our italics] did better educationally and occupationally 13 years after high school."

And which were least likely to catch up? The McCall team found that kids defined as severe underachievers—those who were two or more grade levels below expectations—did not catch up. For these kids, sadly, underachievement is a relatively permanent characteristic, the McCall team concluded.

So, when nothing is done, the patterns of underachievement in childhood and adolescence are likely to persist into adulthood.

The Underachievement Myth and the Workplace of Tomorrow

The frazzled captains of industry in today's leaner, meaner workplace accept The Underachievement Myth as a given. In their lexicon, unproductive equals lazy and unmotivated. The new watchwords of the workplace are "produce or perish." No one has the patience—or the budget—to tolerate underachievers or support them while they make up their minds whether or not to change. "Lazy and unmotivated" today means unemployed tomorrow.

Doing your job, being loyal and working hard used to be the keys to a successful, long-term career and job security. Today, companies still value loyalty and reliability—but these virtues are lower on their priority list.

It no longer does a company any good to have a loyal and reliable employee on the payroll who doesn't make a direct contribution to bottom-line needs. The bottom line includes increasing profits, cutting costs and maximizing efficiency, productivity, quality and sales. This requires workers who can adapt to changing needs, learn new competitive skills, take on increased responsibility, work more effectively with others and, above all, show the highest levels of motivation and initiative. *In short, what the companies of today and tomorrow are looking for are achievers.*

Achievers used to be the cream of the crop, the people who moved to the top of an organization. Today, you have to be an achiever simply to keep your job. The only people whom organizations can afford to keep are the ones who help the company survive, not the ones who just occupy a desk and do the job. The achievers now are the survivors.

All of this leaves underachievers vulnerable in the economy of the '90s and beyond the year 2000.

Transcending Underachievement

It is our heartfelt belief that achievement is important to your child's future. If we did not believe this, we would not have written this book. But not fulfilling *all* your potential does not spell the end of the world. It does, in fact, describe 95 percent of the world as we know it! And it's rare—exceedingly rare—for underachieving kids' lives to spiral into total failure and self-destruction. When this does happen, there's a lot more at work than underachievement, pure and simple.

Strive for balance. ✗

As important as achieving is to your child's future, *do not ever let the issue of achievement take over your relationship with your child.* As in all things in life, it comes down to a question of balance.

Harping on the subject constantly won't do any good anyway. Economists would say you'll experience diminishing returns. This means that after a point, it becomes counterproductive. Your child will turn you off, and you'll lose whatever tenuous influence you may have had. You may even worsen your relationship.

Take a vacation from pounding the achievement issue. Your relationship as a parent is going to last a lot longer than your child's years at school. Don't jeopardize your relationship. Even if your son or daughter is a chronic underachiever, continuously and deeply in academic trouble, don't get trapped into talking with your child *always and only* about achievement. Make sure you have lots of contact and interactions that have absolutely nothing to do with achievement or school.

Don't sabotage your shot at a rounded relationship with your child. Your child needs you as a parent for a thousand things that have nothing to do with achievement. She needs your emotional support. She needs positive give-and-take as part of the family. It's crucially important that you don't make achievement at school the sole subject of communication with your child.

There are hundreds of professionals out there who can focus on your child's special problems and needs. There are teachers, counselors, tutors, psychologists, physicians—all of whom have something to contribute at appropriate moments and appropriate times. But you are your child's only parents. Don't give up that unique and precious role to become just one more teacher or tutor or therapist. *It is important that you be your child's parent first.* Take the time to be a parent, and not just someone who stands over your children to make sure they get their homework done.

If a family vacation is approaching, make it a real vacation. No matter how much unfinished business there is between you and your child about the achievement issue, let it go for the moment. Give yourself and your kid a break. Give the whole family a break from the constant harangue. Before you go away, make a conscious decision that nothing about school will be discussed on the holiday. Announce it as a family-vacation rule, if you wish. Underachievers need vacations too—even chronic, habitual, persistent, hard-core, intractable underachievers, the kind who specialize in driving their parents to distraction. *Everybody* needs time out from The Underachievement Thing.

And you don't have to wait for a major vacation to give the issue a break. Strive for balance within any seven-day period. If the family is going out to dinner on a Friday evening, don't spoil everyone's appetite by focusing the table talk on school only.

Letting up like this may give you an opportunity to renew your relationship with your child on a basis other than school and homework. Never forget that your child is not going to be in school forever. But she's going to be yours forever, your child. That relationship is sacred, something to jealously safeguard and build upon.

Learn to let go.

No matter what your underachiever's problems may be, and no matter how insurmountable his underachieving syndrome may seem, as the weeks and years go by, he will become more independent. Whatever control or influence you have over his life will shrink somewhere in the middle to late teenage years. And no matter how your fledgling adult spreads his wings and flies into the future, as a parent you want to make sure that you learn how to let go. If you do, you'll have a better chance to build a relationship that lasts into your child's adulthood.

So go with the flow. Don't fight the inevitable. Reinforce your child's sense of responsibility and accountability for making her own choices. Learn to let go of your role as chief teller-what-to-do.

You won't always agree with your child's choices. You may *never* agree with your child's choices! You can try to set limits on his decisions, but you cannot pretend he's not making his own choices and independent judgments. It's going to get worse before it gets better!

Day by day, week by week, month by month, the power and responsibility for your child's life will shift from you to him. It's up to you as a parent to recognize the handwriting on the wall and respect the fact that your child is becoming a free agent.

Appreciate and support your child's successes.

Don't fall into the trap of paying attention to your child only when she does poorly or otherwise messes up. Pay attention to things well done, even—perhaps, especially—when they have nothing to do with achievement at school. Never assume things are understood. Vocalize your appreciation and emotional support.

Take time to see and understand the whole picture.

When you see what looks like a familiar, negative situation on the horizon and you're about to shift into automatic pilot and rush in with pronouncements and accusations, make sure you take the time to get all of the details. Train yourself to refuse to react to any situation until you have given yourself the chance to obtain all relevant facts. It will save you from making a lot of mistakes. And if you do decide to put your foot down or intervene or set limits, then you'll know why you're doing it and what you're likely to accomplish.

Learn to listen to your child. And find out about normal stages of development.

Earlier in this book, we discussed the importance of listening to your child. We described listening techniques in detail. We cannot overemphasize the importance of genuinely listening to your child, whatever his underachievement pattern. Learning how to listen gives you a pipeline to your child's heart.

And it's important, too, to have a basic understanding of normal adolescent stages of development. Bookstore shelves are lined with books on human development from birth to adulthood. Get a grip on some of the information in them. What may seem like bizarre behavior may suddenly look normal. As one parent remarked wryly, "From the ages of 13 through 20, every kid receives signals from outer space. And then, as if by magic, the signals become earthbound again."

So learn as much as you can about predictable stages and issues of development. Check with your pediatrician, child-guidance experts, school counselors. There is a great deal of information available to help you understand what your child is going through.

Don't expect to be a perfect parent.

Being a parent is about making mistakes. Every parent makes mistakes. Intentions and relationships are what's important, not the mistakes you unintentionally make. You do the best you can.

You can, of course, try to minimize your mistakes. But none of us knows what a mistake is beforehand. So recognize that, as a parent, you strive to do the best that you can—and then accept your effort and be content with it. If perfection were a requirement for parenthood, no human being would qualify. In fact, being perfect would set a terrible example for our children. It would give them something to live up to that would make them feel forever inadequate.

So give your children your best. Help them as much and as intelligently and in as caring a way as you can. Be as firm as you can to help them achieve their potential. Your goal is to help your children go out and meet the world confidently and successfully. Not only to survive but to lead a meaningful life and to know the satisfaction of achieving one's potential. This is what the great psychologist Abraham Maslow referred to as "self-actualization." It is the fulfillment of who one is, not only in terms of monetary and career success, but realizing oneself as a person. There is no more joy as a parent than to pass along to the succeeding generation the knowledge, wisdom and love that are yours to give.

This is the challenge every parent has. We wish you well along this path.

References

American Psychiatric Association (1994). *Diagnostic and Statistical Manual, 4th Edition*; Washington: American Psychiatric Association.

Coleman, J.S., and Hoffer, T. (1987). *Public and private high schools*; New York: Basic Books.

Cote, J.E., and Allahar, A.L. (1994). *Generation on hold: Coming of age in the late 20th century*; Toronto: Stoddart Publishing Company.

Egan, G. (1976). "Confrontation" in *Group & Organizational Studies*, 1(2); La Jolla, CA: University Associates.

Finch, A.J., Nelson, W.M., and Ott, E.S. (eds.) (1993). *Cognitive-behavioral procedures with children and adolescents: A practical guide*; Boston: Allyn and Bacon.

Ford, M.E. (1992). *Motivating humans: Goals, emotions, and personal agency beliefs*; Newbury Park, CA: Sage Publishers.

Kazdin, A.E. (1987). *Conduct disorder in childhood and adolescence*; Newbury Park, CA: Sage Publishers.

Mandel, H.P. (in press). *Conduct disorder and underachievement*; New York: John Wiley & Sons.

Mandel, H.P., and Marcus, S.I. (1988). *The psychology of underachievement: Differential diagnosis and differential treatment*; New York: John Wiley & Sons.

March, J.L. (ed.) (1995). *Anxiety disorders in children and adolescents*; New York: The Guilford Press.

McCall, R.B., Evahn, C., and Kratzer, L. (1993). *High-school under-achievers: What do they achieve as adults?* Newbury Park, CA: Sage Publications.

Patterson, G.R., Reid, J.B., and Dishion, T.J. (1992). *Antisocial boys;* Eugene, OR: Castalia.

Postman, N., and Weingartner, C. (1969). *Teaching as a subversive activity;* New York: Delacorte Press.

Purkey, S., and Smith, M. (1983). "Effective schools: A review" in *Elementary School Journal,* 83, 427–452.

Rogers, C.R. (1951). *Client-centered therapy;* Boston: Houghton-Mifflin.

Roth, R.M. (1970). *Underachieving students and guidance;* Boston: Houghton-Mifflin.

Roth, R.M., and Meyersburg, H.A. (1963). "The non-achievement syndrome" in *Personnel and Guidance Journal,* 41, 535–540.

Sholevar, G.P. (ed.) (1995). *Conduct disorder in children and adolescents;* Washington: American Psychiatric Press.

Stevenson, H.W., and Stigler, J.W. (1992). *The learning gap: Why our schools are failing and what we can learn from Japanese and Chinese education;* New York: Summit Books.

Webster-Stratton, C. (1992). *The incredible years: Trouble-shooting guide for parents of children ages 3-8;* Toronto: Umbrella Press.

Webster-Stratton, C., and Herbert, M. (1994). *Troubled families— problem children;* New York: John Wiley & Sons.

Weiner, B. (1992). *Human motivation: Metaphors, theories, and research;* Newbury Park, CA: Sage Publishers.

Wilkes, T.C.R., Belsher, G., Rush, A.J., and Frank, E., and Associates. (1994). *Cognitive therapy for depressed adolescents;* New York: The Guilford Press.

Resources for Professionals

The Institute on Achievement and Motivation at York University, Toronto, Canada, is a non-profit organization mandated to provide service to underachieving students and their parents; to educate professionals through internships, workshops and training materials; to develop new approaches and diagnostic tests for the assessment and treatment of academic underachievement; and to conduct research.

Institute on Achievement and Motivation
Founders College – Room 127
York University
4700 Keele St.
North York, Ontario
Canada, M3J 1P3
Tel: (416) 736-5384 Fax: (416) 736-5357

Professionals are invited to contact the Institute for information about workshop topics and the following professional training materials:

1. Mandel, H.P., and Marcus, S.I. (1988). *The psychology of underachievement: Differential diagnosis and differential treatment*; New York, John Wiley & Sons.

2. Mandel, H.P. (1991). *Personality and motivation in under-achievement: A videotape workshop*; York University, Toronto, Institute on Achievement and Motivation.
3. Mandel, H.P., and Mandel, D.E. (1992). *Along the path: Case histories of differentially diagnosed underachievers*; York University, Toronto, Institute on Achievement and Motivation.
4. Mandel, H.P., Marcus, S.I., and Mandel, D.E. (1992). *Helping the non-achievement syndrome student: A clinical training manual*, Revised Edition; York University, Toronto, Institute on Achievement and Motivation.
5. Mandel, H.P. (in press). *Conduct disorder and underachievement*; New York, John Wiley and Sons.
6. Friedland, J., Mandel, H., and Marcus, S. (1995). *The Achievement Motivation Profile (AMP)*; Los Angeles, Western Psychological Services.
7. Friedland, J., Marcus, S., and Mandel, H. (1995). *The Sales Achievement Predictor (SalesAP)*; Los Angeles, Western Psychological Services.
8. Friedland, J., Marcus, S., and Mandel, H. (in press). *Motivation and Achievement Inventory (MAI)*; Los Angeles, Western Psychological Services.

Since 1945, Friedland & Marcus Career Consultants have provided comprehensive career and job-search counseling to more than 50,000 individuals; testing, training and other services to more than 450 businesses; acted as a resource for schools, educators and counselors; and worked with thousands of students to help them improve their motivation and study skills. Professionals, individuals and companies are invited to contact Friedland & Marcus for further information.

Friedland & Marcus
300 W. Washington, Suite 1106
Chicago, IL
U.S.A., 60606
Tel: (312) 641-3050   Fax: (312) 641-3059

Index